Microsoft Dynamics CRM 2015 Application Design

Master professional-level business application designs using Microsoft Dynamics CRM 2015 and its xRM features

Mahender Pal

[PACKT] enterprise 🞲
PUBLISHING   professional expertise distilled

BIRMINGHAM - MUMBAI

Microsoft Dynamics CRM 2015 Application Design

First published: October 2015

Production reference: 1261015

Published by Packt Publishing Ltd.
Livery Place
35 Livery Street
Birmingham B3 2PB, UK.

ISBN 978-1-78439-415-8

www.packtpub.com

Credits

Author
Mahender Pal

Reviewers
Ahmad Saad Masroor
Nishant Rana
Tanguy Touzard
James Wood

Commissioning Editor
Sarah Crofton

Acquisition Editors
James Jones
Larissa Pinto

Content Development Editor
Parita Khedekar

Technical Editor
Deepti Tuscano

Copy Editor
Stephen Copestake

Project Coordinator
Milton Dsouza

Proofreader
Safis Editing

Indexer
Tejal Soni

Graphics
Abhinash Sahu

Production Coordinator
Aparna Bhagat

Cover Work
Aparna Bhagat

About the Author

Mahender Pal is a Microsoft Dynamics CRM technology specialist, trainer, and author. He has worked on various Microsoft technologies. He started working with Dynamics CRM 3.0, and since then he has worked on various Microsoft Dynamics CRM implementations. He has been a Microsoft MVP for Dynamics CRM for five years, loves to contribute to the Dynamics CRM community, and blogs regularly about Dynamics CRM. He wrote his first book, *Microsoft Dynamics CRM 2011 Application Design, Packt Publishing,* which was based on developing xRM solutions using Dynamics CRM 2011.

He is a nature lover and loves to spend vacations in his native place, Himachal Pradesh, India, with his family. He is the founder of HIMBAP, which is a training and consulting company.

I would like to dedicate this book to my late father, Joginder Singh, and my mother, Kamla Devi, because they made me who I am. To my wife, Sonia, for supporting me during the writing of this book, and my kids, Diksha and Arnav, because of their continued unconditional love and amazing understanding about my work throughout the writing of this book.

To my brothers, Jasbir and Vikram, my nephews (Himanshu, Vini, Ayush, and Abhit), and nieces, Nishu and Kriti, for supporting me.

I would like to thank Packt Publishing for giving me the opportunity to write this book. My special thanks go to my technical reviewers Tanguy, Nishant Rana, James Wood, Ahmad Saad and Akashdeep Kundu, and my content development editor for giving me their valuable feedback for drafts.

And finally I would like to thank my friends, my team members, and Microsoft Dynamics CRM community for their support.

About the Reviewers

Ahmad Saad Masroor is a senior solution architect for a Denmark-based Microsoft Dynamics partner, AlfaPeople, where he is responsible for the technology and architecture of AlfaPeople across Dubai and Saudi Arabia. He is currently in the AlfaPeople Middle East presales team and supports sales and customer/prospect engagements.

Ahmad completed his bachelor of information technology degree from Amity University and has a total of 10 years experience in CRM consulting, implementing, and supporting solutions that have diverse technologies and capabilities. He has worked in a number of consulting roles with Microsoft, PWC, and HCL.

He is diligent and committed to the profession and is a supporter of poverty alleviation.

By applying strong business acumen, systems acuity, and leadership talents, Ahmad is very much at home creating operational centers of excellence. He has built a solid foundation of corporate clients through his IT consulting and business advisory services.

Aside from being a CRM solution architect, he is the managing partner at SattvaSoul. It is a professionally-run charitable organization working towards revolutionizing society with a holistic approach. Ahmad also works as a philanthropist.

You can follow him on Twitter at a_saad and write to him at saad.029@gmail.com.

I would like to express my gratitude to the many people who helped me through this book: to all those who provided support, talked things over, read, wrote, offered comments and allowed me to quote their remarks, and assisted me in editing, proofreading, and designing. I would like to dedicate this book to my parents.

I especially want to express my gratitude and deep appreciation for my friends whose knowledge and wisdom has supported, enlightened, and entertained me over many years.

Nishant Rana is a Microsoft Certified Professional who loves working in Microsoft Dynamics CRM, SharePoint, and other Microsoft .NET technologies such as Azure and ASP.NET.. He is currently working as a consultant in Microsoft, India, and actively promotes budding professionals through his weblog, http://nishantrana. me/

He has also been a technical reviewer for Microsoft Dynamics CRM 2011 Application Design, Microsoft Dynamics 2011 Reporting, and CRM 2013 Quick Start.

You can follow him on twitter at https://twitter.com/nishantranaCRM or write to him at nishant_bliss@hotmail.com

Tanguy Touzard is a technical consultant and solution architect at Javista in Paris, France. He has been working with Microsoft Dynamics CRM for more than ten years on various project aspects: development, consulting, and training. He has been a Microsoft MVP for five years.

Tanguy is the creator of XrmToolBox, a set of tools that allows a nondeveloper to customize Microsoft Dynamics CRM with less pain than these tasks normally require. This project also allows other developers to create their own tools for XrmToolBox. The project is available on Github at http://www.xrmtoolbox.com.

I would like to thank my wife, Emeline, who supported me, despite our two-year-old baby boy whose care is also like a full time job, while I did my community work for Microsoft Dynamics CRM.

James Wood is a solution architect at Gap Consulting with skills in the end-to-end implementation of enterprise Microsoft Dynamics CRM solutions. He acts in a hybrid role—that is a combination of technical and functional roles. He is also a developer of bespoke software. He graduated from the University of Huddersfield with a first class honours degree.

He has worked with Microsoft Dynamics CRM for over five years. He has worked on a number of small to large implementations in sectors including local and regional government, insurance, charitable, welfare, and health care.

Outside the workplace, James participates in the Microsoft CRM community with a personal blog that attracts a strong following. He posts on StackOverflow where he is a top poster on CRM-related questions, and he has technically edited a number Microsoft CRM books published by Packt Publishing.

You can read more about James at www.woodswork.co.uk.

I would like to thank my family and friends for everything—especially Rob, Chloë, Jamie, and Josh.

www.PacktPub.com

Support files, eBooks, discount offers, and more

For support files and downloads related to your book, please visit www.PacktPub.com.

Did you know that Packt offers eBook versions of every book published, with PDF and ePub files available? You can upgrade to the eBook version at www.PacktPub.com and as a print book customer, you are entitled to a discount on the eBook copy. Get in touch with us at service@packtpub.com for more details.

At www.PacktPub.com, you can also read a collection of free technical articles, sign up for a range of free newsletters and receive exclusive discounts and offers on Packt books and eBooks.

https://www2.packtpub.com/books/subscription/packtlib

Do you need instant solutions to your IT questions? PacktLib is Packt's online digital book library. Here, you can search, access, and read Packt's entire library of books.

Why subscribe?

- Fully searchable across every book published by Packt
- Copy and paste, print, and bookmark content
- On demand and accessible via a web browser

Free access for Packt account holders

If you have an account with Packt at www.PacktPub.com, you can use this to access PacktLib today and view 9 entirely free books. Simply use your login credentials for immediate access.

Instant updates on new Packt books

Get notified! Find out when new books are published by following @PacktEnterprise on Twitter or the *Packt Enterprise* Facebook page.

Table of Contents

Preface

Microsoft Dynamics CRM 2015 released many new features that makes it a true xRM Framework to develop custom applications. This book will help you to learn all the new features of Microsoft Dynamics CRM 2015 and to use them to develop real-world business applications. You will learn all the technical aspects of Microsoft Dynamics CRM 2015 that are related to customization, extension, and integration using sample applications.

What this book covers

Chapter 1, *Getting Started with Microsoft Dynamics CRM 2015*, provides the basic details of Microsoft Dynamics CRM 2015 such as software and hardware requirements, different deployment models, and available clients. This chapter also provides an overview of the new features introduced in CRM 2015.

Chapter 2, *Customizing Microsoft Dynamics CRM 2015*, will help you to learn customization concepts and different out-of-the-box tools to customize CRM 2015. You will learn how to create a sample application for an IT training company.

Chapter 3, *Client-side Logic with Microsoft Dynamics CRM 2015*, gives the details of the CRM 2015 client object model. You will learn about web resources using client-side scripting, and you will access CRM web services using client-side code and business rules.

Chapter 4, *Working with Processes*, explains the different type of processes with their usages. This chapter will explain how to use these processes to automate different business requirements. You will learn to develop a library management system using processes.

Chapter 5, Working with CRM SDK, explains the Microsoft Dynamics CRM extendibility architecture and the CRM SDK components. You will learn to use CRM web services methods using the early bound and late bound programming models.

Chapter 6, Extending Microsoft Dynamics CRM 2015 will help you to learn plug-in development in CRM 2015 and to understand how they are executed via event execution pipelines. You will learn how to write and deploy plug-ins using different plug-in components.

Chapter 7, Creating a Project Tracking Application, demonstrate the xRM capability of CRM 2015. You will learn to set up another sample application to track and maintain a project life cycle using the out-of-the-box capabilities of CRM 2015.

Chapter 8, Introduction to Mobile Client and Microsoft Dynamics Marketing, explains the different CRM 2015 mobile clients and their features. You will also learn to set up the Microsoft Dynamics Marketing add-on and use it.

Appendix A, Data Model for Client Entities, provides fields that we are using in our client entity form.

Appendix B, Data Model for Account Entities, provides fields that we are using on account entity form.

What you need for this book

You will need the following:

- Microsoft Dynamics CRM 2015 on premise or Online environment
- XrmToolBox Solution from `www.xrmtoolbox.com`
- Microsoft Windows Identity Model
- .Net 4.5.5
- Visual Studio 2012 or later and the .Net 4.5.2 developers pack
- Microsoft Dynamics CRM SDK for 2015

Who this book is for

This book targets skilled developers who want to build business-solution software and are new to application development in Microsoft Dynamics CRM.

Conventions

In this book, you will find a number of text styles that distinguish between different kinds of information. Here are some examples of these styles and an explanation of their meaning.

Code words in text, database table names, folder names, filenames, file extensions, pathnames, dummy URLs, user input, and Twitter handles are shown as follows: "Microsoft Dynamics CRM 2015 application navigation is controlled by `SiteMap.xml`."

A block of code is set as follows:

```
if (typeof(HIMBAP) == "undefined") {
    HIMBAP = {
        __namespace: true
    };
}
```

New terms and **important words** are shown in bold. Words that you see on the screen, for example, in menus or dialog boxes, appear in the text like this: "In case of CRM online, we can check the consumption of the resources by navigating to **Settings | Administration | Resources In User**."

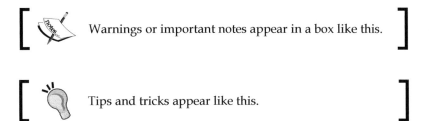

> Warnings or important notes appear in a box like this.

> Tips and tricks appear like this.

Reader feedback

Feedback from our readers is always welcome. Let us know what you think about this book—what you liked or disliked. Reader feedback is important for us as it helps us develop titles that you will really get the most out of.

To send us general feedback, simply e-mail feedback@packtpub.com, and mention the book's title in the subject of your message.

If there is a topic that you have expertise in and you are interested in either writing or contributing to a book, see our author guide at www.packtpub.com/authors.

Customer support

Now that you are the proud owner of a Packt book, we have a number of things to help you to get the most from your purchase.

Downloading the example code

You can download the example code files from your account at `http://www.packtpub.com` for all the Packt Publishing books you have purchased. If you purchased this book elsewhere, you can visit `http://www.packtpub.com/support` and register to have the files e-mailed directly to you.

Downloading the color images of this book

We also provide you with a PDF file that has color images of the screenshots/diagrams used in this book. The color images will help you better understand the changes in the output. You can download this file from `http://www.packtpub.com/sites/default/files/downloads/4158EN_ColorImages.pdf`.

Errata

Although we have taken every care to ensure the accuracy of our content, mistakes do happen. If you find a mistake in one of our books—maybe a mistake in the text or the code—we would be grateful if you could report this to us. By doing so, you can save other readers from frustration and help us improve subsequent versions of this book. If you find any errata, please report them by visiting `http://www.packtpub.com/submit-errata`, selecting your book, clicking on the **Errata Submission Form** link, and entering the details of your errata. Once your errata are verified, your submission will be accepted and the errata will be uploaded to our website or added to any list of existing errata under the Errata section of that title.

To view the previously submitted errata, go to `https://www.packtpub.com/books/content/support` and enter the name of the book in the search field. The required information will appear under the **Errata** section.

Piracy

Piracy of copyrighted material on the Internet is an ongoing problem across all media. At Packt, we take the protection of our copyright and licenses very seriously. If you come across any illegal copies of our works in any form on the Internet, please provide us with the location address or website name immediately so that we can pursue a remedy.

Please contact us at copyright@packtpub.com with a link to the suspected pirated material.

We appreciate your help in protecting our authors and our ability to bring you valuable content.

Questions

If you have a problem with any aspect of this book, you can contact us at questions@packtpub.com, and we will do our best to address the problem.

1

Getting Started with Microsoft Dynamics CRM 2015

This chapter will help you understand the basics of Microsoft Dynamics CRM 2015. We will be discussing an overview of the new features released in CRM 2015 and also we will be discussing the upcoming features of CRM 2015 Update 1. In a later chapter, we will work on these features in detail and will see how we can use them for implementing different requirements. We will discuss the following topics in this chapter:

- Introduction to Microsoft Dynamics CRM 2015
- The deployment options available
- Online versus on-premise
- The available clients
- The software and hardware requirements
- The upgrade options
- The license model in Microsoft Dynamics CRM 2015
- The new features in Microsoft Dynamics CRM 2015

Based on the Microsoft Dynamics CRM road map presented in Microsoft Dynamics Convergence 2014, Microsoft announced general availability of Microsoft Dynamics CRM 2015 code name "Vega" on November 30, 2014. This is a major release for Microsoft Dynamics CRM after Microsoft Dynamics CRM 2013 release. Microsoft Dynamics CRM 2015 introduced many new exciting features for every type of CRM users such as Administrators, Functional and Technical Consultants, and Developers. Microsoft Dynamics CRM 2015 also enhanced some of the features that were released in Microsoft Dynamics CRM 2013. After the CRM 2015 release, another release that is lined up is CRM 2015 Update 1, which will introduce another set of exciting features. We will be discussing more on these features in a later topic.

Similar to the earlier version, this time, the Microsoft CRM development team did not redesign the Microsoft Dynamics CRM interface. All the UI and navigation is the same as that of Microsoft Dynamics CRM 2013, except the new navigation group added with the advance find button and global search box on the top navigation bar. The new navigation group has also added for accessing security features:

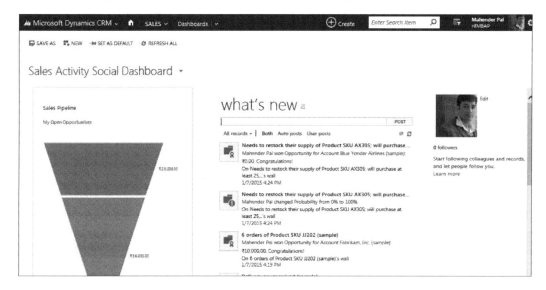

Microsoft Dynamics CRM 2015 mainly added features to Sales with the **Dynamics Marketing** and **Social Listening** components. Microsoft Dynamics CRM 2015 also supports accessing its records using voice commands. **Cortana**, an intelligent personal assistant, which is a part of Windows Phone 8.1, can be used for Microsoft Dynamics CRM 2015. So, the customers who use Windows Phone 8.1 can use voice commands to create activity records, such as appointments, tasks, phone, search and navigate to entity records.

 This app can be downloaded from `http://windows.microsoft.com/en-us/windows-8/cortana`.

Deployment options

The different Microsoft Dynamics CRM 2015 deployment options can be considered based on the resources available. The following are the different options available for Microsoft Dynamics CRM 2015:

- **On-premise**: Microsoft Dynamics CRM 2015 on-premise is installed on our own server, so we need IT and infrastructure support to install and set up CRM 2015 and the related software applications. If we have the infrastructure that is compatible with CRM 2015, we can reuse it; otherwise, we need to set up a new server or virtual servers based on our requirement.

 Refer to the software and hardware requirement section for details on hardware and software requirements for CRM 2015.

The Microsoft Dynamics CRM 2015 on-premise server is available with two editions as follows:

- ° **Workgroup edition**: This is limited to five users and one organization.
- ° **Server edition**: This involves unlimited users and multiple organizations.

 More information on CRM 2015 servers can be found at https://technet.microsoft.com/en-us/library/hh699677.aspx.

- **Online**: Microsoft Dynamics CRM 2015 online, also known as cloud, is hosted on Microsoft's data centers. All the required infrastructure is handled by Microsoft, so we don't require any servers. Microsoft also provides access to nonproduction instances, which can be used for development or testing purposes based on the number of users in our production organization. Currently, we need to have 25 or more professional USLs to get nonproduction instances.
- **Hosted**: Hosted deployment is a mix of on-premise and online deployment. Here, a CRM application is hosted on a third-party vendor instead of Microsoft and the services are dependent on the service agreement with the CRM service provider.

Microsoft Dynamics CRM on-premise versus online

This is a very common question that comes during the initial planning of Microsoft Dynamics CRM implementation on the customer side. Which option should be selected by us depends on various factors, such as cost, data storage, database maintenance, scalability, and company size. For example, if we are a small company with a limited number of resources, it would be easy to set up our CRM online organization compared to on-premise, where first we need a place for the infrastructure. In the upcoming sections we will discuss the different points comparing on-premise and online versions.

Database access

Microsoft Dynamics CRM 2015 on-premise provides full control over the database. Since the application is installed on our own servers, we are always free to access the CRM database for taking backups, restoring in case of failure, profiling, SSRS reporting, accessing records, and so on. We can increase database stores at any time, if required.

 A direct update to the CRM table is not supported by Microsoft Dynamics CRM 2015.

However, in the case of Microsoft Dynamics CRM 2015 online, we don't get flexibility. We cannot access our CRM database, so backup and any type of database troubleshooting is not possible directly; we need to always work with Microsoft support for these activities. Our database might be also hosted outside of our country because there are limited datacentres available. You can check CRM online datacenter lists from `https://www.microsoft.com/online/legal/v2/en-us/MOS_PTC_Geo_Boundaries.htm`. Microsoft Dynamics CRM 2015 online provides a default size of 5 GB, which is increased by 2.5 GB for every professional user's subscription at no extra cost until 50 GB. If we need more space after that, we need to pay for every GB.

 In the case of CRM online, we can check the consumption of the resources by navigating to **Settings** | **Administration** | **Resources In User**.

New updates

In case of Microsoft Dynamics CRM on-premise deployment, we have full control over installing new updates, patches, and upgrades. So, if you are using an older version and want to continue using the same version, you have the choice. However, you will not be able to use the new features that are introduced with the latest version. In case of online, we don't need to take care of installing the new updates. All the new updates, patches installation and upgrades are done by Microsoft. In case of major updates, we can schedule a specific date when we want to update our organization. CRM admins first need to approve the update before the update can occur, whereas all the rollups or hotfixes are applied without any schedule information.

 It is recommend to keep your organization updated with the latest updates.

Integration

Both online and on-premise deployments provide great flexibility to integrate with other applications. We can utilize Microsoft Dynamics CRM web services/SDK for integration. We have the option to run our server side code known as plug-in full trust and partial trust (also known as sandbox) in on-premise, but online deployment only supports partial trust. In case of online deployment, we can only use HTTP and HTTPS protocol to access web resources, whereas in case of on-premise, we don't have any restrictions.

Availability

In any business application, availability is a very critical factor. Microsoft Dynamics CRM on-premise availability is totally dependent on our network resources, whereas Microsoft provides a 99.9 percent uptime service-level agreement, so we don't need to bother about our network downtime.

Security

Microsoft provides a very secure and reliable environment for online deployment. There are security policies applied through Microsoft security programme to keep customer's data highly secure and threat free. To maintain the physical security of the data, multiple security checks are applied at different levels. You can refer to further details about how CRM online maintains security at `https://technet.microsoft.com/en-us/library/jj134081.aspx`. However, in the case of CRM on-premise, we are responsible for the implementation of the security measures for unauthorized data access and privacy.

CRM add-ons

Microsoft Dynamics CRM online deployment comes with some free add-ons such as free Bing Maps key, inside view, and social listening. But we need to pay for these add-ons in the case of on-premise deployment.

 Social listening will be replaced with social engagement, which will provide new and enhanced social media tools.

Extension and customization

Both Microsoft Dynamics CRM on-premise and online provide great flexibility for customizing and extending its capabilities. We can utilize the solutions for deploying changes from one environment to another easily. Microsoft Dynamics CRM provides many out-of-the-box business entities, but if required we can create custom entities to fulfil our specific business requirement. We can create an unlimited number of entities in case of on-premise, but Microsoft Dynamics CRM online only supports 300 custom entities per organization. We can create up to 200 workflows/dialogs in case of online deployment, but there is no limitation in on-premise.

Microsoft Dynamics CRM 2015 clients

The Microsoft Dynamics CRM 2015 application can be accessed using different types of clients with different versions. These clients provide a unique set of features with the common features available to all clients. We will now take look at the clients available for CRM 2015.

Web client

The Microsoft Dynamics CRM 2015 web client provides access to CRM applications through browsers. The following are the web clients that are supported by Microsoft Dynamics CRM 2015:

- Internet explorer 10 and 11
- Mozilla Firefox (latest publicly released version)
- Google Chrome (latest publicly released version)
- Apple Safari (latest publicly released version)

Outlook client

One of the most important reasons for easy adaptability of Microsoft Dynamics CRM is the out-of-the-box integration with Microsoft Office outlook. Microsoft Dynamics CRM 2015 provides flexibility to access CRM 2015 applications using the office outlook client. There are two types of clients available for outlook:

- Online client
- Offline client

For CRM 2015,the following outlook versions are supported:

- Microsoft office 2010
- Microsoft office 2013

Mobile client

We can also access Microsoft Dynamics CRM 2015 using mobile and tablet devices. There are different clients available for different mobile devices:

- Windows mobile client (MOCA)
- iPhone client
- Android client
- Tablet client

Some of the apps for mobile clients are provided by Microsoft and some of the apps are provided by other vendors. We will be discussing mobile client in the last chapter of this book.

Software and hardware requirements

Microsoft Dynamics CRM 2015 does not support many software applications such as Windows Server 2008 and 2008 R2 server with all the versions of Windows Small Business Servers. It also does not support Internet Explorer 8 and 9. Just like its earlier version, Microsoft Dynamics CRM 2015 also supports 64-bit machines. The following table provides minimum software and hardware requirements for Microsoft Dynamics CRM 2015:

The *hardware requirements* are as follows:

Component	Minimum	Recommended
Processor	This needs a x64 architecture or compatible dual-core 1.5 GHz processor	A quad-core x64 architecture 2 GHz CPU or higher
Memory	A 2 GB RAM	An 8 GB RAM or more
Hard disk	10 GM space	40 GM or more

The *software requirements* are articulated in the following table:

Components	Version and Edition
Windows Server	Windows Server 2012 64 bit (Standard, Developer) Windows Server 2012 R2 64 bit (Standard, Datacenter)
SQL Server 2008 64-bit	SQL Server 2012 64-bit Developer Standard Enterprise Datacenter Business Intelligence
Microsoft SQL Server Reporting Services	This is based on supported Microsoft SQL Server editions
Internet Information Services	8.0,8.5

 You can refer to `https://technet.microsoft.com/en-us/library/hh699671.aspx` to get complete details on hardware and software requirements.

Upgrade options

Microsoft Dynamics CRM 2015 provides different upgrade options based on the deployment used. In the case of on-premise, the following are the options available:

- In place
- Migration upgrade

In place

If we are using Microsoft Dynamics CRM 2015 compatible servers, we can go with the in place upgrade option, but this option is not recommended for upgrade because it involves a great risk of downtime in case of any issues occurring during upgrade. It can also corrupt the complete database, so it is always recommended that you create a VM from the existing CRM deployment and do a trial upgrade there instead of directly upgrading the real CRM servers. Also, we should always keep a complete copy of the CRM database before planning an upgrade.

Migration upgrade

This option requires a different server setup, but still this is the recommended method of doing an upgrade because it involves less downtime. We can use two methods of migration upgrade. One option is to use different servers for the CRM application and CRM database. The other option is to use different servers for CRM application and use the existing CRM database server that is compatible with Microsoft Dynamics CRM 2015 SQL server requirements.

We can select the upgrade option based on the infrastructure, but the only possible upgrade path to Microsoft Dynamics CRM 2015 is from Microsoft Dynamics CRM 2013 Service Pack 1 (SP1). This means if we are using Microsoft Dynamics CRM version earlier then 2013, we need to first upgrade to Microsoft Dynamics CRM 2013:

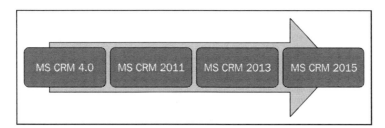

So, let's say if you are using Microsoft Dynamics CRM 4.0 and want to upgrade to Microsoft Dynamics CRM 2015, you need to follow sequential setups explained in the preceding screenshot to upgrade. It is recommended to clean the organization's data before upgrading to CRM 2015. Some of the upcoming functionality depreciated from CRM 2013 version, so if we are upgrading to CRM 2015 from CRM 2011, we need to clean the organization's data based on these points.

Cleaning all 2007 endpoints

Support for Microsoft Dynamics CRM 4.0 web service endpoints (known as 2007 endpoints) is not supported by CRM 2015, so if you are using 2007 endpoints in your code, you need to update your code to use **OData** endpoints or **SOAP using 2011 WCF** endpoints before upgrade.

> You can use the legacy tool to detect 2007 endpoints in your organization. You can download the legacy tool from `http://go.microsoft.com/fwlink/p/?LinkID=309565`.

Support for the Microsoft Dynamics CRM 4.0 object model

Microsoft Dynamics CRM 2015 does not support the CRM 4.0 object model. So, if there is any client-side code written using the CRM 4.0 object model that needs to be changed to a similar CRM 2015 object model, we can use the CRM 2013 custom code validate tool to detect scripting, which is written using CRM 4.0 standards.

> You can download the Microsoft Dynamics CRM 2013 custom code validation tool from `http://www.microsoft.com/en-in/download/details.aspx?id=30151`.

Licensing model for Microsoft Dynamics CRM 2015

Microsoft Dynamics CRM 2015 have a flexible licensing model for both on-premise and online customers, which enables customers to mix and match new licenses based on how they use the CRM 2015 functionality. CRM 2015 on-premise and online deployment offers the following types of licenses:

- Enterprise (online only)
- Basic
- Professional
- Essential

The following table provides details about these license-type features:

License type	Description
Enterprise	This license provides full access to Sales, Marketing and Service features, Microsoft Dynamics Marketing, and Parature.
Basic	This license is essential and provides access to system entities, such as accounts, contact, case, lead, reporting, and personal dashboard.
Professional	This license provides full access to Microsoft Dynamics CRM 2013 functionality and any custom application.
Essential	This license includes access to the Microsoft Dynamics CRM 2013 system, activities, custom entities, and any custom application. This license also provides access to SDK.

Access to Microsoft Dynamics CRM 2015 using different clients is available in all license types. Now, in CRM 2015, there is no need to buy external user licenses for external users (the users who are not employees or affiliates) unless they are not using Microsoft Dynamics CRM 2015 clients to access applications, an external user license is covered under server license for on-premise. So, if we are required to develop any portal application to expose CRM data to our customers, it can be done without an external user license.

 You can download the licensing guide from PartnerSource at
`https://www.microsoft.com/en-us/download/details.aspx?id=45904.`

The new features in Microsoft Dynamics CRM 2015

Microsoft Dynamics CRM 2015 introduced many new features with some new enhancements to the existing features, such as business rules, business process flow, dashboard capability in the tablet client, and global search for web and outlook clients.

Global search

Although this feature was originally introduced in Microsoft Dynamics CRM 2013 for CRM for the tablet client, Microsoft Dynamics CRM 2015 made it available to the web and outlook clients. Global search is based on the old method of searching CRM records using the quick find view, where we can add find columns in the quick find view on the basis of the columns we want to search the entity record using global search.

We can use global search using the search textbox under the top navigation bar in the web client and using the **Search** option under the **Home** tab in CRM for the outlook client. At present, the maximum number of entities allowed in search is 10. We can configure it by navigating to **Settings | Administration | System Settings | Set up Quick Find**:

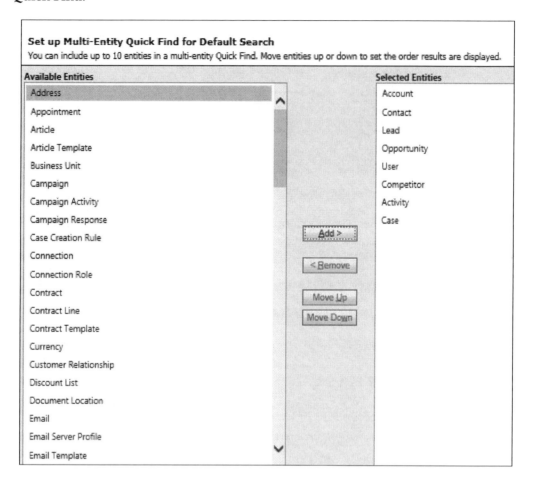

We can also configure the quick find record limit using **Enable Quick Find record limits** under **Settings | Administration | System Settings | Set up Quick Find**. By default, **Yes** is selected; this means when more than 10,000 records are found during search, it will display a message box to make the search more selective. Once we have the result, we can also filter it based on a specific entity using the **Filter With** drop-down menu:

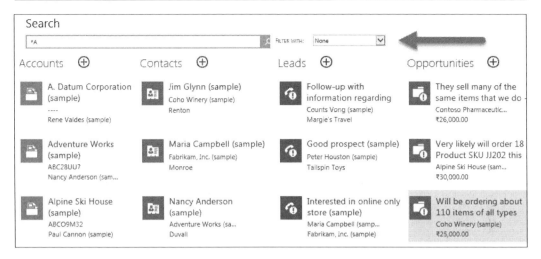

Once the result is listed, you can open the entity record by simply selecting the record or can create the new entity record using the plus sign.

Business rules enhancement

This feature was also released in Microsoft Dynamics CRM 2013 initially, which helps nontechnical CRM users to implement no code business logic. While working on different business requirements, we need to implement many business-specific validations. But still, there are some generic data validations, such as hide/show form fields, making fields based on some business logic, and setting the field's default values. The business rules help us to implement these types of validation from CRM UI. The business rules can be added/modified by navigating to **Settings | Solution | Components | Entities | Entity | Business Rules**. We can also create/ modify the business rules from the entity form editor using the **Business Rules** button under the **Home** tab in the entity form:

The business rule in Microsoft Dynamics CRM 2015 now provides the following features:

- Support for both server and client-side logic
- Both AND and OR logical operators are available now
- If and else conditionals for branching
- It supports the following actions:
    - Show an error message
    - Set the field value
    - Set the business required
    - Set visibility
    - Set the default value
    - Lock or unload the field:

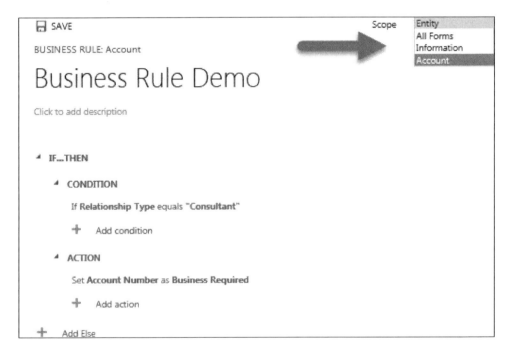

Once the business rule is defined, we need to set up its scope. A new option, **Entity**, is added under the scope drop down to make business logic available on the server side. If the entity option is selected, the business logic will fire on the server during the operation on the records from all the clients including any custom integration code.

Property exception handling should be implemented in the server side code, if **Show error message** is used in the business rules actions.

Business process flow

Every business has some predefined business process workflows that they follow in day-to-day business. Let's take a very common scenario of the approval process. Let's assume you are a technical consultant and working in a multinational company. You need to apply for a one week vacation. As soon as you apply for leave, it will initiate a leave approval behind the scenes, which may contain different stages and subapproval of your team lead, your project manager, your project delivery manager. We can implement similar business requirements in Microsoft Dynamics CRM 2015 using the business process flow. The business process flow was introduced in CRM 2011 Polaris release initially and enhanced in Microsoft Dynamics CRM 2015. Business process flow is basically a guided approach to complete any business process, which may have different stages based on business requirements. Microsoft Dynamics CRM 2015 provides a rich editor to design for designing business process flow. You can create a business process flow by navigating to **Settings | Process | New** and selecting **Business Process Flow** under the **Category** drop-down menu. We can have up to 30 stages and 30 steps per business process flow:

We can include multiple entities in the same business process flow and take the process flow from one entity to another entity. We can include up to five maximum entities in the business process flow. The following is the screenshot of the out-of-the-box **Lead to Opportunity Sales Process** business process flow:

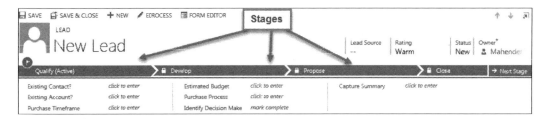

Microsoft Dynamics CRM 2015 added support for branching logic, which allows us to switching the process stage using if conditions, the logical AND and OR operator support, which allows us to group multiple conditions and support for interacting with the business process flow using client-side scripting for developers.

You can access `https://msdn.microsoft.com/en-us/library/dn817874.aspx` to get details about the scripting method available for the business process flow.

Hierarchy visualization

Another new feature added in Microsoft Dynamics CRM 2015 is hierarchy visualization of your data. In Microsoft Dynamics CRM, we can associate entities using entity relationships. Hierarchical visualization provides logical visualization of the 1:N relationship or self-relationship between entities. At present, we can have only one hierarchical relationship per entity. While setting up a relationship, we can select whether we want to use this relationship as hierarchical using the **Hierarchical** dropdown.

Once the relationship is set up, we can navigate to **Hierarchy Settings | New** under the entity node to create the hierarchy setting. As soon as the hierarchy setting is created per entity, the new button will not be available anymore because we can set up only one hierarchy setting per entity:

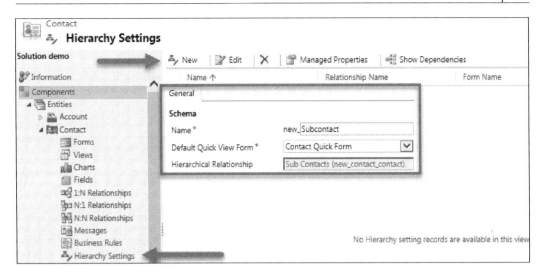

Once the hierarchy setting is set up and the record is associated, we can see a logical relationship visualization using the hierarchy icon on the entity grid view or entity form. The following screen represents the hierarchy visualization for the parent account. We can see that Adventure Works (Sample) is a parent account and it has two child accounts. Data is represented in tiles, where a maximum of four fields are allowed. The data fields are represented from a default quick view form. If it has more than four fields, then only the first four fields are used for display:

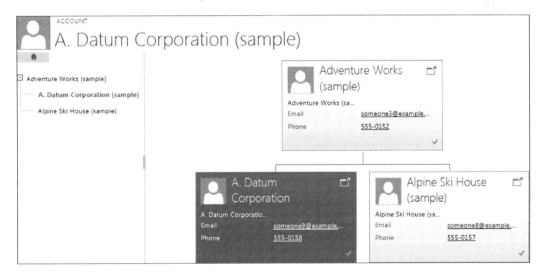

Two new query operators are also added for querying hierarchical data, which are explained as follows:

- **Under**: This is used to get the list of entities, which are child entities of a specific entity, for example, list out all subaccounts under a particular account
- **Note Under**: This is used for reverse of the under operator

Hierarchical security

Microsoft Dynamics CRM provides a robust security model, but sometimes developers still need to write custom extensions to the security model to fulfil complex business requirements. Microsoft Dynamics CRM 2015 introduced a new hierarchical security feature that works with the existing security model and reduces the development and maintenance costs for implementing complex security requirements. There are two security models available in hierarchical security in Microsoft Dynamics CRM 2015, which are as follows:

- Manager
- Position

Manager hierarchy

The manager hierarchical security model is based on the reporting hierarchy that can be implemented using the manager lookup in the system user entity:

This security model facilitates managers to access the data that their reports have access to. Let's take an example of two business users Mahender Pal and Vikram Singh. Both are in the same business unit and Vikram Singh is a sales person who has user level create and read access on the account entity. Now, let's say to implement the reporting hierarchy, we need to assign Vikram as the manager of Mahender.

However, since Vikram has only user level read access on the account entity, he can't access entity records owned by Mahender's unless it is shared or assigned to him or a team where he is a member. So, if he tries to access **Active Accounts**, it will only show records owned by him. Now, let's enable the hierarchy security by navigating to **Settings | Security** and then click on **Save and Close**:

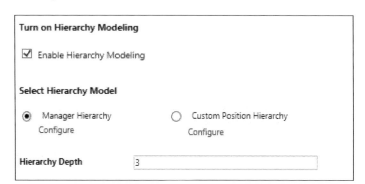

As soon as the manager hierarchical security model is applied, Vikram will be able to access the record owned by his report:

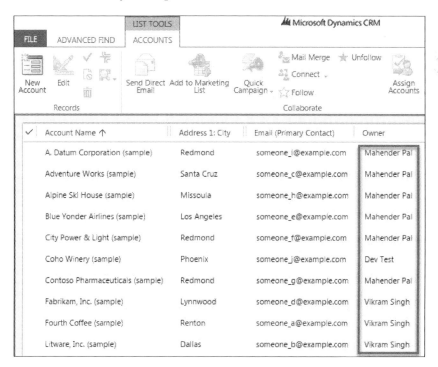

Now, Vikram will have **Read**, **Write**, **Update**, **Append**, **AppendTo** access to Mahender's data, who is direct report to Vikram, and read only access to Dev Test's data, who is non direct report to Vikram. While configuring the hierarchy security settings, we can define the depth property, which decides up to what level we can access the records.

Position

The position hierarchy security model is based on the new position hierarchy that is added in Microsoft Dynamics CRM 2015. A CRM admin can define different job positions based on the business requirement and can assign the user from a different business unit to a particular position. We can add multiple users to any position, but any user can be associated with only one position. A higher position user can access the data of a lower position user similar to manager hierarchy security model irrespective of their business units. So, the higher positions will have **Read**, **Write**, **Update**, **Append**, **AppendTo** access to the lower positions' data and nondirect higher positions will have read-only access to the lower positions' data. We can define positions by navigating to **Settings** | **Security** | **Position**:

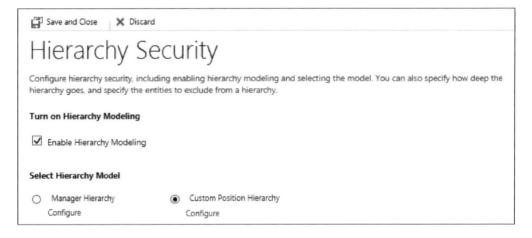

Once the positions are defined, we can configure the position hierarchy security module by selecting **Custom Position Hierarchy** as shown in the preceding screenshot.

New fields for calculation

While working on business requirements, most of the time we need to calculate values using different attributes and need to store them in other fields. For these type of requirements, CRM admins need to depend on CRM developers to write code. However, with the release of Microsoft Dynamics CRM 2015, CRM admins can utilize calculated and rollup fields for calculation. Next, we will introduce two new types of fields.

Calculated fields

Calculated fields are very useful to set the calculated value to any field. Calculated fields can be used with the following data types:

- **Single Line of Text**
- **Option Set**
- **Two Options**
- **Whole Number**
- **Decimal Number**
- **Currency**
- **Date and Time**

While we create a new field, we can select **Field Type** as **Calculated** to set up a calculated field, as shown in the following screenshot:

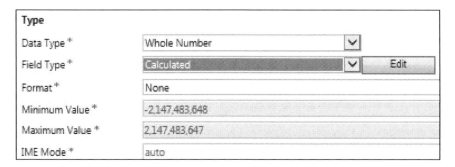

To set up a calculated formula first, we need to save the field definition and then we can click on the **Edit** button to set up the formula. Calculated provides an editor similar to the business rules. Let's take a scenario where we are a service-based company and allow our customers to set trail for thirty days. So, we can create two fields: trail start and trail end.

Now, we want to implement the logic when the trial date is saved, trial end data should be calculated automatically with an addition of 30 days. We can easily implement this using the calculated field, so we can set the trail end date as the calculated field and can use the formula as shown in the following screenshot to calculate the value of the trail end date field:

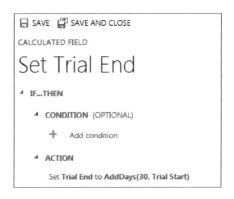

The calculated fields are calculated in a synchronous manner. So, as soon as we create our entity record, if the trail start date is there, the trail end date will be calculated automatically. The calculated fields are always read only:

Trial Start	3/1/2015
Trial End	🔒 3/31/2015

We can refer to the calculated fields in charts and view, but at present we can only use up to 10 calculated attributes in charts and views. The calculated fields are also not available offline at present.

Rollup field

This is another type of calculated field added in Microsoft Dynamics CRM 2015, which is used for record-level aggregation from related entities record. Rollup fields are calculated using asynchronous system jobs after a 12-hour interval. If the required system administrator can configure it to run during a different interval, we can use the rollup field with the following data types:

- **Whole Number**
- **Decimal Number**
- **Currency**
- **Date and Time**

Rollup fields can be created similar to the calculated fields. We just need to select **Rollup** under the **Field Type** dropdown as shown in the following screenshot:

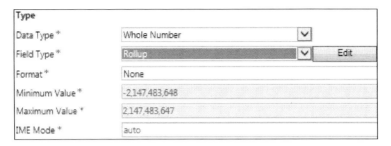

Microsoft Dynamics CRM 2015 automatically adds two more fields for every rollup field that is created:

- <Field SchemaName>_**Date**: This is a date time field, which stores the date/time information when the rollup field was last calculated

- <Field SchemaName>_**State**: This is the integer field that stores the state of the rollup field

Rollup fields are also available as read only in entity form. Once the rollup field is created, we can click on the **Edit** button to set up the formula for the rollup field. The rollup field can be used in different scenarios, for example, let's say we want to count the number of contacts for a particular account. We can simply create a rollup field and setup the formula as shown in the following screenshot:

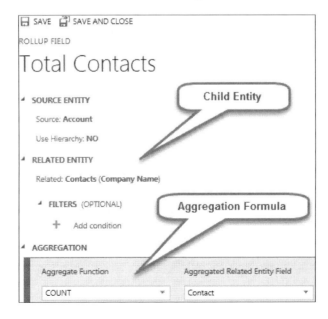

We can have 100 rollup fields per Microsoft Dynamics CRM 2015 organization and the entity can have up to 10 rollup fields, which can be used in charts, views, and reports.

New capability for mobile client

With the release of CRM 2015, new offline capabilities are added in CRM for the mobile client. This feature allows us to create the record in draft mode, which is not saved to the server yet. When the device is connected to server, the record will be synched to the server. The new dashboard support is also added to tablets. We will be discussing more on the mobile client in a later chapter.

Product catalog enhancement

Microsoft Dynamics CRM also provides a product catalog to store the product or service information. This product catalog provides different out-of-the-box features such as configuring products, defining discount list, setting unit groups, and maintaining a price list based on the different scenarios.

With CRM 2015, many new product catalog enhancement features have been released such as:

- Support for Product Families
- Define Product Properties at Family level
- Define Product Bundles
- Price List based on Territory
- New System Setting for Product
- Custom Price Calculation
- Support for Cross Sell and Up Sell

With CRM 2015, we can use the product family for grouping. The product family allows us to define product properties as well, which is inherited by products when added to the product family. The product family is useful especially when we want to combine similar category products in one group:

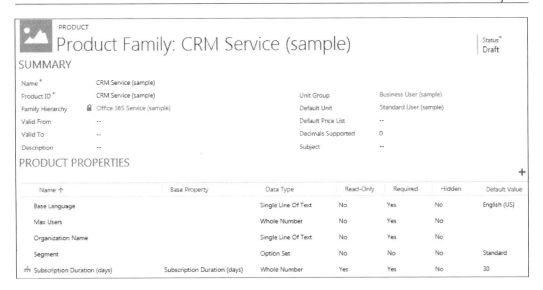

In the preceding screenshot, we can see an example of the product family, where we have different properties such as base language and max users. Another enhancement in the product catalog is the product bundle which is similar to product kits. The bundle provides more flexibility than kits used in the earlier version. We can configure if the product is required or not while selling the bundle.

Microsoft Dynamics CRM 2015 added another feature to set up product suggestions that can be used for cross sell and up sell. While setting the product, we can add related products and define their **Sales Relationship Type** as shown in the following screenshot:

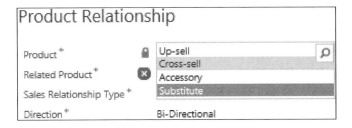

When the product is added in opportunity or quote or order, all the related products available under the suggestion box can be displayed by clicking on the **Suggestion** link. Microsoft Dynamics CRM 2015 also added new settings for the product catalog. For example, we can configure to set the default pricelist based on the in-built rule, which will set the pricelist based on the default price list defined for territories:

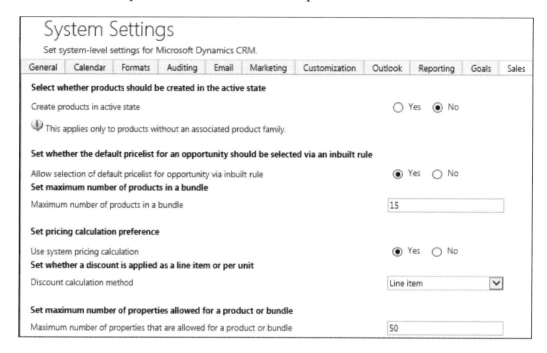

Microsoft Dynamics CRM 2015 also added a new method to define the custom pricing. Now CRM developers can write SDK code to use custom pricing, when the default system pricing is overridden.

Field-level security enhancement

Sometimes we may want to hide some specific field values from a specific CRM user or group of users. Field-level security helps us to implement this requirement. This feature was initially released with Microsoft Dynamics CRM 2011, but it was applicable to custom fields only. With the release of Microsoft Dynamics CRM 2015, we can now use field-level security with the system field as well. We manage field-level security by creating field-level security profile and adding user or team to that profile. We will find a default **System Administrator** profile, which has access to all the secured fields:

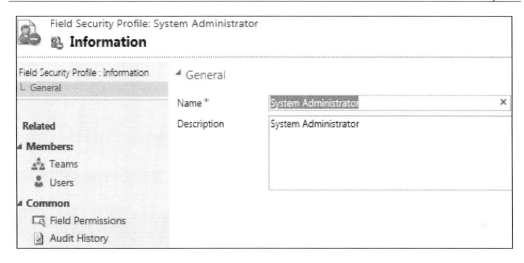

By default, all users with the system administrator role are added to this profile automatically. This profile can't be modified or deleted.

Creating custom help

Microsoft Dynamics CRM 2015 added another true xRM feature, which allows the CRM admin to configure custom help URL in CRM UI. We can navigate to **Settings | Administration | System Settings | General** and configure custom help URLs:

Once this is configured, when a user clicks on the **Help** button from any entity record or grid, a new tab opens that displays the custom help dialog. We can also configure entity-level custom help URL settings by navigating to **Settings | Customizations | Customize the System**:

This is where we can select our entity where we want to use our **Use custom Help** dialog. First, we need to enable the **Use custom Help** option as shown in the preceding screenshot. After this, when the CRM user clicks on the **Help** button for that entity, your custom help will be displayed.

Disabling the welcome screen

Microsoft Dynamics CRM provides an overview wizard with the welcome screen for the user when they start Microsoft Dynamics CRM the first time. Although the welcome screen contains an option to select **Don't show me this again**, it will still appear if you start CRM from another machine or use a new browser window:

Microsoft Dynamics CRM 2015 introduced a new setting, which can be used to disable this screen for complete organization. We can navigate to **Settings** | **Administration** | **System settings** | **General** | **Set whether users see navigation tour**.

Nested quick create forms

The quick create form feature was also released with CRM 2013, which allows us to create entity records quickly by entering key fields, which we can customize. We can use a quick create form using the **Create** button on the top navigation bar and **New** button from the lookup and subgrids.

Quick create forms support form scripts and business rules.

By default, quick create forms are only enabled for some of the entities, such as account, case, contact, competitor, lead, and opportunity. We can enable the quick create feature by navigating to **Settings | Customizations | Customize the System**. This action will open the default solution and then we can select our entity definition under **Components | Entities** and enabling the option **Allow quick create** under the **Data Services** section. Once this option is available, our entity will be visible under the quick create entity lists:

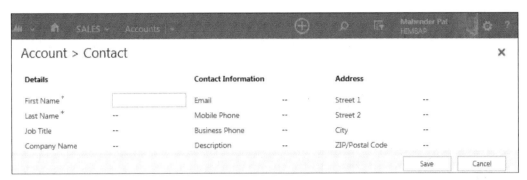

Microsoft Dynamics CRM 2015 enhanced the quick create feature by allowing nested quick create options. Let's take an example. If we are creating the account record and want to create a primary contact record on the fly, we can select the **New** option under the lookup window and it will open a new quick create form for the contact instead of opening the contact's main entity form.

New outlook configuration wizard

Microsoft Dynamics CRM 2015 introduced a new redesigned outlook configuration wizard. This configuration process is similar to the process in the previous version, but it is a more simplified version to CRM for outlook installation.

 You can download CRM for outlook from `http://www.microsoft.com/en-us/download/details.aspx?id=45015`.

Service Level Agreement enhancement

Microsoft Dynamics CRM 2015 also added a new enhancement to **Service Level Agreement (SLA)**. In Microsoft Dynamics CRM 2015, the new option pause and resume added SLA with timer support. This helps to track how long a case was on-hold or awaiting a customer response.

We can configure the status of the cases when SLA will be paused. To check this status, navigate to **Settings | Administration | System Settings** and configure the settings as shown in the following screenshot:

As we configured to status **On Hold** and **Waiting for Details**, the SLA timer will be paused during these statuses and when the status will be moved back to **In Progress** or **Researching**, the SLA timer will again start working.

Synchronization between CRM and Outlook or Exchange

Microsoft Dynamics CRM 2015 also added new fields for configuring the synchronization setting. New fields for appointment attachments, additional contact, and tasks can be configured as shown in the following screenshot:

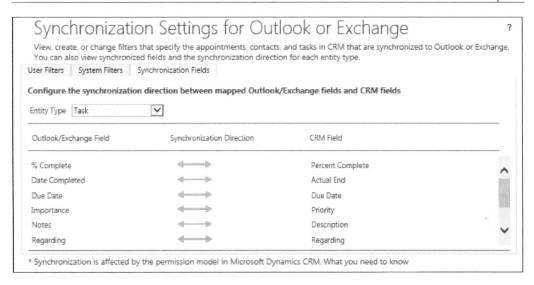

Navigate to **Settings** | **Email Configuration** | **Email Configuration Settings** to configure the additional fields.

Summary

In this chapter, we learned about new Microsoft Dynamics CRM 2015 features such as nested quick create enhanced business process flow and business rule enhancement. We discussed different deployment options with clients that we can use to access CRM 2015. We also discussed software and hardware requirements for CRM 2015 with different upgrade options. Finally, we discussed the new license model introduced in CRM 2015.

In the next chapter, we will learn the customization feature in MS CRM 2015 and start creating a sample application for the training company.

2
Customizing Microsoft Dynamics CRM 2015

This chapter is going to help you learn the customization features of Microsoft Dynamics CRM 2015. We will discuss different customization concepts and we will learn how we can customize Microsoft Dynamics CRM 2015 using tools available in the CRM UI. In this chapter we will be creating a sample application for a training company. We will discuss the following topics:

- Training solution scope
- Training solution design
- Understanding the customization concept
- Customizing Microsoft Dynamics CRM 2015
- Setting up a training catalog
- Understanding security
- Testing customization

Training solution scope

In this chapter, we are going to create a solution for a training company called **Diksha Trainers**. Diksha Trainers specialize in Microsoft technologies. They run different online and corporate training programs on different Microsoft technologies such as .Net, ASP.NET, Testing Automation, Microsoft Dynamics CRM, Ax, and GP trainings. They want to use Microsoft Dynamics CRM 2015 to manage their different training programs and other training requirements.

HIMBAP, a team of Dynamics CRM experts, is going to help Diksha Trainers and will use Microsoft Dynamics CRM as a platform to build a solution for them. We will be using Microsoft Dynamics CRM 2015 out-of-the-box features to customize and implement training application requirements. In the initial solution they want the following features:

- Capture training requests using e-mail, phone, and direct entry
- Should able to attach course contents to training requests
- Maintain a list of the corporate clients
- Maintain a list of the contacts from clients
- Maintain a list of trainers
- Maintain different technology training
- Send notification to client and trainers
- Complete solution for executing training requests

Training solution design

Microsoft Dynamics CRM 2015 provides a set of generic business entities, which provides specific attributes to map business requirements. For example, CRM contains an account entity that provides set of attributes best suited to storing data related to company, individual, clients, vendors, advertisers, agencies and so on. Similarly their CRM also has other out-of-the-box entities that can be reused to store different types of data. It is always recommended to first analyze customizable out-of-the-box entities to map our requirements, instead of creating new custom entities. Some out-of-the-box entities are also available that can be reused but can't be customized.

All of the required features for training solutions can be accomplished using out-of-the-box features only, so we are going to customize out-of-the-box entities to capture training-related information. We are going to map the following business entities with a custom training solution requirement.

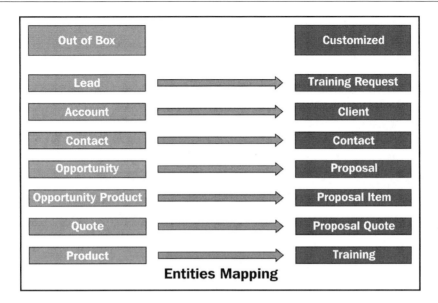

Entities Mapping

Business entities are out-of-the-box entities that are available in the Microsoft Dynamics CRM default installation without any customization.

We have mapped these entities based on the existing out-of-the-box fields and functionality. A **Lead** entity is used to capture basic information about the customer and their requirement details. We have different ways to collect this information; for example it can be collected from a sales person directly, who is working with the customer to win this sale. It can be also collected from the company website, most of the time via the contact us page. Apart from this, the lead can be also created from other communication channels such as phone calls or e-mails. Once the lead is qualified it can be converted to an **Opportunity**, which is a potential sale. In an **Opportunity**, we can attach a quotation for the project or service that we are going to sell to our customer. We are using leads to capture our training requirement-related information such as proposed timings for training, company details, number of attendees, technology in which training is required, and other basic details. Once the training request is qualified, we will be converting it to a proposal (opportunity) to add training- and pricing-related information. Once training is done we can close the proposal as Won.

Microsoft Dynamics CRM 2015 provides three status options for Opportunity: Open, Won, and Lost.

The **Account** and **Contact** entities in Microsoft Dynamics CRM 2015 are used to store customer information, where **Account** represents a particular organization or individual. So for example if we want to store any company details in Microsoft Dynamics CRM 2015, we can use an account entity and it has out-of-the-box fields to define company information. The **Contact** entity is used to store individual information: who is normally associated with company and works as an intermediate between vendor and company. We will be using the **Account** entity to store our client information and **Contact** entity will be used to store individuals from the company and other vendor information.

Microsoft Dynamics CRM 2015 allows us to store product or service-related information under the **Product** catalog. We are going to utilize the **Product** catalog to store our different training programs and pricing information.

The following diagram provides the training program process flow that we are going to implement in our training solution.

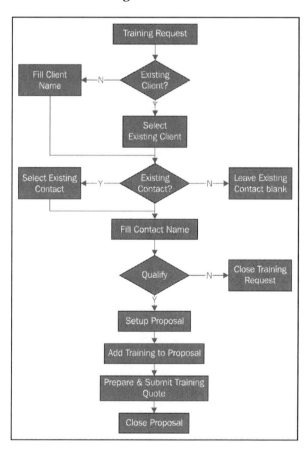

Training requests will be created from different sources to record the training requirements of the client. While creating the training request, we will be selecting a client from an existing lookup (if we are getting the new training requirement from an existing client); otherwise, if it's a new client, we will record their details. We will be also setting existing contact lookups if we are going to deal with an individual who is already part of our database for this training opportunity.

After the training request is qualified, we will create a training proposal and will add a training program to this proposal. We will be also adding a quotation to this proposal and will share this with client; once they agree on the pricing, we will execute training sessions. Once the training session is completed we will be closing the proposal record by changing the status to Won.

Understanding the customization concept

The customization feature in any business application helps us to modify it without writing any code. Just like earlier versions, Microsoft Dynamics CRM 2015 also provides great flexibility to **System Customizers** and **System Administrators** to customize CRM application capability and behavior using out-of-the-box tools. Just like other business applications available on the market, Microsoft is also making their CRM product more and more customizable for business users, who are basically non-technical users.

Most of the new features introduced in Microsoft Dynamics CRM 2015 can be customized from out-of-the-box designers available in the application and don't require any coding skills. If you are a Microsoft Dynamics CRM developer and have worked in it since the earlier versions, you might have noticed how Microsoft Dynamics CRM is moving to no-code customization. For example, using business rules a business user can define simple form field validation using an out-of-the-box designer, business process flow can be designed using the process designer, and global searches can be configured to search data in multiple entities.

While working in Microsoft Dynamics CRM 2015 we customize different components to map these components with our specific business processes. The following are the components that can be modified from the Microsoft Dynamics CRM 2015 application:

- Entity metadata, business rules, and solutions
- Business process flow, workflow, dialogs, and actions
- Dashboards, reports, and charts
- Sitemaps and command buttons

- Field-level security profiles and security roles
- Templates
- Web resources

[You need to have the System Customizer or System Administrator role to customize the Microsoft Dynamics CRM 2015 application.]

We will be working on customization features in later topics, where we will learn how we can change the Microsoft Dynamics CRM 2015 application UI, navigation, and other components.

Customizing Microsoft Dynamics CRM 2015

Now we have our design ready for our training solution, so we are going to customize Microsoft Dynamics CRM 2015 components. We will be customizing different components from those we discussed in the first topic.

Understanding application navigation

Microsoft Dynamics CRM 2015 has an easy user-friendly navigation. Microsoft Dynamics CRM 2015 follows the single-window concept, which means you don't need to switch your window to navigate to other parts of the application. We can use the top navigation bar in order to switch to different areas of the application.

Microsoft Dynamics CRM 2015 application navigation is controlled by SiteMap.xml, which defines the complete structure of application. Microsoft Dynamics CRM 2015's top navigation bar is divided in nodes called **Areas**.

In the earlier screenshot, **Sales**, **Service**, **Marketing**, **Settings** and **Help Center** all are examples of default areas. We can also set up our own custom area or can modify existing areas based on project requirements; a common example is to hide unwanted areas and give existing area more business-specific names.

Areas are further divided in **Groups** and **Sub Areas**. In the following screenshot, **My Work** and **Customers** are examples of groups and **Dashboards**, **What's New**, **Activities**, **Clients**, and **Contacts** are examples of sub areas.

You can also add your own custom groups and sub areas, or modify properties or existing groups or sub areas. You can refer to the Site Map XML from `https://msdn.microsoft.com/en-us/library/gg334430.aspx` to get for more details on Site Map structure.

The visibility of sub areas in the Site Map can be controlled using security roles and privilege. If all the sub areas of the group will be hidden, CRM will not show the corresponding group in navigation.

 You can refer to `https://msdn.microsoft.com/en-us/library/gg309286.aspx` for details on controlling sub areas using privileges.

We will be modifying Microsoft Dynamics CRM 2015 application navigation in a later topic.

Understanding solutions

Solution is a basic component of Microsoft Dynamics CRM 2015 and acts like a container for all customizable components.

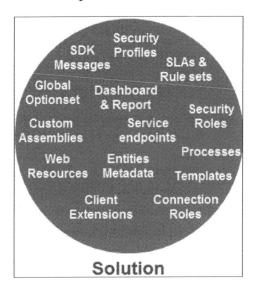

We can consider solution as a packager, used to take all of our customization and other customization components from one environment to another environment. Every Microsoft Dynamics CRM 2015 organization has one default solution that contains all the components that can be customized. Being a base solution all the customization done on the components is also reflected in the default solution.

Let's take an example. Say, we are working in a Microsoft Dynamics CRM 2015 implementation and we have set up three environments: development, QA and production. It is always recommended to create our own custom solution and do all of our customizing in our own solution, so that we can easily take only customized components from one environment to another.

There are two types of solution: managed and unmanaged. Unmanaged solutions allow us to create new and add existing components for customization. Once all the customization is done we can export our solution in a managed or unmanaged state.

Managed solutions can be uninstalled easily but there is no direct way to uninstall unmanaged solutions. While uninstalling or deleting unmanaged solution components, we need to keep in mind that data from related components will be deleted by CRM, so make sure you back-up your data first.

Managed solutions are normally locked solutions, which does not allow adding or modifying any new components, which is part of the managed solution. We can configure **Managed Property** for all unmanaged components (custom components created by **System Customizer** or **System Administrator**), as in the following screenshot.

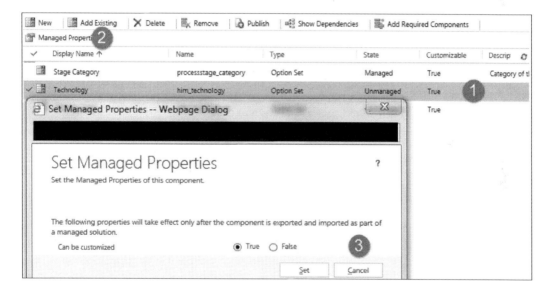

If we have selected **Can be Customized** as **False**, **System Customizer** and **System Administrator** won't be able to customize this component when it is exported as a managed solution.

Managed solutions are only recommended if you are an independent software vendor. But if you are developing solutions for yourself, it is recommended to use unmanaged solutions while transferring solutions from one environment to another—for example, from development environments to QA environments.

Currently, solutions also supports compatibility with earlier versions, so solutions exported from Microsoft Dynamics CRM 2013 or later can be imported into later CRM versions, but can't be imported in earlier versions of Microsoft Dynamics CRM—for example Microsoft Dynamics CRM 2011.

 You can get detailed information about solution compatibility from `https://msdn.microsoft.com/en-in/library/gg334576.aspx`

Creating the publisher

Before creating a solution, let's set up publisher. Publisher basically helps us to differentiate our customization from other vendors. It is required for creating solutions. Every organization contains a default publisher with the name of the organization. Solution publisher is also very critical in solution release management. A managed solution can only be updated with the same publisher. Let's take an example. Say we developed a solution in our development environment A and imported it as a managed solution into our QA environment. Now, if we want to do some more enhancements to our existing solution, we can edit our existing solution in the development environment. Once our change is done we can export it as a managed solution and import it to our QA environment only if the same publisher is used; we can't update our QA solution with a different publisher. While creating solutions we can define the following properties:

Property	Required	Description
Display Name	Y	Display label of the solution
Name	Y	Logical name of solution, used in programming
Description		Details about publisher
Prefix	Y	Customization prefix that we want to use
Option Value Prefix	Y	Used for option set values; it is generated automatically based on prefix characters

 You can't use **mscrm** as a prefix; it is a reserved keyword.

Use the following steps to create our publisher:

1. Navigate to **Settings** | **Customizations** | **Publishers** | **New**.

2. Use the following properties to create our publisher:
   ○ **Display Name**: HIMBAP
   ○ **Name**: **himbap** (It will be filled automatically after tabbing out from the display name field.)
   ○ **Prefix**: him
   ○ **Option Value Prefix**: Keep it default.

3. Click **Save and Close**.

Creating our solution

It is always recommended to create our custom solution and do all the customization there instead of customizing directly into the default solution. While creating the solution, we need to define some required properties. The following table provides a list of solution properties:

Property	Required	Description
Display Name	Y	User-friendly name of the solution.
Name	Y	Logical name of the solution that is used in code.
Publisher	Y	An entity that identifies the vendor of the solution. In publisher we can set up our unique prefix property with which we want to prefix all the custom objects and attributes created by us.
Configuration Page		A custom web resource to provide more detailed information about solutions.
Version	Y	Version information of the solution; we can define version up to four numbers separated by decimals and this version will be appended to the solution name when exported.

Property	Required	Description
Description		Details about solutions.
Installed On		Date information when the solution is installed or created.
Package Type		State of solution: managed or unmanaged.
Market Place		Market place information, if the solution is available on Microsoft market place.

Use the following steps to create your training solution:

1. Navigate to **Settings | Solutions | New** from the top navigation bar.
2. Enter the following solution properties:
   - **Display Name: Training Solution**
   - **Name: TrainingSolution** (It will be filled automatically, after tabbing out from the display name field)
   - **Publisher: HIMBAP**
   - **Version: 1.0.0.0**
3. Click on **Save**.

Adding components to our solution

Once our solution is created, we can create new or add existing components to our solution. Let's first add an account entity to our solution so that we can customize it to store our client information. Follow these steps to add an account entity:

1. Select **Entities** and click on the **Add Existing** button.

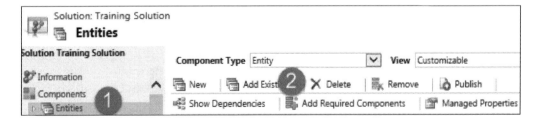

2. Select the **Account** entity under the entity list and click on the **Ok** button.
3. Select the **No, do not include required components** option in the **Missing Required Components** dialog and click on **Ok**.

When an existing component is added to a custom solution, CRM automatically detects related components and will display a dialog listing all the related components corresponding to the selected component. When a solution is imported into the target organization, all the related components should exist in the target system, as the account entity is available in every CRM installation, so we don't need to include dependencies But if any of the related components are missing from the target organization and are also not available in the source solution, the import process will fail. So, if related components are not available in the target organization, we should include them in our solution.

> We can also include required components using the **Add Required Components** button in the solution command bar.

While exporting solutions, CRM will also show the **Missing Required Components** dialog if the current solution is missing any related components.

Customizing entities

We need to do a different customization to entities, such as renaming the entity, changing entity form layouts, customizing fields or creating new fields, and changing navigations. So let's start customizing our out-of-the-box entities one by one.

Renaming entities

First we are going to rename all of our selected business entities based on the entity mapping diagram; for example we need to rename account to client, lead to training request, product to training, and opportunity entity to proposal. While renaming an entity, we need to modify the entity reference from all places such as entity information, in the attribute list if there is an attribute referencing entity name, all entity forms, entity views, entity-related messages (these messages are used by CRM to display information to the user; we can check entity messages by navigating to **Entity | Messages** under the solution), reports, and the navigation area.

We could rename entity references globally one by one or the other option we have is to use translations. We could export a translation XML file from Microsoft Dynamics CRM 2015 and rename labels based on the mapping table; we can re-import it back to Microsoft Dynamics CRM 2015.

Use the following step to use translation to rename business entities:

1. Navigate to **Settings | Solution** under the top navigation bar.

2. Double-click on **Training Solution** to open it.

3. Click on the **Export Translations** button solution command bar and save the file when prompted.

4. Extract the **CrmTranslations** folder, open **CrmTranslations.xml** and select the **Display Strings** sheet.

5. Click on the **Unprotect Sheet** ribbon button under the **Changes group** in the **REVIEW** menu.

6. Select **column C** and press *Ctrl + f* to open the **Find and Replace** dialog.

7. Search all entities one by one and rename them based on the **Entity Mapping** diagram.

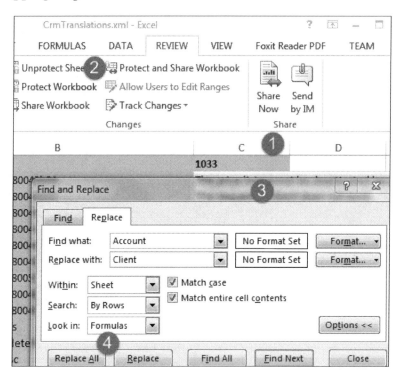

8. Follow steps 7 to 9 on the **Localized Labels** sheet as well.

9. Select all the files under the **CrmTranslations** folder and ZIP them; we need to keep the name of the ZIP file the same as the exported **CrmTranslations** folder.

10. Navigate to **Training Solution** and click on the **Import Translation** button to import our modified translations ZIP file.

> Make sure you review the translation file before import to verify all references are changed — for example, account to client and accounts to clients.

After completing the earlier steps make sure you click on **Publish All Customization** in the solution command bar to publish your changes. This operation will change the entity references; you could also include reports if you want to rename them as well.

> Renaming entities will change the display name and plural name where applicable, but it won't change the name (also known as logical name) field; this field is used during coding.

We can also edit components individually one by one; for example, we can rename entity forms using the **Form Properties** button on the entity editor ribbon bar. In a similar manner we can rename entity views through their definition. We can open the view definition using the steps in the following screenshot.

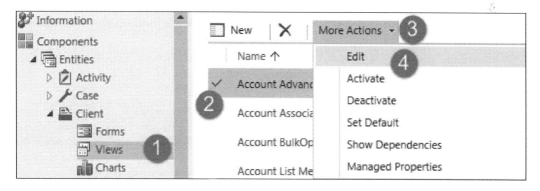

After that we can change the view name using the **View Properties** button available under **Common Tasks**.

After renaming entities, let's set up our entity data structure training solution.

Data types in Microsoft Dynamics CRM 2015

Microsoft Dynamics CRM 2015 provides different data type options to handle different types of information. We are going to use out-of-the-box entities to implement our training process, but we will be also creating some new fields, so let's discuss what the data types available in Microsoft Dynamics CRM 2015 are. The following table represents Microsoft Dynamics CRM 2015 data types:

Single line of text

Single line of text is used for single lines of text information—for example, first name, last name, city, state and any other information where we need to capture one line of input. This field supports a maximum of 4,000 characters. While creating this field we can also define the following formatting options:

- **Email**: This option validates text for a valid e-mail address. It also makes e-mail addresses hyperlink-enabled, which opens the default e-mail software when clicked.

- **Text**: Provides a simple text field.

- **Text area**: This option also provides a simple text field but with scrolling support.

- **URL**: This option allows you to store URLs with hyperlink-enabled.

- **Ticker Symbol**: This option is used to store a stock ticker symbol.

- **Phone**: This option provides a phone integration option with Skype and Lync when the country code is prefixed with a phone number.

Option sets

An **Option Set** in Microsoft Dynamics CRM 2015 is like a drop-down that can be used to provide different options for selection. Only one value can be selected at a time. This field stores text and corresponding index values for the text. Entity table just stores index values of this field and all other details related to the option set are stored in the **stringmap** table. We can create two types of option sets:

- **Global**: This option is created directly from solutions and can be referenced while creating a local option set in all entities

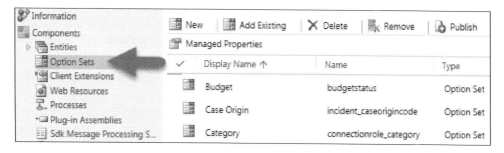

- **Local**: This option set is limited to a specific entity only

While creating a local option set, we can select **Use Existing Option Set** if we want to reference a global option set. We can also set default values for an option set, which will be selected as default while we create a new entity record.

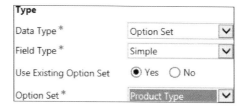

Two options

Two options are used to store Boolean type values. By default two options have **Yes** and **No** options, but if required we can rename them as needed. We can also set up a default selected option. Once this field is created we can change the two option set control type after placing the field form; we can double-click on the two options field to open the field property and can set the **Control Formatting** option under the **Formatting** tab.

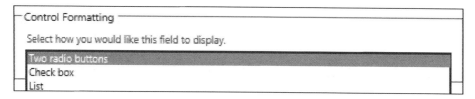

 The **Two radio buttons** option does not display a radio button control. It is displayed like a label, which works like a toggle button.

Images

Image field is used to store an image of the entity record. We can only create one image field per entity. Currently there are 24 system entities where an image field is available. We can't add an image field to a system entity, but we can create an image field for our custom entity.

We can upload images in the following formats:

- BMP
- GIF
- JPG
- JPEG
- PNG
- TIFF
- TIF

We can upload images up to 5120 KB by default based on the CRM configuration. Once an image field is added to our custom entity, we can set the property of the entity form to display an image placeholder. We can open the **Form Property** dialog and select the **Show Image** in the form checkbox under the **Display** tab. More information on the image field can be obtained from `https://technet.microsoft.com/en-us/library/dn531187.aspx#BKMK_ImageFields`

 All the images stored in the image entity and image field act like a lookup to store image references.

Whole numbers

This data type is used to store whole integer values. This field allows us to store integer value between -2147483648 and +2147483647. This field also provide the following different formatting options:

- **None**: This is the default integer format.
- **Duration**: This option provides a drop-down field with value options for minutes, hours, and days; this option should be only used when we want to represent time: **durationTime** zone. We can use this formatting option to provide different time zone options.
- **Language**: This option can be used to select language options based on the language packs installed.

Floating point numbers

The floating point numbers field is used to store fraction values. We can store up to five decimal numbers in the range from -100000000000 to +100000000000.

Decimals

The decimal field also allows us to store decimal numbers, but we can store up to 10 decimal numbers between -100,000,000,000.00 and 100,000,000,000.00.

Currency

The currency field is used to store money values. We can store up to four decimal numbers between -922,337,203,685,477.0000 and 922,337,203,685,477.0000. When a currency field is added to an entity for the first time, CRM creates the following four fields:

- `prefix_fieldname`: This field is used to store the value entered by the user
- `Currency`: A lookup field is created for currency, which allows us to select configured currencies
- `ExchangerateStores`: The exchange rate value, based on the currency setup
- `Prefix_fieldname_base`: The value of the amount that is entered in the first field in the base currency

 Base currency is configured while setting up a new organization in Microsoft Dynamics CRM 2015.

Multiple lines of text

This data type is used to capture multiple lines of text. While creating this, we can set up the maximum length of the field. This field can be used to store up to 1,048,576 characters of text.

> If we have a requirement to store long text, we can use notes to store this information instead of the multiple line of text field.

Date and time

The date and time type field is used to capture date and time information such as the training start date and training end date. It provides calendar control. We have the following formatting options in this field:

- **Date Only**: We can set up this format to capture only the date part
- **Date Time**: This format is used to capture both date and time

Microsoft Dynamics CRM 2015 stores date and time information in the **Coordinated Universal Time (UTC)** format but for display purposes it is automatically converted to the date and time format selected in the user's personal settings.

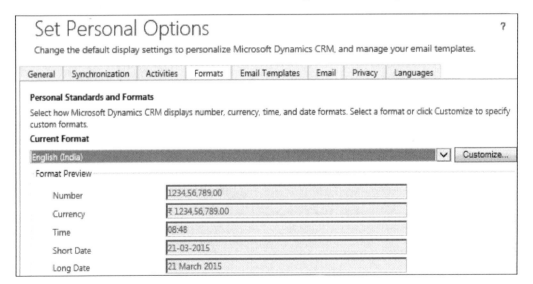

We can access the user's personal settings by selecting **Options** from the **Setting** button over the top navigation bar.

You can refer to `https://technet.microsoft.com/library/73d691c7-344e-4c96-8979-c661c290bf81.aspx` for more details on the date time field format.

Lookup

The lookup data type is used to setup n:1 relationships between entities. We can select our target entity to set a relationship and, once lookup is created, it is available as a lookup control that provides a list of available and related records for selection when clicked.

Field properties

While creating fields, there are some basic properties that we need to configure for entity fields. The main properties are as follows:

- **Display Name**: The label of the field, visible in all the places where field is referenced such as forms, views, and reports.
- **Name**: The logical name of the field; it is used while coding for Microsoft Dynamics CRM 2015.
- **Description**: This is used to provide additional information or setup tooltips for the field.
- **Field Requirement**: The requirement level of the fields. It has three options: **Business Required**, which is mandatory; **Business Recommended**, which means it is recommended for business: and **Optional**.
- **Searchable**: This property defines whether we can query the entity record based on this field or not using advanced find.
- **Field Security**: Used to protect fields based on the field level security profile; we can configure the field level security for both custom and system fields.
- **Auditing**: Used to keep track of the changes in field value; provides two options, **Enable** or **Disable**.
- **Date Type**: Available data types in Microsoft Dynamics CRM 2015; we can select them based on the data that we want to store in a field.
- **Field Type**: Dependent on the data type selected. It has three options: **Simple**, **Calculated**, and **Rollup**. We will discuss this in greater detail in a later topic.
- **Format**: Allows us to format fields based on the data type selected.

Setting data structures for a training solution

Now we are going to set up a data structure for a training solution. We are going to map some of the existing fields with our training solution requirement and will just change their display names. Please refer to *Appendix B, Data Model for Account Entities* for data structure details.

Creating a new attribute

Every entity in Microsoft Dynamics CRM 2015 represents a table in the SQL server and every attribute of each entity represents a column. Microsoft Dynamics CRM 2015 allows us to set up entity fields from the UI, instead of doing it from a database, and all the attributes are available as a control to place over entity forms. We will learn how to place fields on entity forms while discussing the form customization topic.

Let's create new attributes for a training request entity. Use the following steps to create a new attribute:

1. Open **Training Solution** and navigate to **Entities | Training Request | Fields**.

2. Click on the **New** button on the field toolbar.

3. Enter properties in line with the following screenshot:
    - **Display Name: Proposed Start**
    - **Field Requirement: Business Required**
    - **Name: him_proposedstart** (after tabbing out from the **Display Name** field)
    - **Searchable: Yes**
    - **Field Security: Disable**
    - **Auditing: Disable**
    - **Data Type: Date and Time**
    - **Field Type: Simple**
    - **Format: Date Only**
    - **IME Mode: auto**

4. Click on **Save** to create the field.

 Input Method Editor (IME) is basically used for entering Chinese, Japanese, and Korean characters.

After entering the preceding properties, the **Field** window should look like following:

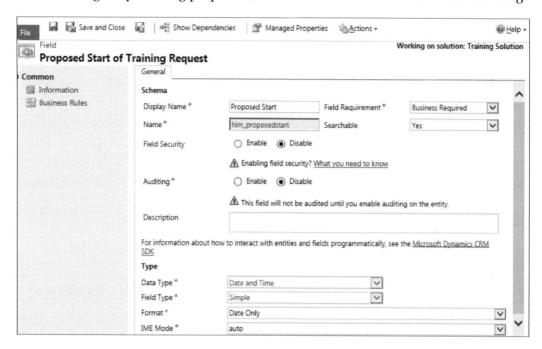

We are using contact entity to represent three types of contacts: employee, trainer and client contact. We will be providing a lookup control over a training request entity to select proposed trainer, so let's create a lookup on the training request entity. Follow the next steps to create a lookup field:

1. Click on the **New** button on the field toolbar.

2. Enter properties in line with the following screenshot. Click on **Save and Close**.

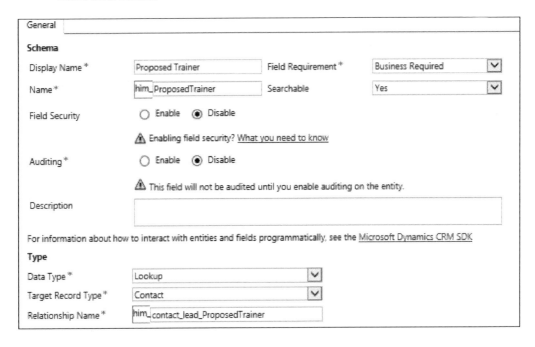

We need to create the same field in our proposal entity as well, so follow the earlier steps to create the same relationship in the proposal entity. However, let's keep the field name as **Trainer** instead of **Proposed Trainer**.

Setting field mapping

When two entities are related we can use field mapping to map data from the source entity to the target entity. Let's say we have a 1:n relationship between the contact and the training request entity. While creating a 1:n to a relationship we get lookup control on the related entity (n side entity). In the primary entity we get an associated view, where we can see a list of related entity records that is associated with the current primary entity record instance.

Associated view provides us with the option to create related entity records from the primary entity itself. If we want to carry some of the primary entity information to the related entity while creating a record we can set up field mapping. In our solution we want to carry the selected proposed trainer from the training request entity to the proposal entity, when the training request is converted to the proposal. We can do that using field mapping. Follow the next steps to set field mapping between proposed trainer in the training request entity and trainer in the proposal entity that we created in the last step:

1. Navigate to **Training Request** under our **Training Solution** and select 1:N relationship.

2. Double-click on the **opportunity_originating_lead** relationship to open it.

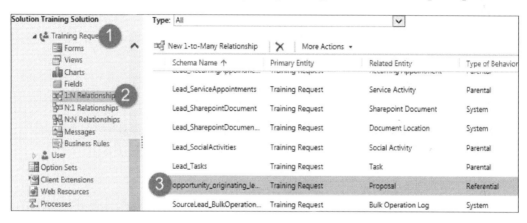

3. Select **Mapping** | **New** and select source the **him_proposedtrainer** and target **him_trainer** fields and click on **OK**.

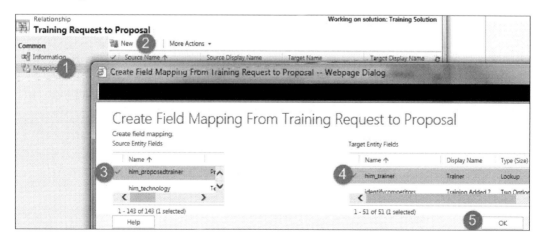

4. Click on the **Save and Close** button and publish your changes.

We can follow the same steps to create other custom fields for our training request entity; please refer to *Appendix B, Data Model for Account Entities* for the complete data structure of the training request entity.

To customize existing fields we can double-click on them to open their definition. We can modify the following properties for existing fields:

*   **Display Name**
*   **Field Requirement**
*   **Searchable**
*   **Field Security**
*   **Auditing**
*   **Description**
*   **Maximum Length**
*   **IME Mode**

There are other field-specific properties that can be also changed; for example, in the case of an option set we can add or remove option set items. But while removing option set values we should keep in mind that there should not be records refereeing that value.

Using the following procedure we can create and modify the data structure for all of our business entities. Please refer to *Appendix B, Data Model for Account Entities* for the data structure for other required entities.

Customizing entity forms

Now we have our data structure ready, let's modify our entity forms. Microsoft Dynamics CRM 2015 allows us to set up multiple forms for entity. Microsoft Dynamics CRM 2015 forms provide a responsive web design experience, which means Microsoft Dynamics CRM 2015 screens will be adjusted according to the screen resolution of the device used to access the application. So the same entity form can be used for a variety of devices without any changes.

If we have multiple forms, we can control their visibility based on user security roles. We can define which form will be visible to which type of users. For example we can create one main form for the **Sales Person** security role and another for **System Administrator** roles. We can also set a default fall-back form that will be displayed to the user when there is no form associated with the user's security role.

We can create the following types of forms for Microsoft Dynamics CRM 2015:

- **Main Form**: This is the form that is used for Web, Outlook, and CRM for tablet clients
- **Mobile Express**: This form is used for mobile express clients
- **Quick Create**: This form is available when users try to create a record using the **Quick Create** button over the top navigation bar
- **Quick View**: This form is associated with the lookup field and shows parent-related information in the child entity form

The main form

Every updated entity in Microsoft Dynamics CRM 2015 has one default main form available with the name of the entity. For example, in account we have one **Account** main form. Main forms are used for Microsoft Dynamics CRM 2015 web clients, Outlook clients, CRM for phone, and for tablet clients. If required we can create multiple forms by navigating to the **New** button under the **Forms** toolbar.

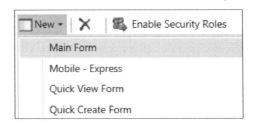

While designing the main form we can place different types of controls such as tabs, sections, sub grids, iframes, web resources, fields, and spacer. We can add these field from the **Insert** tab in the form editor.

The following is the default main form editor for the lead entity.

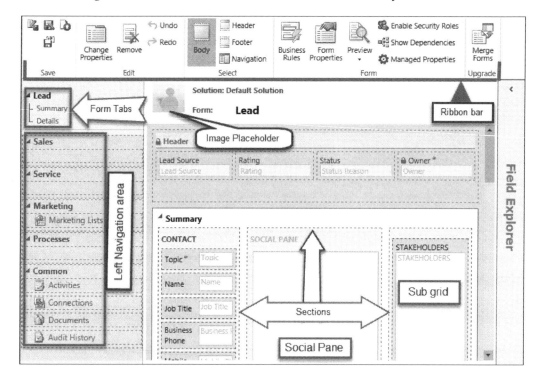

We can simply drag-and-drop fields from **Field Explorer** to the appropriate section. We can also select an existing field and double-click on it in **Field Explorer**; then it will be added after the selected field section. The **Remove** button is used to remove any unwanted control from an entity form.

While designing the form, we can select different areas such as **Body**, **Header**, **Footer**, and **Navigation** to place controls in the respective area. The **Form Properties** button can be used to configure different settings such as managing form and field events and setting the form's display properties with other settings. The **Merge Forms** button can used to place controls from other forms.

 Make sure you have created and customized existing fields based on *Appendix B, Data Model for Account Entities* before starting to design entity forms.

Understanding the social pane

The social pane is basically a tab control that act as a center point for interaction with the customer. It includes four tabs:

- **Post**: This tab provides record activity feed details, just like our social network feeds
- **Activities**: Lists all the activities related to the current record
- **Notes**: A free text area; we can also attach documents from here
- **Yammer** (if configured): Provides yammer feed details

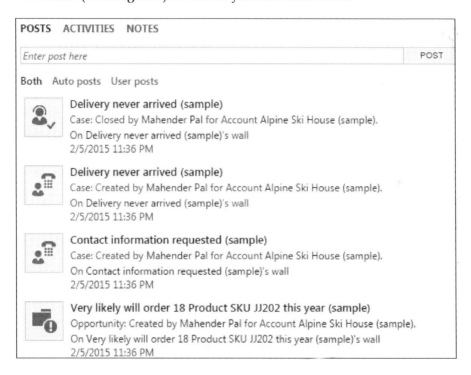

We can't change the order of the **Social Pane** tab, but if required we can set up a default tab for social pane. Also we can change social pane's default size; if we have a requirement to reduce the size of the social pane we need to remove the default social pane and add it again to the form. While doing so, we can change **Default** tab property under the **Display** tab and **Row Layout** under the **Formatting** tab.

Select a control and click on the **Change Properties** button under the form editor's ribbon button bar to change properties for any control.

Understanding the sub grid

The sub grid control is a list control that displays data from a related or non-related entity. By configuring the sub grid property we can select if we want to see a list of the data or a chart under the sub grid, but we can see one at a time. We can add a sub grid via the **INSERT** tab in the form editor.

While adding a sub grid we can define its data source. We can specify if we want to see only a list of the records associated with the current record or we want to see all the records. We can also add searching capability to the sub grid by selecting the **Display Search Box** check box button under **Additional Options**.

The **Display Index** provide an A to Z index at the bottom of the sub grid to filter data based on the letter selected. This option is only available in classic forms (old entity forms that lacks the new layout and controls such as command bar, process control, and the Quick View form), We can also configure if we want to show a specific view or allow users to change views in the sub grid using the **View Selector** option.

Let's design our training request entity main form. Use the following steps to customize the main form:

1. Navigate to **Components | Entities | Training Request | Forms** and double-click on the **Training Form** to open the form editor under our **Training Solution**.

2. Double-click on the header area and remove all existing fields. We need to add the **Proposed Start, Proposed End, Budget Amount** and **Technology** fields.

3. Rearrange sections and fields in the **Summary** tab based on the following screenshot.

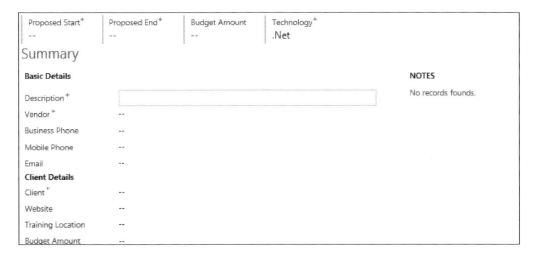

4. Double-click on the **Details** tab and re-label it to **Requirement Details**.

5. Customize the existing section and rearrange the fields based on the following screenshot.

Requirement Details

		Specific Topics	More Details	--
Proposed Start *	--			
Proposed End *	--	--		
Technology *	.Net		Industry	--
Version	--		Currency	रुपया
Study Material Requi	No		Evaluation Required	Yes
Training Level	--		Evaluation Date	--
No. of Employees	--		Proposed Trainer *	--

6. Double-click on **Footer** and add the **Created By, Created On** and **Modified By** fields.

7. Click on the **Form Properties** button under the ribbon bar and deselect the **Show image in the form** checkbox under the **Display** tab.

8. Click on the **Save and Publish** button.

 We can preview forms using **Preview** under the ribbon bar to preview form changes before publishing.

Mobile express forms

Mobile express forms are used by Microsoft Dynamics CRM 2015 for mobile express clients. There is one default mobile express form available per entity but if required we can add more than one mobile express form. In mobile express forms we can't place any control; we can just add a list of the fields under the **Selected Attributes** list that we want to see over mobile forms. We are not going to use Microsoft Dynamics CRM 2015 for mobile express clients so we are not going to modify mobile forms for our training solution.

Quick create forms

Quick create forms provide an option to create an entity record quickly with critical information. We can also create multiple types of Quick Create forms. While designing a Quick Create form, we are limited to placing a single tab with three columns. We can only place one single column section in each column of the tab and these sections can contain a field and spacer only. The following is an example of an account Quick Create form.

We can quickly create forms using the **New** button over the forms toolbar. There is an existing quick create form in the training request entity called **Lead Quick Create**; we are going to modify this form. Use quick create following steps to modify it:

1. Double-click on the **Lead Quick Create** form to open it.

2. Click on **Form Properties** and change **Form Name** and **Description** to **Training Request Quick Create** under the **Display** tab.

3. Remove and add fields to the form based on the following screenshot.

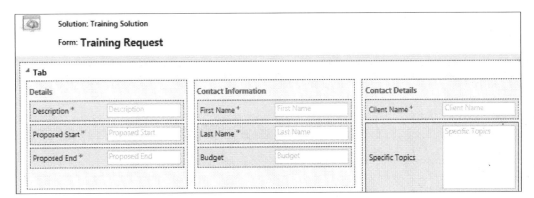

 The size of the multiple line of text field can be increased or decreased by modifying the **Number of Rows** property under the **Formatting** tab.

4. Click on **Save and Close** and click on **Publish All Customizations** to publish all the changes.

Quick view forms

Quick view form is associated with lookup control and used to see additional information for the related record. Quick view form can be only added to the main form type. It is available as a control and can be place on the form from the **Insert** tab under the entity editor ribbon bar. Quick view form provides read-only information that can't be edited.

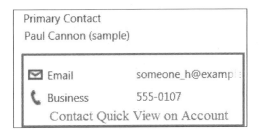

While designing a quick view form we can't place all types of control over it. We are limited to including one tab that has one column and that column can contain one or more single-column sections. We can only include fields, spacers, and a sub grid on quick view forms.

Designing other forms

We have completed the design of our training request entity forms; now we need to follow the same process for our other business entities. We need to customize other forms based on the following designs.

Client main form design

Customize the existing main form of a client entity based on the following screenshot:

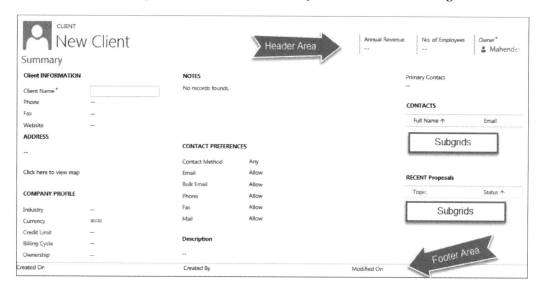

 We can rename existing tabs and sections by changing their properties, instead of adding new tabs and sections.

Client quick create form design

Customize an existing client quick create form based on the following screenshot.

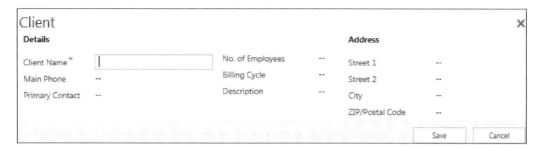

Contact main form design

Customize the existing main form of a contact entity based on the following screenshot.

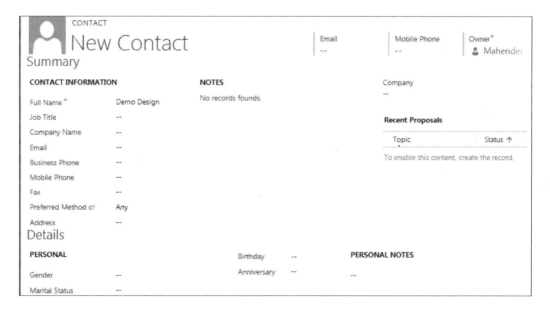

Proposal main form design

Follow the next screenshot to customize an existing proposal (opportunity) main form:

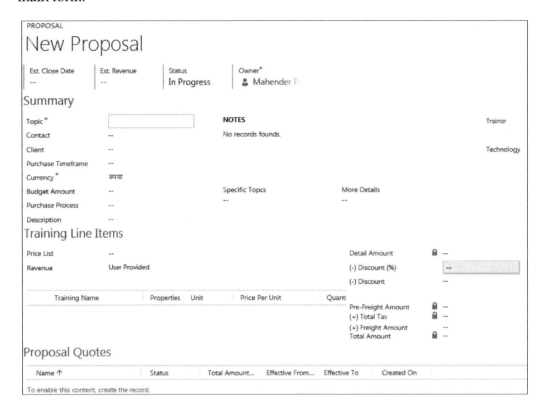

We are going to use all other entity forms without modification.

Customizing application navigation

Microsoft Dynamics CRM 2015 navigation can be easily modified by customizing the sitemap file. We can modify a sitemap manually in any XML or text editor such as Notepad++ or Visual Studio; alternatively, we can use custom tools. We are going to use **XrmToolBox**, which is an excellent (and free) tool developed by Tanguy Touzard, Microsoft Dynamics CRM MVP. This tool is available at: `http://www.xrmtoolbox.com` or can be downloaded from `https://github.com/MscrmTools/XrmToolBox`.

Name	Action	Description
Sales	Rename to	Training solution
Marketing	Hide	
Service	Hide	
Setting	Rename to	Configuration

Download XrmToolBox from the preceding location and unblock the ZIP file first. To unblock the file, right-click on the ZIP file then click on **Properties**. After that click on the **Unblock** button, then extract the ZIP file. After extraction, use the following steps to customize navigation:

1. Run the `XrmToolBox.exe` file and click on **Connect to CRM**.

2. Click on **New Connection** and enter your organization's details.

3. Click on the **Get Orgs** button to get your organization, select your **Organization** drop-down and click **OK**.

4. Click on **SiteMap Editor** and the **Load SiteMap** button.

5. Select **Area (SFA)** and change **Title and Description** as follows:

   Title: Training Solution

   Description: **Training Solution Application**

6. Click on **Save** to save the changes.

7. Right-click on the following **Group**, **Area** and select **Disable**.

Name	Location
Group (MyWork)	Area (SFA)
SubArea (nav_comps)	Area (SFA) | Group (SFA)
SubArea (nav_orders)	Area (SFA) | Group (Collateral)
SubArea (nav_invoices)	Area (SFA) | Group (Collateral)
SubArea (nav_saleslit)	Area (SFA) | Group (Collateral)
Group (MA)	Area (SFA)
Group (Goals)	Area (SFA)
Group (Tools)	Area (SFA)
Area (CS)	
Area (MA)*	

8. Select **Area (Settings)** and the following settings from the right-hand side of the property window:

   Title: Configuration

   Description: To configure training solution

9. Select **SubArea (nav_productcatalog)** under **Area (Settings) | Group (Business_Setting)** and change the following setting from the right-hand side of the property window:

   Title: Training Catalog

   Description: To configure training catalog

10. Click on the **Update SiteMap** button to update the changes in Microsoft Dynamics CRM 2015.

Refresh the Microsoft Dynamics CRM 2015 application and we should be able to see changes like the following:

Setting up a training catalog

Microsoft Dynamics CRM 2015 allows us to store our product or service information under a product catalog. We have mapped the product entity with the training entity, which will store information and price details about training. Microsoft Dynamics CRM 2015 provides different options to set up products or services. We can set up a discount list for different discount options depending on the quantity of sale. We can set up a multiple discount list and, while creating a product, we can select which discount list we want to apply. We can set up discount list by navigating to **Configuration | Training Catalog**.

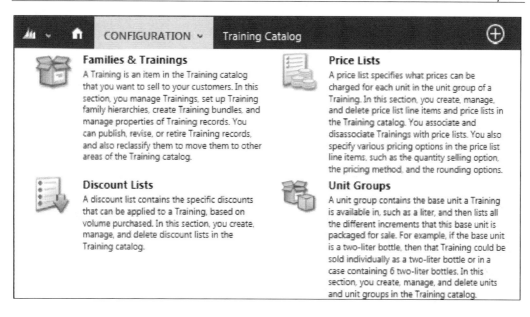

A unit group is a group of all the measurement units in which we can sell our product or service. While creating unit groups, we need a primary unit that acts as base for all unit groups—for example, gram is the primary unit for kilogram. We are developing a solution for a training company, so we will be setting up our unit groups to measure training service in term of hours, days and weeks. Follow the next steps to configure unit groups:

1. Navigate to **CONFIGURATION | Training Catalog** and click on **Unit Groups**.

2. Click on the **New** button and enter the following details in the **Create Unit Group** dialog:

    Name: Training Service

    Primary Unit: Hour

3. Click on **Units | Add New Unit** and enter the following details; click on the **Save and Close** button.

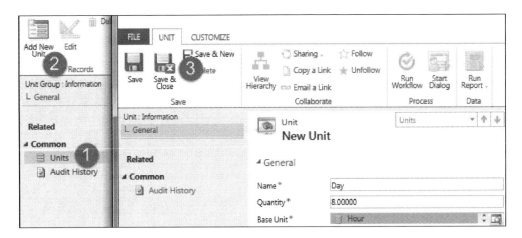

4. Follow the same steps to set up other units as follows:

Name: **Week**

Quantity: **40**

Base Unit: **Hour**

Once unit groups are defined we can set up our products or services. Microsoft Dynamics CRM 2015 allows us to set up standalone products or product groups as a product family, which shares common features. We can use different product families to categorize them in different groups. We can also add product properties at the product family level, which helps us to differentiate a product from another product. When a product is added to a product family it inherits all the properties from the product family. We can set up a product hierarchy using the product family and can visualize it using the hierarchy visualization feature. Let's set up our Microsoft Dynamics training family for our training programs based on the following table:

Name	Members
Microsoft Dynamics	Microsoft Dynamics CRM Function,
	Microsoft Dynamics CRM Customization ,
	Microsoft Dynamics CRM Extending
	Microsoft Dynamics Ax Function ,
	Microsoft Dynamics Ax Technical
	Microsoft Dynamics GP Functional,
	Microsoft Dynamics GP Technical

1. Navigate to **CONFIGURATION | Training Catalog** and click on **Families and Training**.

2. Click on **ADD FAMILY** to enter the following details and click on the **Save** button:

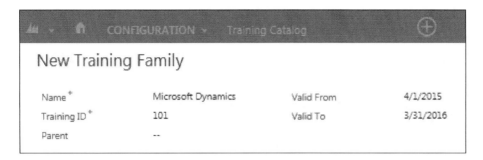

 There is no out-of-the-box business logic available in Microsoft Dynamics CRM 2015 to expire a product family after the **Valid To** date.

Now we have added our training family, let's add the following common properties to our Microsoft Dynamics family:

Name	Data type	Value	Description
Level	Drop down	Level I, Level II, Level III	Training level
Category	Drop down	Online, On the Job	Training type

Use the following steps to add the properties:

1. Open a Microsoft Dynamics family record and click on the **+** sign on the property's sub grid to create a property.

2. Enter the following details and click on the **Save** button.

   Name: Level

   Required: Yes

   Description: Training Level

3. Click on the **+** sign on the **Property Option Set Items** sub grid and enter the following details:

4. Close the property window.
5. Follow steps 1-3 to set up the category property.

All the pricing-related information for products or services is configured using another entity called **Price List**. We can set up different price lists for different scenarios; for example, we may have different price lists for different regions or for different retailers or wholesalers. Once a price list is created, we can set up a price list item for different units. We can also set up a price list item from the product entity. Use the following steps to create a price list for our CRM training.

1. Navigate to **CONFIGURATION | TRAINING Catalog** and select **Price Lists**.
2. Click on the **+New** command button, enter the following details, and click on **Save**.

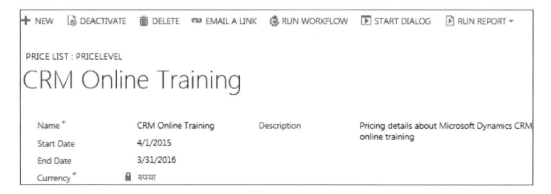

3. Close the price list window.

We can also set default price list to **Territory**, if you are doing business based on territories.

Use the following steps to add training to training family:

1. Navigate to **CONFIGURATION | TRAINING Catalog** and select **Families and Trainings**.

2. Select the Microsoft Dynamics family record and click on the **ADD TRAINING** button over the command bar.

3. Enter the following details and click on the **Save** command button.

4. Click on the **+** sign on **PRICE LIST ITEMS** under **ADDITIONAL DETAILS** and enter the following information and lead keep fields as default:

   Price List: CRM Online Training

   Unit: Day

   Amount: 5000

5. Click on **Save & Close**.

We can follow the same steps to add another price list item based on a different unit—for example, week. Use the earlier steps to set up other training and price lists based as required.

Once we have added our products we need to publish them so that we can use them while creating opportunities. A product can be published individually or with the product family using **Publish | Publish Hierarchy** under the product family record. Perform the following steps to publish our **Microsoft Dynamics family**:

1. Navigate to **CONFIGURATION | TRAINING Catalog** and select **Families and Trainings**.

2. Open the Microsoft Dynamics family record.

3. Select **Publish Hierarchy** under the **Publish** drop-down button.

Understanding security

User management is an essential part of any business application. Microsoft Dynamics CRM 2015 provides out-of-the-box support for user management and security. If you are using Microsoft Dynamics CRM 2015 on premise, a user can be added to Microsoft Dynamics CRM 2015 after being added in Active Directory. In the case of Microsoft Dynamics CRM 2015, online users can be managed using Office 356 portal.

Access to the Microsoft Dynamics CRM 2015 application can be managed using an entity called **Security Role**. Once a user is added to Microsoft Dynamics CRM 2015 he should have at least one security role or should be part of the owner team (the owner team should have at least one security role assigned). User security is handled in Microsoft Dynamics CRM 2015 in three ways:

- Role-based security
- Record-based security
- Field-level security

 You can refer to https://msdn.microsoft.com/en-us/library/ gg309524.aspx to get more information about the CRM 2015 security model.

Role-based security

Role-based security is handled by security roles, which are basically a grouping of a set of privileges and five access levels. Privileges define which action a user can perform on a specific entity; for example, we can configure whether a user can create an account entity record or not. Access level defines up to what level the user can perform a particular action on a specific entity; for example, if a user can read data created by himself, created under his business unit, from a child business unit of his business unit, or from the organization level.

The business unit is a base of the security model, which is a group of users and a team. Every organization contains one root business unit. We can set up parent and child business units to map the security requirements of the organization.

Record-based security

Record-based security is used to control security for specific entity records using access rights. Access rights work on the basis of privileges only, so an access right will only work if users have appropriate privileges on a specific entity; for example, a user can only access a record that is shared with him if he has read privileges.

Field-level security

Field-level security allows us to control specific field security on the basis of the field level security profile. In field-level security, we can define read, create, and update access to a particular field in which the field level security is enabled. In Microsoft Dynamics CRM 2015 we can enable field-level security for both system and custom fields. We will cover field-level security in detail in a later chapter.

For our training solution application, we are going to use the following three security roles:

Name	Description
Sales Person, Sales Manager	To create and manage training requests and execute training programs
System Customizer	To implement any changes in training solutions
System Administrator	For the power admin user

 You can refer to `https://technet.microsoft.com/en-us/library/hh699698.aspx` to get more details on Microsoft Dynamics CRM 2015 security management.

Testing customization

We can test our entity form designs and fields that we have created. We can start capturing training request information by creating a new training request record by navigating to **TRAINING SOLUTION | Training Requests**.

Perform the following steps to test a training solution:

1. Create a **Training Request** record and enter the following details. As we are creating a request for a new client we won't be selecting **Existing Client?** and **Existing Contact?**.

We can capture additional information and attach a file in the **NOTES** tab in the social pane.

We will see the default business process flow while creating a record. Business process flows help us to implement a guided approach to following any business-specific process flow. We have not yet modified business process flows (we will be working with these in detail in the next chapter).

2. After completing the required fields, click on the **Save** button and then click on the **Qualify** button over the command bar.

3. This action will create a **Proposal** record from the **Training Request** record and will map all the entered fields. It will close the **Training Request** record.

4. Select our **CRM Online Training Price List** and click on the **Save** button available at the bottom-right of the record status bar.

 Use the **Next Stage** button at the end of the business process flow to move to the next stage in the business process flow.

5. Click on the **+** sign on the **Training Line** items sub grid to add **Training**.

 A price list is required to add a product in **Opportunity**.

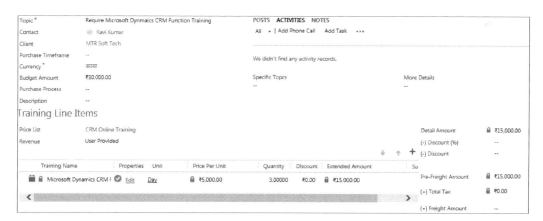

6. Set up **Training** properties using the **Edit** button in the editable grid view and enter a **Quantity** value.

7. Click on the **+** sign on the **Proposal Quote** sub grid to create a quote for the proposal.

8. Enter a billing address and click on the **Activate Proposal Quote** button.

9. Click on **Close Proposal Quote**, select **Do not revise Proposal Quote**, and click on **OK**.

10. Complete the business process flow and click on the **CLOSE AS WON** button on the command bar to close the proposal.

Summary

In this chapter we learned about Microsoft Dynamics CRM 2015 customization features. We learned about different components and how to customize them. We also created a sample application for managing training, where we utilized only out-of-the-box features. We discussed various data types available in Microsoft Dynamics CRM 2015 with their different formatting options. We also discussed the security mode of Microsoft Dynamics CRM 2015. In our sample application, we also learned how to work with the Microsoft Dynamics CRM 2015 product catalog, using the out of product catalog feature to manage our training programs.

In the next chapter we will be learning about implementing client-side logic in Microsoft Dynamics CRM 2015 and we will also enhance our training solution application.

3

Client-side Logic with Microsoft Dynamics CRM 2015

In this chapter, we will learn about implementing client-side logic in Microsoft Dynamics CRM 2015. We are going to learn about various client-side extensions in Microsoft Dynamics CRM 2015. We will start by creating JavaScript Web resources and will learn about consuming CRM web services using client-side code. We will also discuss business rules in Microsoft Dynamics CRM 2015 with their new enhancements and we will keep working on our training solution that we created in the previous chapter.

In this chapter we will be discussing the following topics:

- Understanding the client scripting object model
- Understanding web resources
- Accessing forms and controls using client-side code
- Understanding client-side events
- Using CRM web services in client-side code
- Understanding Business Rules

Understanding the client scripting object model

In the client scripting object model, we utilize client-side programming to write code that runs on browsers. We can embed our client-side code in different places in Microsoft Dynamics CRM 2015. We can write client-side code to interact with entity forms and their controls. To work with client scripting object models, there are events exposed for forms and controls that we will be discussing in later topics.

Using client scripting object model, we can customize the behavior of command buttons; for example, let's say that we want to enable a command button for specific security role users or we may want to show a button when a specific value is entered in a text box. These types of requirement can be implemented by writing custom JavaScript actions for command buttons with enable and display rules.

 We can refer to `https://msdn.microsoft.com/en-us/library/gg309639.aspx` to get details about enabling and displaying rules.

We can also write our client-side code or create a client-side library using web resources. We will be discussing web resources in later topic. Once web resources are saved and published, we can attach a reference to them in entity forms and command bar buttons by modifying `RibbonDiffXML`, and in other web resources. Client-side object models can also be used to create HTML web resources to develop custom web pages.

 The `RibbonDiffXML` file is an XML file that is used to customize command button definitions. Refer to `https://msdn.microsoft.com/en-us/library/gg328409.aspx` for more details on RibbonDiffXML.

Understanding web resources

Web resources are reusable components that are stored as files in Microsoft Dynamics CRM 2015. We have different choices for creating web resources; once created, they can be called using their unique URL. They can be referenced in multiple places such as in sitemaps, in entity forms, in dashboards, and command buttons.

We can create the following different types of web resources in Microsoft Dynamics CRM 2015:

Web Resource Type	Extensions	Descriptions
Webpage (HTML)	`.htm` or `.html`	Used to create HTML Web pages
Style Sheet (CSS)	`.css`	Can be used to create a style sheet to refer to in other web resources
Script (JScript)	`.js`	Used to create scripting Web resources
Data (XML)	`.xml`	Can be used to store some data using XML strings
Image (PNG)	`.png`	Used to upload Portable Network Graphics
Image (JPG)	`.jpg`	Used to upload Joint Photographic Expert Group graphics
Image (GIF)	`.gif`	Used to upload Graphic Interchange Format graphics
Silverlight (XAP)	`.xap`	For creating Silverlight web resources
StyleSheet (XSL)	`.xsl, .xslt`	Web resources to transform XML data
Image (ICO)	`.ico`	Used to upload icon images

Web resources can be referenced via absolute and relative paths. But it is always recommended to use relative paths. While adding web resources you are advised to set a virtual directory structure for different components; for example, for scripts we can use `/Scripts/Account.js` and for images we can use something like `/Images/ SMS_16.png`.

While adding web resources an automatic prefix is applied by CRM based on the publisher setup. So, if we want to follow the preceding virtual directory structure, the name of the web resource will be something like `prefix_/Scripts/Account. js`. It is not required to append a file extension at the end of a web resource but it is recommended to follow this practice. Please refer to *Chapter 2, Customizing Microsoft Dynamics CRM 2015*, for details about creating the publisher.

It is common to refer to one web resource in another web resource while working on extending a CRM application. In order to reference one web resource in another, we should use a relative path only. So for example if we have created a JavaScript web resource named `him_/Scripts/CommonScripts.js` and want to refer this in another HTML web resource, we need to reference our JavaScript web resource as follows:

```
<script src="Scripts/CommonScripts.js"
  type="text/javascript"></script>
```

We should use the same technique to reference other resource as well, such as referencing HTML web resources. The maximum default size of the file that can be uploaded as a web resource is 5 MB, but if required it can be changed by navigating **Settings** | **System Settings** | **Email** | **Set Maximum file size (in kilobytes)**.

Always use the $webresource directive while referring to web resource in command buttons or SiteMap because, when the $webresource directive is used, CRM will create or update solution dependencies.

Creating our first web resource

Let us create our first web resource. It is always recommended to create your web resource in a custom solution so that it can be easily exported and deployed to other environments. We can create web resources by carrying out the following steps:

1. Open our demo solution and navigate to **Components** | **Web Resources** | **New**.

2. Enter the following details:

    Name: Helloworld.js

    Display Name: Helloworld.js

    Type: Webpage (HTML)

    Language: English

 A prefix will be added to **Name** automatically based on publisher being selected while creating the solution.

3. Click on the **Text Editor** button to open the editor.

4. Design your first HTML web page contents in the **Rich Text** editor.

5. Use the **Rich Text** editor toolbar to modify the content style.

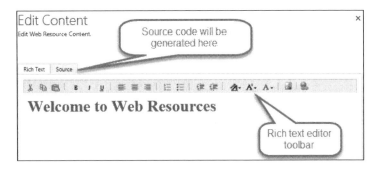

6. Click on **Ok** to close the **Text Editor**.
7. Click on the **Save** and **Publish** buttons.
8. Click on the **PREVIEW** button on the top to preview our HTML web resource.

Accessing forms and controls using client-side code

In order to work with the client object model, first we need to understand the Xrm.Page object model. The Xrm.Page object is used to interact with forms and related controls. It is a top hierarchal object that has three namespaces:

*   Context
*   Data
*   UI

The following namespaces provide different methods that we can use to manipulate data at different levels.

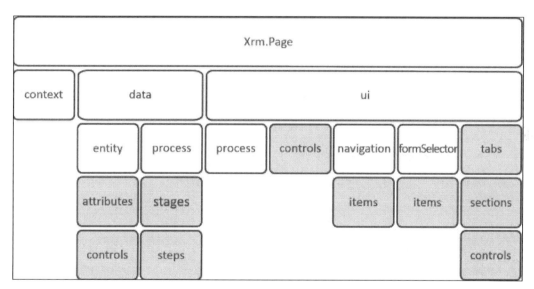

Image source: msdn.microsoft.com

Context namespaces

Context namespaces provide different methods to access client-side contexts. These methods help us to get different contextual information related to the organization, user, client, and other details. We can utilize these methods to write generic code; for example, if we need an organization name in our JavaScript program, we can utilize the getOrgUniqueName method to get the current organization instead of hard-coding the organization name. In a similar way, if we need to know the current user security roles using client-side code, then we can utilize the getUserRoles method. The following table provides common methods for context namespaces.

Method	Description
Xrm.Page.context.getClientUrl()	This method is used to get the URL of the server
Xrm.Page.context.getOrgUniqueName()	This method is used to get the unique name of the organization
Xrm.Page.context.getUserId()	This method is used to access current user GUID
Xrm.Page.context.getUserName()	This method provides the current user's full name
Xrm.Page.context.getUserRoles()	This method is used to get current user security roles
Xrm.Page.context.getClient()	This method is used to get the client name where the script is executing— for example browser, Outlook or mobile

 You can get more details about client-side contexts from
https://msdn.microsoft.com/en-us/library/gg334511.aspx.

Data namespaces

Data namespaces help us to get entity-related information and provide a method to get data on entity forms.

The following table provides common methods for entity objects:

Method	Description
Xrm.Page.data.entity.getEntityName()	This method is used to get the logical name of the current entity
Xrm.Page.data.entity.save()	We can utilize this method to save entity form data
Xrm.Page.data.entity.getId()	This method is used to get the current record GUID
Xrm.Page.data.entity.getIsDirty()	This method is used to detect if a form is modified or not

 You can refer to https://msdn.microsoft.com/en-us/library/gg334720(v=crm.6).aspx for more details on entity methods.

Microsoft Dynamics CRM 2015 includes support for handling processes using client-side code. Following is a list of common methods that we use to interact with business process flow:

Method	Description
Xrm.Page.data.process.getActiveProcess()	We can utilize this method to get active processes
Xrm.Page.data.process.setActiveStage(staged, callbackfunctionname)	We can utilize this method to set the active stage
Xrm.Page.data.process.getActivePath()	To get a collection of stages in the active path
Xrm.Page.data.process.addOnStageChange(function name)	Used to call a method when the stage changes
Xrm.Page.data.process.addOnStageSelected(function name)	Used to call a method when a stage is selected

 More information about business process flow methods can be found at https://msdn.microsoft.com/en-in/library/dn817874.aspx.

We can access form data using attribute collections or the `getAttribute` shortcut method. Next is the common method used to access form data using the `getAttribute` shortcut:

Method	Description
`Xrm.Page.getAttribute("FieldName").getRequiredLevel()`	Used to get the requirement of the field; possible options are: none, required, recommended
`Xrm.Page.getAttribute("FieldName").setRequiredLevel(Requirement Level)`	Used to set the requirement level of the field; possible parameter are: none, required, recommended
`Xrm.Page.getAttribute("FieldName").getSubmitMode()`	Used to check if field will be submitted or not when record is saved
`Xrm.Page.getAttribute("FieldName").setSubmitMode(parameter)`	Used to set submitted mode based on parameter
`Xrm.Page.getAttribute("FieldName").getValue()`	Used to get the value of a field
`Xrm.Page.getAttribute("FieldName").setValue(Value)`	Used to set the value of a field
`Xrm.Page.getAttribute("FieldName").addOnChange(function name)`	Used to associate the method with on change event
`Xrm.Page.getAttribute("FieldName").removeOnChange(function name)`	Used to remove the method from on change event
`Xrm.Page.getAttribute("FieldName").fireOnChange()`	Used to fire on change event on a field

 More information on attribute methods can be found at `https://msdn.microsoft.com/en-us/library/jj602964(v=crm.6).aspx`.

UI namespaces

This namespace contains methods that can be used to fetch data about user interfaces. Following are the common methods used:

Syntax	Description
`Xrm.Page.ui.close()`	Used to close entity forms
`Xrm.Page.ui.getFormType()`	Used to get the entity form type
`Xrm.Page.ui.setFormNotification(message, level, uniqueid);`	Used to show custom notification of entity forms

Syntax	Description
`Xrm.Page.ui.clearFormNotification(unique id)`	Used to clear form notifications
`Xrm.Page.ui.refreshRibbon()`	Used to refresh the command bar

 You can refer to `https://msdn.microsoft.com/en-us/library/gg327828(v=crm.6).aspx` for more details on UI methods.

Understanding client-side events

Microsoft Dynamics CRM 2015 exposes events for forms, fields, and other controls. These are the event handlers where we can call our custom JavaScript methods. We can configure our client-side code to execute on specific events or dynamically associate our method to a corresponding event. Let's first understand events related to forms.

Form events

Two events — `OnLoad` and `OnSave` — are exposed for entity forms where we can write our client-side code.

OnLoad event

The `OnLoad` event handler executes code when the entity form is loaded. We can utilize this event for controlling the behavior of entity forms and this event is useful for different scenarios. For example, we may want to hide/disable some fields based on other fields or based on the user security role. Business rules also utilize the `OnLoad` event to execute logic. We will be discussing business rules in a later topic. If we are not working in updated entity forms then `OnLoad` is executed whenever the form is loaded — for example, at the time of initial creation and after data is saved. But if we are using updated entities then the `OnLoad` event is only executed at the time of initial creation. Let's take an example; say we want to set a default credit limit of 50,000 while creating our new clients in our training solution. We can write a simple JavaScript to implement this example.

 Updated entities are those entities that provides a new form layout with command buttons instead of ribbon buttons.

We can create an individual web resource or a common JavaScript library where we can add all of our common methods. Let's add this library in the training solution that we created in *Chapter 2, Customizing Microsoft Dynamics CRM 2015*. Open our training solution by navigating **CONFIGURATION | Solutions** and perform the following steps to create our JavaScript Web resource:

1. Click on **Web Resources | New** and enter the following properties:

   Name: **him_/Scripts/Common.js**

   Display Name: **Common.js**

   TypeL Script: **(JScript)**

2. Click on **Text Editor** and use the following code.

   To create a JavaScript library, it is always a best practice to use namespaces. Namespaces allow us to group our code under one unit and help us to avoid any confusion. We can create namespaces using the following code:

```
if (typeof(HIMBAP) == "undefined") {
    HIMBAP = {
        __namespace: true
    };
}
```

   The preceding code will define the HIMBAP namespace if it is not defined already. Now we can add the following generic method, which will take two parameters for the field name and default value. We can write our methods as follows:

```
//Common methods for
HIMBAP.CommonScripts= {
//Method to set default field value
SetDefaultValue(): function(fieldName,defaultValue)
{
    //Set value
    Xrm.Page.getAttribute(fieldName).setValue(defaultValue);
},
__namespace: true
};
```

It is always a best practice to add fields under the **Non-Event Dependencies** list under **Form Properties** referenced in the script.

3. Click on **Ok** and **Save** and **Publish** our web resource.

   Now we need to add a web resource for our client entity where will be utilizing our common JavaScript library. Perform the following steps to add a Web resource for the client entity:

4. Click on **Web Resources | New** and enter the following properties:

   Name: him_/Scripts/Client.js

   Display Name: Client.js

   Type: Script (JScript)

5. Click on **Text Editor** and use the following code:

```
//Set credit limit to 50000
function SetCreditLimitDefault() {
    //Call method from common library
    HIMBAP.CommonScripts.setDefaultValue("creditlimit", 50000);
}
```

6. Click on **Ok** and save and publish the web resource.

   Now we can add these web resources to our client entity form and use them. Perform the following steps to utilize these web resources:

7. Navigate to **Components | Entities | Client | Forms** and double-click on the **Client** main form to open the form editor.

8. Click on the **Form Properties** button under the form editor ribbon bar and click on the **Add** button under **Form Libraries**.

9. Search for our web resources and click on **Add**.

 We can use our publisher prefix to search for web resources quickly.

10. Click on the **Add** button under **Event Handler**, select our **Client.js** web resource library, and use our function name under **Function** text box. It should look like this:

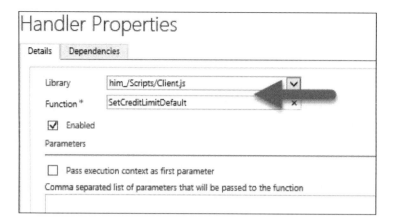

11. Click on **Ok**. The **Events** table should look like the following:

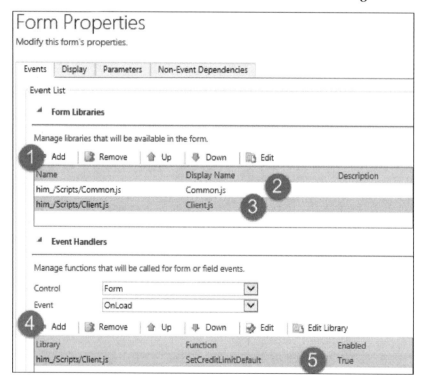

12. Click on **Ok** and save and publish our client form.

Now, when we create a new client record, it will set a default value of 50000 in the **Credit Limit** field.

OnSave event

The OnSave event is executed when the entity form is saved; for example it is executed when the user clicks on the **Save** button in the lower-right corner of the screen. It is also executed automatically after 30 seconds if auto-save is enabled.

It can also be executed using the following methods:

```
Xrm.Page.data.entity.save
Xrm.Page.data.save
Xrm.Page.data.refresh
```

We can also stop the save event, if required. Let's take an example. When all the data has been entered on the entity form and the user wants to save it to the CRM database, but before sending it to the server, let's say we want to validate the data by the user; if the validation fails, you can cancel the save event. We can use following code to cancel the save event:

```
Xrm.Page.context.getEventArgs().preventDefault();
```

 This method will only cancel the save event if all other events will be executed accordingly. You can find details about save events at https://msdn.microsoft.com/en-us/library/gg509060.aspx.

Field events

All entity fields have one event exposed: the OnChange event. The OnChange event fires when focus from the field is lost. So, as soon as we tab out from a CRM field by entering or selecting some value, our custom JavaScript code associated with the OnChange event will fire.

This statement is not true for set value fields if they are formatted as a radio button or checkbox. The OnChange event for these fields fires immediately instead of executing after the focus is lost.

Let's say we want to implement a validation on our proposed start and proposed end dates in a training request entity form. We want to make sure that the user should not select a proposed end date before a proposed start date. It should also validate this when the user tries to change value from the proposed start date if the proposed end date is available. We can add a new method in our common library as follows for this validation. Perform the following steps to update the `common.js` library:

1. Click on **Web Resources** under **Training Solution** and double-click on **Common.js** to open it.

2. Click on **Text Editor** to add the following method between the last method and the `__namespace: true` line.

```
ValidateProposedDates: function(startDate, endDate) {
    var startDateValue = Xrm.Page.getAttribute(startDate).
getValue();
    var endDateValue = Xrm.Page.getAttribute(endDate).getValue();
    if (startDateValue > endDateValue) {
        alert("End Date Should be greater than Start Date")
        Xrm.Page.getAttribute(endDate).setValue(null);
        //Set focus on end date field
        Xrm.Page.getControl(endDate).setFocus();
    }
}
```

3. **Save** and **Publish** the web resource.

   This method will take two parameters: `startDate` and `endDate`. This method will also clear the value from the end date field and will set the focus on the end date if validation fails. To call this method we need to create another local web resource for the training request entity as for the client entity. We can create a new JavaScript web resource and use the following code to call this method:

```
//To validate dates
function ValidateProposedDates() {
    HIMBAP.CommonScripts.ValidateProposedDates
                ("him_proposedstart", "him_proposedend");
}
```

   Once we have saved and published our web resource, we need to attach both web resources to our training request entity form and call our `ValidateProposedDates` method on the `OnChange` event handler for both the `him_proposedstart` and `him_proposedend` fields. After attaching these web resources to our training request entity form, it should look as follows:

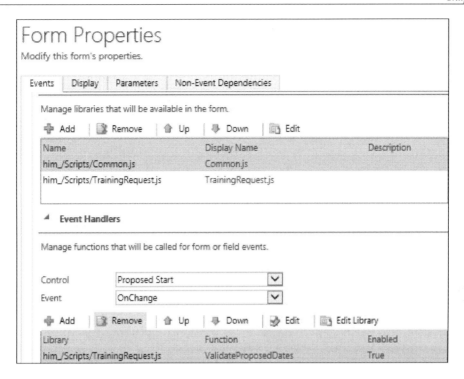

4. Save and publish the training request entity and form. Now, if we try to select an end date smaller than the start date, we will get an alert:

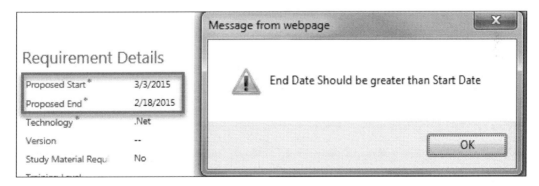

Control events

Apart from form and field events, there are specific control events that we can use for implementing client-side logic. Following are the other common events.

TabStateChange

The `TabStateChange` event is associated with the display state of tab control, so it fires when the tab control display state changes. We can use this event to control fields and other controls such as loading the IFRAME control.

OnReadyStateComplete

This event is associated with the IFRAME control and occurs when the content of the IFRAME is loaded fully.

PreSearch

This event is associated with lookup controls. We can utilize this to filter lookup controls based on our specific requirements. We can't configure this event through the UI; instead, we use `addPreSearch` and `removePreSearch` to associate our JavaScript function with the `PreSearch` event.

We are using the contact entity in our training solution to represent multiple types of record client contact (employee, trainer, and vendor) and we have trainer lookup over the proposal entity form. By default, when we click on **Trainer** lookup it will show all types of contact records:

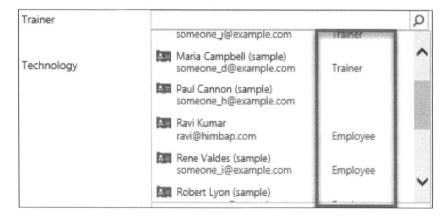

Let's say we want to filter this lookup to show only the trainer type of contact. We can use the `PreSearch` event to filter this lookup. We can pass our custom filter string to the `addCustomFilter` method. This filter string can be designed by ourselves or we can utilize Advanced Find to get this filter. Advanced Find is an out-of-the-box query engine that we can use to design our query criteria. Once designed, we can execute this query to get the result and it can be also exported as a `FetchXML` string.

Perform the following steps to design our query:

1. Click on the **ADVANCED FIND** button on the top navigation bar.

2. Select the **Contact** entity under the **Look For** drop-down and select **[new]** in the **Use Saved View:** drop-down.

3. Select **Contact Type** in the field drop-down and make sure the **Equals** operator is selected.

4. Select the **Trainer** option by clicking on the ellipses and click on **Results**.

5. Click on the **Download Fetch XML** button.

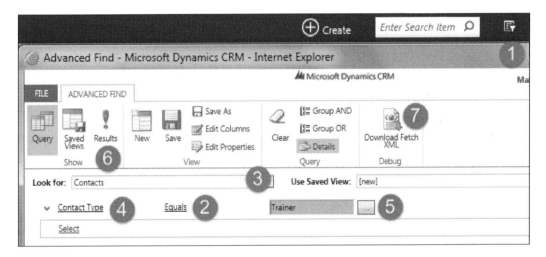

6. Open the `FetchXML` file in any XML editor and copy the filter part.

Now we have our filter string to filter the trainer lookup control, so we can add a new method in our common library and call the method from another JavaScript web resource that we will create for the proposal entity.

```
FilterLookup: function(LookupControl, Filter) {
   Xrm.Page.getControl(LookupControl).addPreSearch(function() {
        Xrm.Page.getControl(LookupControl).
addCustomFilter(Filter);
     });

},
```

These methods will take two parameters: lookup control name and filter string. After that we use the `addPreSearch` method to call the `custom` method, which will use `addCustomFilter` to lookup the control. Once this method is added to our `common.js` library, save and publish the web resource.

Now we need to create another web resource for our proposal entity. Use the following properties to set up a new JavaScript web resource as we did earlier:

7. Click on **Web Resources | New** and enter the following properties:

Name: him_/Scripts/Proposal.js

Display Name: Common.js

Type: Script (JScript)

8. Click on **Text Editor** and use the following code:

```
//to filter trainer lookup
function AddLookupFilter() {
    HIMBAP.CommonScripts.FilterLookup("him_trainer",
"<filter type='and'><condition attribute='new_contacttype'
operator='eq' value='100000001'/></filter>");
}
```

Now we need to associate our common.js and proposal.js library with the proposal entity form. We will be calling our AddLookupFilter method in OnLoad for the proposal entity form. After the web resource is added to our form, when we click the **Form Properties** button under the entity editor ribbon button, it should look like the following:

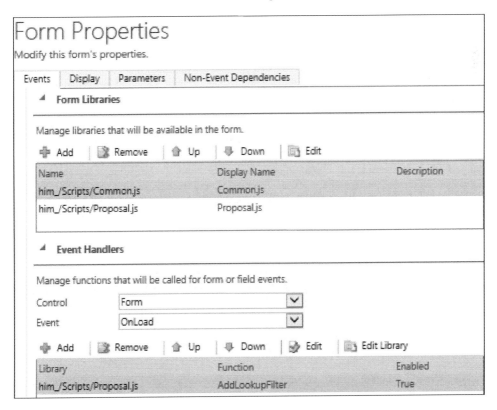

After saving and publishing the proposal entity form, when we click on **Trainer** lookup on the proposal form it will only show records where the contact type is equal to trainer, as follows:

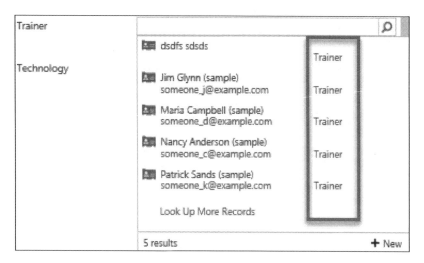

Using CRM web services in client-side code

Apart from interacting with entity forms, fields, and controls, we can also use client code to access the CRM database. This is especially necessary when we want to fetch data from another related or non-related entity. We can work with CRM web services using the client-side to get and post data to CRM. We have two endpoints available to work with Microsoft Dynamics CRM 2015:

* OData
* Modern SOAP

OData

According to OData's official website (http://www.odata.org/)

> *"An open protocol to allow the creation and consumption of queryable and interoperable RESTful APIs in a simple and standard way."*

REST stands for **Representational State Transfer**, which is based on the principle that everything is a resource and can be accessed by using a unique URI. OData can use ATOM or **JavaScript Object Notation (JSON)** to send and receive data.

ATOM is an XML language used for RSS feeds. We can use ATOM to access entity records feeds. We can append EntitySchemanName + Set to an organization data service to access specific entity record feeds. For example, for an account it will be as follows:

```
Server URL /XRMServices/2011/OrganizationData.svc/AccountSet
```

 We can find the organization service URL under **Settings | Customization | Developer Resources | Organization Data Service**.

JSON is a lightweight data interchangeable format. We use JSON to serialize JavaScript objects. We will be using JSON in our OData query samples.

 We have to use the schema name of the entity and fields in an OData query and we need to keep in mind that schema names are case-sensitive.

OData query options

While writing an OData query, we can use different options. For example, we can define filter criteria to retrieve records based on condition. We can use the following options while writing our query.

$select

Using this option we can limit the number of columns returned from the entity. We can define which specific columns we want to fetch instead of unnecessarily fetching all the columns. The following is an example of using the $select option:

```
/AccountSet?$select=Name,Address1_City,Address1_Country
```

This statement will fetch Name, Address1_City, Address1_Country fields from the account entity.

$filter

We can use this option to specify a conditional expression to fetch data. We can use logical and conditional operators in our filter expression. The following are some filter expressions:

Query	Filter Syntax
Get proposal entity records based on trainer lookup ID	/OpportunitySet?$filter=him_Trainer/Id eq (guid'" + Trainer GUID + "')

Query	Filter Syntax
Get training request records where state equals Himachal Pradesh	`/LeadSet?$filter=StateFieldSchemaName eq 'Himachal Pradesh'`
Get contact records where contact type is equal to trainer	`/ContactSet?$filter=new_ContactType/Value eq 100000001`
To get client records where the credit limit is greater than 50,000	`/AccountSet?$filter=CreditLimit/Value gt 50000`

$top

This option is used to limit the number of records in the result set. For example, if we just want to fetch the top 10 records from the account entity, we can use code as follows:

```
/AccountSet?$top=10
```

 OData returns 50 record per page; if we have more than 50 records in our entity we need to use the **Next** link to return additional pages. This is used to get the next page in the result set returned.

$orderby

This option is used to return results in a specific order such as ascending or descending. If no order is specified externally it will return data in ascending order. While writing an OData query we can specify one or more column names under order by. For example, if we want to return client data in descending order by name and city, we can write our statement as follows:

```
/AccountSet?$select=Address1_City,Name&$orderby=Name,Address1_City desc
```

$skip

This option is used to skip some entries while fetching the result set. We can define a number in this option and this is also used for paging results.

$expand

This option is used to fetch data from a related entity. To fetch related records we require the relationship name that we can check under the relationship view. The following is an example of fetching contact records related to an account:

```
/AccountSet?$expand=contact_customer_accounts
```

In the preceding query, `contact_customer_accounts` is the name of the relationship between account and contact.

We can get more details about OData query options from `https://msdn.microsoft.com/en-us/library/gg309461.aspx`.

Working with organization data services

We can use organization data services via JavaScript, AJAX, and JQuery. We can write our own custom JavaScript libraries to get data from CRM databases or we can use existing libraries that come with Microsoft Dynamics CRM 2015 SDK.

Microsoft Dynamics CRM 2015 SDK comes with the `SDK.REST.js` library, which contains all CRUD (create, retrieve, update, and delete) methods. We can upload this library as a web resource and can consume it in our JavaScript methods. We are going to write our own methods for consuming organization data services.

 We can find `SDK.REST.js` in the `SDK\SampleCode\JS\RESTEndpoint\JavaScriptRESTDataOperations\JavaScriptRESTDataOperations\Scripts` location in Microsoft Dynamics CRM 2015 SDK.

Let's take a common requirement to auto-populate fields in a child entity from a parent entity based on parent entity lookup selection. Let's say we want to auto-populate address information on a contact entity from a client based on the **Company Name** selected in the contact record. To fulfill this requirement, we need to consume organization data services to get data from the client entity based on the client ID that we can get from the **Company Name** lookup on the contact entity form. Let's first write a JavaScript function to get the client id from the company name lookup.

```
//Get client details
function GetClientID() {
    if (Xrm.Page.getAttribute("parentcustomerid").getValue() != null)
{
        var clientID =
Xrm.Page.getAttribute("parentcustomerid").getValue()[0].id;
        PopulateAddressInformationBasedOnAccount(clientID);
    }
}
```

In the preceding function, we are validating if the **parentcustomerid** field value
not equal to null and we are reading its value. The **Lookup** field represents an
array that contains three properties: ID, name, and entitytype. ID is the GUID of
the record, name is the value of name field in the record selected, and entitytype
represents the lookup source entity. Now we need to write our next function
PopulateAddressInformationBasedOnAccount where we will be passing our
client record ID.

```
function PopulateAddressInformationBasedOnAccount(clientID) {
    var clientUrl = Xrm.Page.context.getClientUrl();
    var odataPath = clientUrl + "/XRMServices/2011/OrganizationData.
svc/";
    //Make sure to use schema name
    var type = "AccountSet";
    var req = new XMLHttpRequest();
    req.open("GET", odataPath + type + "(guid'" + clientID + "')",
true);
    req.setRequestHeader("Accept", "application/json");
    req.setRequestHeader("Content-Type", "application/json;
charset=utf-8");
    req.onreadystatechange = function() {
        if (this.readyState == 4 /* complete */ ) {
            req.onreadystatechange = null;
            if (this.status == 200) {
                successCallback(JSON.parse(this.responseText).d);
            } else {
                alert("Error while fetching client data");
            }
        }
    };
    req.send();
}
```

In these methods we are using the getClientUrl method to get the server URL.
When retrieving data based on primary key fields we can use this syntax:

```
/EntitySchemaName+Set(guid'" +primaryid+ "')
```

 You can also use the codeplex utility to write OData request:
https://crmrestbuilder.codeplex.com/.

Now we need to write our last method where we will be processing our result set. You will notice here that, on the left-hand side we are using the logical name of the entity form and on the right-hand side we are using the schema name of the field because we use schema names in OData.

```
function successCallback(ResultSet) {
 Xrm.Page.getAttribute("address1_line1").setValue(ResultSet.Address
1_Line1 != null ? ResultSet.Address1_Line1 : null);
    Xrm.Page.getAttribute("address1_line2").setValue(ResultSet.Address
1_Line2 != null ? ResultSet.Address1_Line2 : null);
    Xrm.Page.getAttribute("address1_city").setValue(ResultSet.Address1
_City != null ? ResultSet.Address1_City : null);
    Xrm.Page.getAttribute("address1_country").setValue(ResultSet.Addre
ss1_Country != null ? ResultSet.Address1_Country : null);
    Xrm.Page.getAttribute("address1_stateorprovince").setValue(ResultS
et.Address1_StateOrProvience != null ?
ResultSet.Address1_StateOrProvience : null);
    Xrm.Page.getAttribute("address1_postalcode").setValue(ResultSet.Ad
dress1_PostalCode != null ? ResultSet.Address1_PostalCode : null);
}
```

Now we can create our web resource for the contact entity and paste the earlier methods. We need to call our `GetClientID` method on the `OnChange` option of the **parentcustomerid** field and it should look as follows:

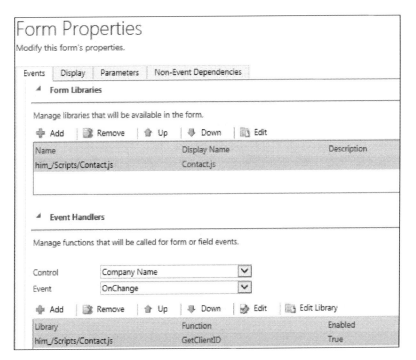

Once all our changes are saved and published when we select **Company Name** in the contact entity form, it will populate address information from the selected client in the contact form.

Modern SOAP

We can also use modern **Simple Object Access Protocol (SOAP)** endpoints to access Microsoft Dynamics CRM 2015 data. In modern SOAP we use organization services and all organization service methods can be implemented using modern SOAP.

SOAP is an XML-based protocol and it uses XML request and response for communication. Similarly to REST.SDK.js, the modern SOAP.SDK.js can be downloaded from `https://code.msdn.microsoft.com/SdkSoapjs-9b51b99a`. We can use this library or can write our own SOAP requests.

Microsoft Dynamics CRM 2015 SDK comes with the `SOAPLogger` utility, which can be used to convert server-side code to a SOAP request. This is a .net console application, so we need Visual Studio 2010 or later with .Net 4.5.2 to work with this utility. We are going to demonstrate how we can use this utility to write SOAP requests.

Let's say we want to write our earlier example using a SOAP request; perform the following steps to create a SOAP request using `SOAPLogger`:

1. Navigate to `SDK\SampleCode\CS\Client\SOAPLogger` and open the solution file.

2. Open the `SOAPLogger.cs` file and navigate to the **Run** method; we need to paste our code in the using block.

```
using (StreamWriter output = new StreamWriter("output.txt"))
{
 SoapLoggerOrganizationService slos = new
     SoapLoggerOrganizationService(serverConfig.OrganizationUri,
     service, output);
 //Add the code you want to test here:
 // You must use the SoapLoggerOrganizationService 'slos' proxy
 //than the IOrganizationService proxy you would normally use.

        Paste Your Code Here
}
```

3. We need to paste the following code here:

```
Guid accountID = new Guid("8F029291-F0B9-E411-80DB-
C4346BADB590");
Entity _account = slos.Retrieve("account", accountID, new
ColumnSet(new string[] { "name", "address1_line1",
"address1_line2", "address1_city", "address1_country",
"address1_postalcode", "address1_sateorprovince"}));
```

In this code we need to pass the GUID of the account record. We can get the account ID in different ways. One is to select the client account and use the **Copy a Link** option from the account view.

When prompted, select **Allow access for clipboard prompt**. Open any text editor and copy the GUID part as follows:

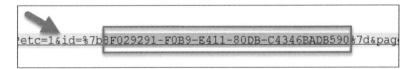

Downloading the example code

You can download the example code files from your account at `http://www.packtpub.com` for all the Packt Publishing books you have purchased. If you purchased this book elsewhere, you can visit `http://www.packtpub.com/support` and register to have the files e-mailed directly to you.

We are using the `Retrieve` method for organization web services; we will be working on organization web services in detail in later chapters. The `Retrieve` method is used to fetch data based in the primary key.

1. Build SOAPLogger and run it.

2. It will ask for your server and credentials as follows:

```
Enter a CRM server name and port [crm.dynamics.com]: crm5.dynamics.com
Is this organization provisioned in Microsoft Office 365 (y/n) [n]: y

 Enter Username:                      .onmicrosoft.com
 Enter Password: *********

List of organizations that you belong to:

(1) HIMBAP (                )

Specify an organization number (1-1) [1]: 1
Press <Enter> to exit.
```

3. After executing the application it will write an equivalent SOAP request in
`SDK\SampleCode\CS\Client\SOAPLogger\SOAPLogger\bin\Debug`.

4. Copy the complete SOAP envelope as follows:

```xml
<s:Envelope xmlns:s="http://schemas.xmlsoap.org/SOAP/envelope/">
    <s:Body>
        <Retrieve xmlns="http://schemas.microsoft.com/xrm/2011/
Contracts/Services" xmlns:i="http://www.w3.org/2001/XMLSchema-
instance">
            <entityName>account</entityName>
            <id>8f029291-f0b9-e411-80db-c4346badb590</id>
            <columnSet xmlns:a="http://schemas.microsoft.com/
xrm/2011/Contracts">
                <a:AllColumns>false</a:AllColumns>
                <a:Columns xmlns:b="http://schemas.microsoft.
com/2003/10/Serialization/Arrays">
                    <b:string>name</b:string>
                    <b:string>address1_line1</b:string>
                    <b:string>address1_line2</b:string>
                    <b:string>address1_city</b:string>
                    <b:string>address1_country</b:string>
                    <b:string>address1_postalcode</b:string>
                    <b:string>address1_stateorprovince</b:string>
                </a:Columns>
            </columnSet>
        </Retrieve>
    </s:Body>
</s:Envelope>
```

5. Now we need to prepare the SOAP request and send it as follows:

```
function GetClientInformation() {
    //get client id
    var id = Xrm.Page.getAttribute("parentcustomerid").getValue()
[0].id;
    var clientUrl = Xrm.Page.context.getClientUrl();
    //set organization service URL
    var ServiceURL = clientUrl + "/XRMServices/2011/Organization.
svc/Web";
    var requestMain = ""
    requestMain += "<s:Envelope xmlns:s=\"http://schemas.xmlsoap.
org/SOAP/envelope/\">";
    requestMain += "  <s:Body>";
    requestMain += "    <Retrieve xmlns=\"http://schemas.
microsoft.com/xrm/2011/Contracts/Services\" xmlns:i=\"http://www.
w3.org/2001/XMLSchema-instance\">";
    requestMain += "      <entityName>account</entityName>";
    requestMain += "      <id>" + id + "</id>";
    requestMain += "      <columnSet xmlns:a=\"http://schemas.
microsoft.com/xrm/2011/Contracts\">";
    requestMain += "        <a:AllColumns>false</a:AllColumns>";
    requestMain += "        <a:Columns xmlns:b=\"http://schemas.
microsoft.com/2003/10/Serialization/Arrays\">";
    requestMain += "          <b:string>name</b:string>";
    requestMain += "          <b:string>address1_line1</
b:string>";
    requestMain += "          <b:string>address1_line2</
b:string>";
    requestMain += "          <b:string>address1_city</b:string>";
    requestMain += "          <b:string>address1_country</
b:string>";
    requestMain += "          <b:string>address1_postalcode</
b:string>";
    requestMain += "          <b:string>address1_stateorprovince</
b:string>";
    requestMain += "        </a:Columns>";
    requestMain += "      </columnSet>";
    requestMain += "    </Retrieve>";
    requestMain += "  </s:Body>";
    requestMain += "</s:Envelope>";
    var req = new XMLHttpRequest();
    req.open("POST", ServiceURL, true)
        // Responses will return XML. It isn't possible to return
JSON.
    req.setRequestHeader("Accept", "application/xml, text/xml,
*/*");
    req.setRequestHeader("Content-Type", "text/xml;
charset=utf-8");
```

```
        req.setRequestHeader("SOAPAction", "http://schemas.microsoft.
com/xrm/2011/Contracts/Services/IOrganizationService/Retrieve");
        req.onreadystatechange = function() {
            successCallback(req);
        };
        req.send(requestMain);
}
```

In the preceding methods, first we get the selected client ID record and then prepare the service URL. You will notice that this time we are using the organization service URL instead of the organization data service URL, because we are writing a SOAP request. Now we need to write our `successCallBack` method where will process the result set. We need to use the following code:

```
function successCallback(req) {
    //if request is execution completed
    if (req.readyState == 4) {
        //if status is OK
        if (req.status == 200) {
            //load data in xml document object
            var xmlDoc = new ActiveXObject("Microsoft.XMLDOM");
            xmlDoc.async = "false";
            xmlDoc.loadXML(req.responseXML.xml);
            var KeyValuePairs = xmlDoc.getElementsByTagName("a:Key
ValuePairOfstringanyType");

            //clear address fields
            Xrm.Page.getAttribute("address1_line1").
setValue(null);
            Xrm.Page.getAttribute("address1_line2").
setValue(null);
            Xrm.Page.getAttribute("address1_city").setValue(null);
            Xrm.Page.getAttribute("address1_stateorprovince").
setValue(null);
            Xrm.Page.getAttribute("address1_postalcode").
setValue(null);
            //traverse resultset
            for (i = 0; i < KeyValuePairs.length; i++) {
                //compare address fields and get corresponding
value
                if (KeyValuePairs[i].childNodes[0].text ==
"address1_line1")
                    Xrm.Page.getAttribute("address1_line1").
setValue(KeyValuePairs[i].childNodes[1].text);
                if (KeyValuePairs[i].childNodes[0].text ==
"address1_line2")
                    Xrm.Page.getAttribute("address1_line2").
setValue(KeyValuePairs[i].childNodes[1].text);
```

```
                        if (KeyValuePairs[i].childNodes[0].text ==
"address1_city")
                               Xrm.Page.getAttribute("address1_city").
setValue(KeyValuePairs[i].childNodes[1].text);
                        if (KeyValuePairs[i].childNodes[0].text ==
"address1_stateorprovince")
                               Xrm.Page.getAttribute("address1_
stateorprovince").setValue(KeyValuePairs[i].childNodes[1].text);
                        if (KeyValuePairs[i].childNodes[0].text ==
"address1_postalcode")
                               Xrm.Page.getAttribute("address1_postalcode").
setValue(KeyValuePairs[i].childNodes[1].text);
                }
        } else {
            alert("Error while retrieving client record");
        }
    }
}
```

6. Now we can create the JavaScript web resource and can paste our earlier code there.

7. Attach the web resource to the contact form and call **GetClientInformation OnChange** in the **parentcustomerid** field in the contact entity.

8. **Save** and **Publish** changes.

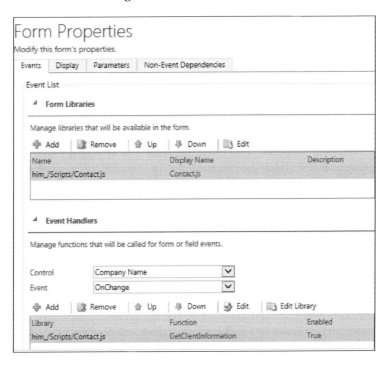

You can also use `SOAP.SDK.js` to work with modern SOAP endpoints. You can find it here at `http://code.msdn.microsoft.com/SdkSoapjs-9b51b99a`.

OData versus Modern SOAP

We can use both endpoints to get data from Microsoft Dynamics CRM 2015 databases. Although SOAP supports more methods, OData is easy to develop with. The following table shows the differences between OData and Modern SOAP:

OData	Modern SOAP
Only supports CURD, Associate and Disassociate methods	Supports all methods
Can't access metadata	Metadata can be accessed
Returns 50 records per page	Returns 5,000 records per page
Schema names used for entities and fields while writing queries	Logical names used while writing queries
Easy to write and provides a better development experience	Comparatively hard to write

Understanding business rules

Business rules help us to implement business logic without any coding requirement. System administrators or business users can use the out-of-the-box business rule designer to design business specific validations in a declarative manner.

Business rules were initially released in Microsoft Dynamics CRM 2013, but we got new enhancements in Microsoft Dynamics CRM 2015. Business rules can be used for simply setting default value or doing complex calculations using formulas. While creating a business rule, we can define its scope. We have the flexibility of applying business rules to specific entity forms or all entity forms (if we are using multiple entity forms).

Business rules are portable so we can take them from one environment to another. When we include our entity in the solution, business rules are also included in it. We can create business rules from different places such as from entity forms, field property forms, and entity trees.

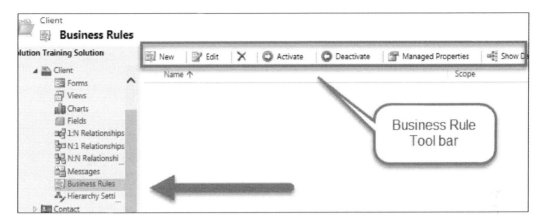

While creating business rules we will be getting the business rule designer as follows, where we can define conditions and their corresponding actions. We can use the Scope drop-down to select options for our business rule scope.

 Business rules can be applied to quick create forms specifically; when the business rule scope is selected as **All Forms**, it is also applied on quick create forms.

Business rules can be only applied to entity fields, currently we can't use business rules for other controls. Microsoft Dynamics CRM 2015 allow us to write both server-side and client-side business rules. We will be discussing more on this in later topic. Client-side business rules are executed on OnChange of the field and OnLoad of entity form.

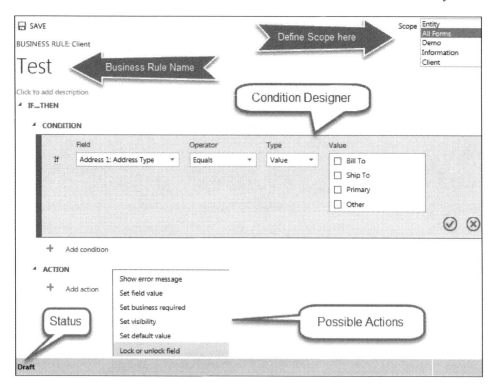

 A client-side business rule will only be executed if the field is available on entity forms.

Actions in business rules

We can use business rules for different requirements. Following are the six business rule actions that we can use for applying business validations.

Showing error messages

We can show an error message using a business rule when any business-specific validations fails. Let's take an example in our training solution: the **Job Title** field should be completed by the user if **Contact Type** is employee. We can design our business rule like following to display an error message on the **Job Title** field:

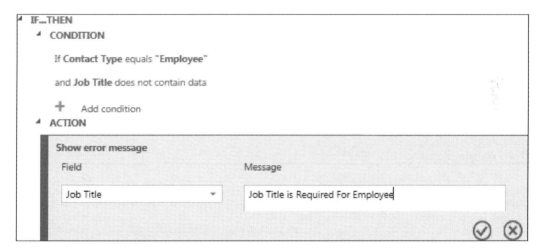

Once activated, it will show an error message as follows if the **Job Title** is blank for an employee.

Setting business requirements

We can also send business requirements using business rules. It may be that, if a specific field is selected, we dynamically want to make some another field required. For instance, in the previous example we can add another action to make the **Job Title** field required. But we also need to remove the requirement level if **Contact Type** is not **Employee** as follows:

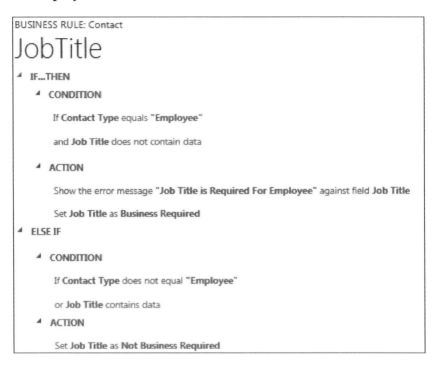

Now it will also show an error message and will remove the requirement level if **Contact Type** is not **Employee** or **Job Title** is completed by the user.

Setting field values

Business rules also contain actions for setting field values. To set a field value we can utilize three options—value, field, or formula—based on the field datatype. We can assign specific values to the target field or we can select a field option to copy another similar datatype field value to the target field. We can set values using the following options:

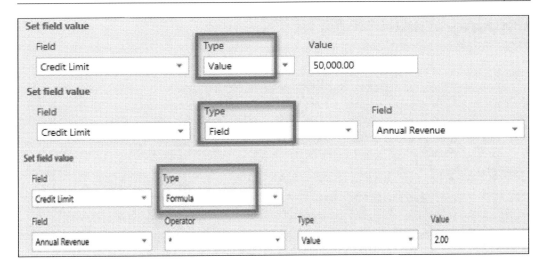

Setting visibility

Now we don't need to write JavaScript to hide the field; we can use business rules to set the visibility of the field based on a condition.

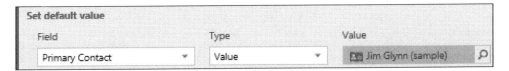

Setting default values

Another new enhancement was added in Microsoft Dynamics CRM 2015 to business rules. We can use business rules to set up default values when a record is created. For example you may want to set a pricelist as the default. Keep in mind, while you are deploying business rules from one environment to another, that the default lookup will only work if a source record exists in the target system with the same GUID.

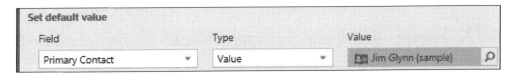

 You can import data in Microsoft Dynamics CRM 2015 from one environment to another and can keep the same record GUID.

Locking or unlocking fields

This option is used to disable or enabled a field based on a condition.

 Showing error messages and setting value actions can't be used without conditions.

Server-side versus client-side business rules

Initially, business rules were only available to run on the client-side, but Microsoft Dynamics CRM 2015 added the ability to run business rules on the server-side as well. If business rules are activated using the **Entity** scope they are executed on both the server-side and client-side.

For example if we have created a business rule to set up some fields and activated our business rule using the **Entity** option, it will be executed when we try to create a record using the CRM SDK or through any other server-side process.

When any business rule scope is set to **Entity** and an entity record is created or edited using entity forms, the business rule will be executed twice, the first time on the client and the second time on the server. Because of this, CRM won't allow us to create a circular reference to the field if the business scope is **Entity**.

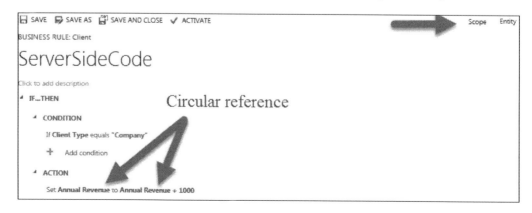

For example, in the preceding example we are using the **Annual Revenue** field on both sides and the scope of the business rule is **Entity**. This will double the value of the **Annual Revenue** field, so CRM won't allow us to activate this business rule. When we try to activate this rule, it will show an error as follows:

Summary

In this chapter we learned about the Microsoft Dynamics CRM 2015 client-side model. We learned about creating different web resources and using them in entity forms. We discussed the Xrm.Page object mode and its object methods. We discussed how can we consume OData endpoints and SOAP endpoints to get Microsoft Dynamics CRM 2015 data using the client-side. We also discussed business rules and new enhancements in Microsoft Dynamics CRM 2015. In the next chapter, we are going to create a new sample application for library management using Microsoft Dynamics CRM 2015.

4
Working with Processes

Microsoft Dynamics CRM 2015 provides different automation options to automate business-specific processes. In this chapter we are going to learn about processes and their use. We will be discussing different processes and new enhancements to them. We are going to create a new sample application for library management. We will demonstrate how we can leverage CRM 2015 processes to automate library management activities. Following are the topics that we are going to discuss in this chapter:

- Understanding processes
- Building library management solutions
- Understanding business process flow
- Understanding workflows
- Creating asynchronous workflows
- Creating synchronous workflows
- Understanding dialogs
- Understanding actions
- Business process flows versus workflows, dialogs, and actions
- Testing library management solutions

Understanding processes

Automation is a critical requirement for any business application. Every business has predefined business activities that they want to automate. Microsoft Dynamics CRM 2015 helps us to automate our business-specific requirements using different types of processes.

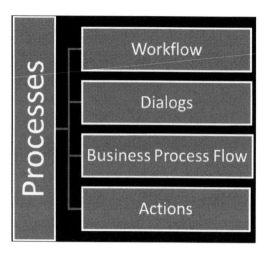

Workflows are based on a Windows **Workflow Foundation (WF)** framework; this provides the required framework for writing workflows. It basically includes the run time engine, which is responsible for the overall process execution.

 Refer to https://msdn.microsoft.com/en-us/library/ versustudio/ms734631%28v=versus.90%29.aspx for more details on Windows Workflow Foundation.

Workflow can be set up as synchronous or asynchronous. Asynchronous processes help us to run our automation in the background. Asynchronous processes work with the asynchronous queue manager, which is responsible for the execution of asynchronous processes based on event execution order. They can be executed after a short delay or can take longer to execute, depending on the number of asynchronous processes in the queue manager.

Synchronous processes do not execute in the background; instead they are executed instantly. If you are looking for instant results, you should consider using synchronous processes for implementing your automations. We can use workflows, dialogs, and actions for implementing synchronous processes in Microsoft Dynamics CRM 2015.

Dialogs provide the flexibility to execute processes with user interaction. During execution we can take some input and provide output to the user if required. These processes are always synchronous in nature.

Business process flows are graphical representations of our process that help us to track the status of our process at different levels. We can also use branching logic to change business processes based on some user input.

Actions are a way of defining our custom events like out-of-the-box events; then we can call them using client-side code or server-side code. We can also register our custom logic on these events. We will be discussing actions in a later chapter.

Building a library management solution

We will be building a library management system solution in this chapter, where we will utilize our out-of-the-box entities such as **Contact** and **System User** and will also create custom entities to map different requirements of the library management system. We will be utilizing different processes to automate our requirements. We will be implementing the following functionality in our solution:

- Maintaining records of members, books, and book issue/return details
- Automating processes to generate an auto ID for books, members, and for book issue/return
- Providing interactive ways to check the book inventory before issuing books
- Maintaining the book inventory at the time of book issue/return
- Setting default values for specific fields

Library management solution design

We will be customizing some of the existing entities and will be creating new custom entities. The following table shows the entities and their mapping information:

Name	Mapped With	Description
Contact	Member	To store library user information
Book	Custom entity	To store book details
Book issue	Custom entity	To store issue and return details
Auto number configuration	Custom entity	To store details about auto numbering
Employee	User	To store employee details

Let's first create our solution by following these steps:

1. Navigate to **Settings | Solutions | New** from the top navigation bar.
2. Enter the following solution properties and click on **Save**:

   Display Name: Library Management

   Name: TrainingSolution (it will be filled automatically, after tabbing out from the display name field)

   Publisher: HIMBAP

   Version: 7.0.1.128

 We need to set up **HIMBAP** publisher first; please follow the steps in the *Creating publisher* section in *Chapter 2, Customizing Microsoft Dynamics CRM 2015.*

Adding components to solution

Let's add our existing entities to the solution so that we can keep our customization in a separate solution and export it easily. We need to add the **Contact** and **User** entities to our solution. We can follow these steps to do this:

1. Select **Entities** and click on the **Add Existing** button.
2. Select the **Contact** and **User entities** and click on **OK**.
3. Select the **No, do not include required components** option under the **Missing Required Components** dialog and click on **OK**.

Customizing entities

 Let's first rename our existing entities, views and other places. We can follow the same approach that we used in *Chapter 2, Customizing Microsoft Dynamics CRM 2015* in the *Renaming entities* section to rename entities using translations. Please follow the same steps to rename entities based on the following screens.

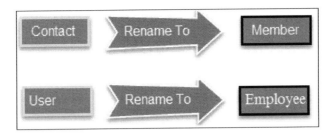

After renaming the entities, let's create our custom entities. We need to create three custom entities: book, book issue, and auto number configuration. We will use the book issue entity to store book issues and return details. In the auto number configuration entity we will store configuration about the auto number setup for the book and member entities.

Customizing member entity

We are using the contact entity to store library member information. We will be reusing all the out-of-the-box fields of the contact entity. We will just be customizing the **Main Form** and **Member Card** quick view forms. Follow these steps to customize the member entity form:

1. Navigate to **Entities | Member | Forms** under our library solution and double-click on the **Main Form**.

2. We need to rearrange fields based on the following design:

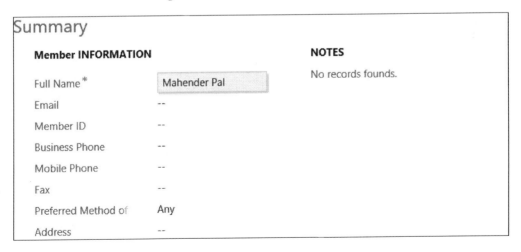

3. Click on the **Save and Close** button on the entity editor command bar.

We also need to modify the **Member Card** form; we will be using this form in our book issue/return entity. Double-click on the **Member Card** form and rearrange the fields as follows; then click on the **Save and Close** button. After that we need to publish the member entity.

MEMBER DETAILS

Mahender Pal

Email	--
Mobile	--
Business	--

Recent Issues Books

Book	Book Issue ID ↑

To enable this content, create the record.

Creating a custom entity

We can create a custom entity in Microsoft Dynamics CRM 2015 to map our custom business requirements. But it always recommended to consider using out-of-the-box entities before a creating custom entity. Custom entities can be created as a standard custom entity or activity type custom entity. A standard custom entity is similar to an out-of-the-box business entity such as account, contact, lead, and opportunity. When custom entities are created, the system creates some default attributes and views. We can't delete these attributes such as `createdon` and `modifiedon` and views such as `lookup` and `associated` views but we can further customize entities and can add custom attributes and custom views if required.

While creating a standard custom entity we have the option to set up ownership as **User or Team** or **Organizations**. By default our custom entity is available only for the System Administrator role so we need to configure individual security roles to provide access to our custom entity. We can configure them under the **Custom Entities** tab in security role editor.

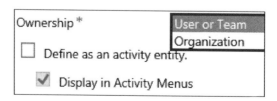

We can also configure the **Managed Property** of a custom entity to restrict customization on it when exported as part of **Managed Solution**.

Custom activity type entities are similar to existing activity entities such as e-mail, task, phone call, and others. When we create a custom activity type entity some standard activity-related fields are created such as `actualstart` and `actualend`, `subject`, `duration`, `scheduledon`, `to`, `from`, `bcc`, `cc` and others. In the custom activity type entity we always have the subject as the primary field; we can't change it.

Actually, all of the activity type entities are connected to one special type of system entity called **ActivityPointer**, which provides common activity fields and views. We can only set ownership of the custom activity type entity as **Organizations**; if we try to create a custom entity with organization ownership, we will get the error "A custom entity defined as an activity must be user or team owned". All activity type entities share the same set of privileges, so we can't configure individual custom activity type entity privileges. When a custom activity type entity is created it is available to other users who have access to other existing activity type entities.

While creating an entity we need to configure the following areas.

Entity definition

This section stores basic entity definition details such as the display name of the entity; based on the display name, the logical name is auto-populated. It also has a field to select a primary image. To set the primary image first we need to create image type attributes in our entity and then we can update this field. In the entity definition we can select if we want to create a standard or activity type entity.

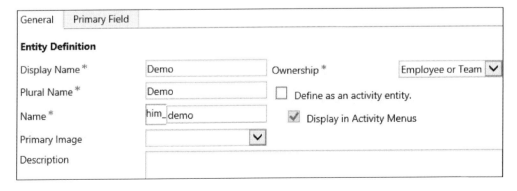

A prefix key word based on the publisher selected is prefixed before the entity name for custom entities.

We need to also define ownership of the entity, which helps us to implement security requirements. We have the two following options:

- User or team
- Organization

When an entity is created with ownership as **User or Team,** an additional field is added to handle ownership for the team and user. We also have the option to set privileges using five access levels: none, user, business unit, parent child business unit, and organization. But when an entity is created with ownership as Organization, we can set two access levels: none or organization.

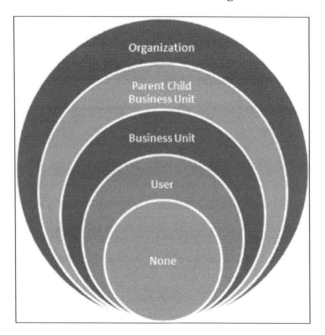

Let's look at the different levels in the preceding image:

- **Organization**: Using this access level, data from a complete organization can be accessed
- **Parent Child Business Unit**: Using this access level, data from current and child business units can be accessed

- **Business Unit**: Using this access level, data from the current business can be accessed
- **User**: Using this access level, data created by the user, shared to that user, and assigned to that user can be accessed
- **None**: Using this access level, no data access is available

 You can refer to https://msdn.microsoft.com/en-us/library/gg334717.aspx for more details on access levels.

Areas that display this entity

Under this section we can select in which module we want to show our entity. We can select any individual module or select all modules if we want to show our entity in all modules.

Areas that display this entity

☑ Sales ☑ Service ☐ Marketing ☐ Settings
☐ Help

Process

Under this section we can configure if we want to use business process flows for our entity. We will be discussing business process flows in detail in later topics. If this option is selected, a different process field is created. Once this option is selected it can't be disabled.

Communication and collaboration

Under this section we can configure different options used for different communication methods such as Activities, Notes, Sending e-mails. and other options.

Setting	Description
Notes (includes attachments) +	Enabling this options allows us to add notes using the free text area to entity records; we can also attach documents using this option
Activities +	Enabling this options allows to create different types of activity record (such as e-mail, task, and phone call) for entity records
Connections +	When this option is enabled it allows us to relate entity records with other entity records

Setting	Description
Sending e-mail	Allows us to send direct e-mails to entity records; enabling this option creates one e-mail field if it is not already created for the entity
Mail merge	If enabled this entity can be used in mail merges
Document management	Allows us to store documents related to the entity in SharePoint. To enable SharePoint integration refer to: `https://technet.microsoft.com/en-us/library/dn531154.aspx`
Access Teams	To enable this entity for access teams
Queues +	To enable this entity for queue management

All the options with a **+** sign can't be disabled once they are enabled, so we can leave these options and enable them later, if required.

Data services

Under this section we can select if we want to use quick create forms for our custom entity. Even if we created a quick created form, the form won't be listed in the quick create bar unless this option is not selected. We can also enable the duplicate detection and auditing features from this section.

Data Services
- [ ] Allow quick create
- [x] Duplicate detection
- [ ] Auditing

Outlook and mobile

This section allows us to enable our entity for Outlook and mobile clients. We can also enable the entity for CRM for tablet clients as well.

Outlook & Mobile
- [ ] CRM for phones
- [ ] CRM for tablets
  - [ ] Read-only in CRM for tablets
- [x] Reading pane in CRM for Outlook
- [ ] Offline capability for CRM for Outlook

Now let's create our custom entity; we need to navigate to our library management solution and follow these steps to create our custom entity.

1. Navigate to **Entities** under our solution and select the **New** option.
2. Enter the following properties:

   Display Name: **Book Issue/Return**

   Plural Name: **Book Issue/Return**

   Name: **him_bookissue**

   Ownership: **User or Team**

   Areas that display this entity: **Sales**

   Business process flows: **Selected**

   Notes: **Selected**

   Activities: **Deselected**

3. Keep all other options as defaults and click on the **Save** button.

Now we need to set up a data structure for the entity. Please refer to *Appendix A, Data Model for Client Entities* and *Appendix B, Data Model for Account Entities* setup field for our entity.

Form design

Once our data structure is set up, we need to customize the **Main Form** of the entity and place the field over the form. Use the following steps to customize the form:

1. Navigate to **Entities** | **Book Issue/Return** | **Forms** under our library solution and double-click on the **Main Form**.
2. Double-click on the **Header** tab to activate it and drag the following fields from **Field Explorer** to the **Header** tab:

   Book Issue ID

   Issue To

   Issue On

   Returned Date

3. Double-click on the body area to activate it and rename the **General** section to **Details**.

4. Select the **Details** section and click on **Quick View Form** under **INSERT**.

5. Select the quick view properties as follows and click on **Ok**. After that we need to save and publish our changes.

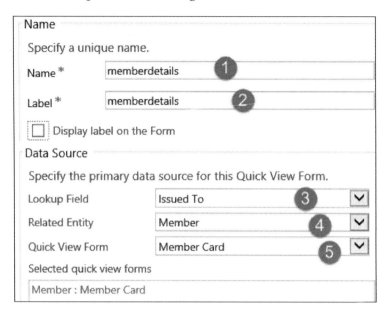

We need to add another quick view for book information based on the book lookup. We will design that view while creating the book entity.

Creating entity views

Views are basically a list of records for a specific entity. For example if we navigate to the account entity we will see the default public view **My Active Accounts**, which basically display a list of records that include records owned by current user and records assigned to current user. We can customize views and change their different properties based on requirements such as columns, sorting records based on specific fields, and changing view filter criteria, and so on.

 We can configure sorting for any view up two fields from the primary entity only.

When we create a new custom entity, different system and public views are created automatically. The following is a list of the views for the book issue / return entity.

- **Active Book Issue**: This is the default view of the book issue entity. Every entity contains one default public view that is available when we try to access that entity record.

- **Book Issue Advance Find View**: This view is presented when users try to search records based on different conditions under the advanced find view.

- **Book Issue Associated View**: This view is available in the parent entity record and used to show all related child records under parent entity records. For example if the A and B entities are related with a 1:N relationship then the associated view will be available under entity A to show all related B entity records.

- **Book Issue Lookup View**: This view is associated with the lookup field and presented when the lookup field is clicked. This view lists all the records that can be associated with the target entity.

- **Inactive Book Issue**: This view display all the disabled records of the entity.

- **Quick Find Active Book Issue**: As the name suggest, this view is used to find quick records based on the field configured under find columns.

Let's set up two views, **Issues Books** and **Returned Books**, for our entity. Perform the following steps to set up the views:

1. Navigate to **Entities | Book Issue/Return | Views** under our library solution and click on the **New** button.

2. Enter the following properties and click on **OK**:

   Name: **Issued Books**

   Description: **View for issued books**

3. Click on **Add Columns** and add the following fields:

    Book

    Book Category

    Issued On

    Issued To

    Status

4. Click on **Edit Filter Criteria** to add a condition as follows and click on **OK**:

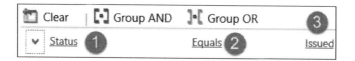

5. Click on the **Save and Close** button.
6. Repeat the preceding steps to set up another view with the name **Returned Book**.
7. Configure criteria to check the status is equal to **Returned** with the following fields:

    Book

    Book Category

    Issued On

    Issued To

    Returned Date

    Status

8. Click on **Publish All Customization** to publish changes.

In a similar way we can also customize existing views to add the preceding columns to them.

Creating book entity

We need to follow the preceding steps and create our book entity to store book information. Use the following information to create the book entity and keep the other settings at their defaults:

Title	Value
Display name	Book
Plural name	Books

Title	Value
Name	him_book
Area	Sales
Communication and collaboration, Data services, Outlook and mobile, Help	Deselect all options

Once the entity is created we need to refer *Appendix A, Data Model for Client Entities* and *Appendix B, Data Model for Account Entities* to create data structure for book entity.

Form design

After setting up the data structure we need to place book entity fields into the main form as follows:

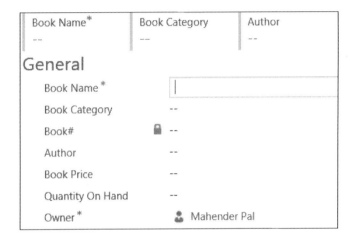

1. Double-click on the **Book#** field, select **Field** is read-only under **Field Behavior**, and click on **OK**.
2. Double-click on the **Autoid** field and deselect the **Visible by default** option.
3. Save and publish your changes.

Creating an auto number configuration entity

We need to set up another custom entity to store auto number configuration details. Use the following details to set up this entity just like we set up our previous entity.

Title	Value
Display name	Auto number configuration
Plural name	Auto number configurations

Title	Value
Name	him_autonumberconfiguration
Area	Settings
Communication and collaboration, Data services, Outlook and mobile, Help	Deselect all options

Setting a relationship with the member and book entities

We want to implement auto numbering functionality in the member and book entities to set a unique identification number for both of these entities records. For that we need to set up a N:1 relationship between the member, book, and auto number configuration entities. Perform the following steps to set up the relationship:

1. Navigate to **Entities | Auto Number Configuration | 1:N Relationships**.

2. Click on **New 1-to-Many Relationship** and enter the **Relationship Definition** and **Lookup Field** properties as follows (and keep the other details as defaults):

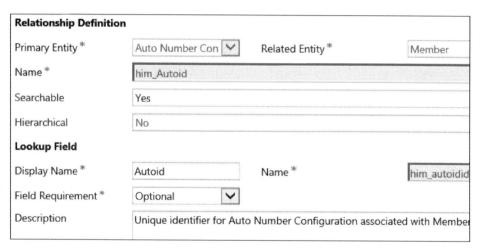

3. Click on **Save and Close**.

4. Repeat step 2 to set up a 1:N relationship with **Book** and enter **Relationship Definition** and **Look Field** properties as follows (and keep the other details as defaults):

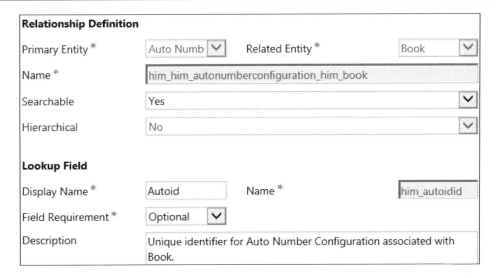

5. Click on **Save and Close** and click on **Publish All Customization** to publish our changes.

A new **him_autoid** field will be created in member and book entity, we need to place this field over member and book entity form, we will be using this field while creating workflow.

Understanding business process flow

Business processes are a very critical part of any business application. Business process flow is one of the business process implementation tools in CRM 2015 that allows us to implement different kinds of processes with different stages. So we can divide our processes into small stages such as qualify, develop, process, and close. We can enable business processes for system entities as well as for custom entities. The following screenshot displays the out-of-the-box **Lead to Opportunity Sales Process**; this process is enabled by default for the lead entity.

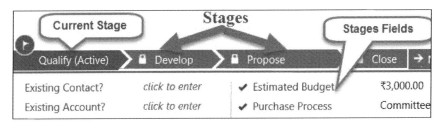

Microsoft Dynamics CRM 2015 comes with three out-of-the-box business process:

- **Lead to Opportunity Sales Process**
- **Opportunity Sales Process**
- **Phone to Case Process**

But we can also design our own custom business process flow. Business process flow is designed by using the out-of-the-box process designer. We can navigate to **Settings | Process | New** and select **Business Process Flow** as a category to create a new business process flow. We can only create a business process flow for an entity if the **Business Process Flow** option is selected under the entity definition.

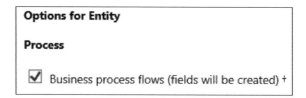

As soon as this option is enabled for an entity, CRM creates two fields named **Process Id** (to store the unique business process flow GUID) and **Stage Id** (to store the unique business process stage GUID). Currently we can create a new business process flow for 27 system entities and our custom entities. CRM allows us to create an unlimited number of business processes but we can only activate up to 10 business process flows per entity. We can also create multi-entity business process flows where more than one entity will be used in the business process flow; for example the **Lead to Opportunity Sales Process** is a multi-entity business process flow that will start from lead and will be redirected to opportunity once lead is qualified. We can use a maximum of five entities per business process flow.

You can get a list of system entities enabled for business process flow from: `https://technet.microsoft.com/en-us/library/dn531164.aspx`.

Business process flow is designed by using the out-of-the-box process designer; we can navigate to **Settings | Process | New** and select **Business Process Flow** as a category.

Using stages

Every business process flow consists of one or more stages, which logically divide our business process flow into different sub processes. We can create up to 30 stages per entity.

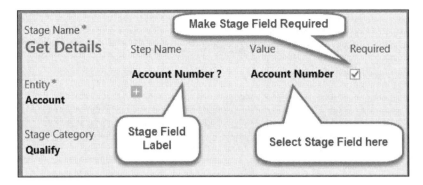

Every stage contains a set of fields that should be considered before moving on to the next stage. We can also make them required just like other entity form fields. Using these stages we can easily identify the current status of the business process flow.

Using branching logic

New enhancements in business process flow now allow us to use branching in the business process flow to jump from one stage to another based on criteria. While designing business process flows, we can define criteria to change the stage. We can also use branching to change the stage from one entity to another entity using a 1:N relationship. So, for example, in the following screen based on the **Relationship Type** selection, we can jump to a different state where the main entity is **Appointment**.

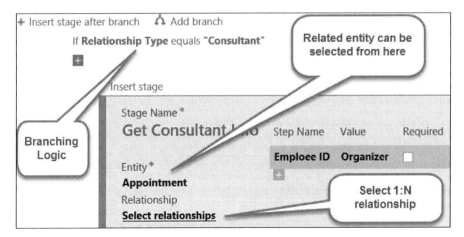

Controlling and ordering business process flows

If we have designed multiple business process flows for an entity, we can control their order using the **Order Process Flow** command button and select which process will be visible to the user first. We can also control the visibility of the business process flow by associating a security role with the business process flow; for example we can enable one business process flow for a sales person and another for a sales manager.

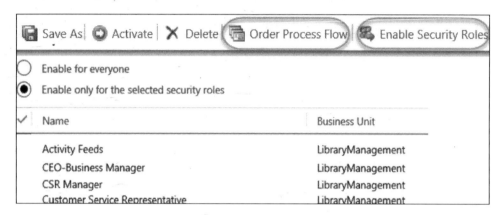

We can change business process flow using the **Switch Process** button available under the more commands (...) option in the entity record command bar.

Creating business process flow

Now we have an understanding of business process flows, so let's set one up for our book issue/return entity, so that we can manage the issue and return process. Perform the following steps to create a business process flow:

1. Navigate to **Components** | **Processes** | **New** in our solution.
2. Enter the following properties and click on **OK**:

   Process name: Book Issue Return Process

   Category: Business Process Flow

   Entity: Book Issue/Return

   Type: New blank process

3. Enter **Issue Book** under **Stage Name** and click on **Select** to enter a data field under **Value** to select entity fields. We need to select the following fields:

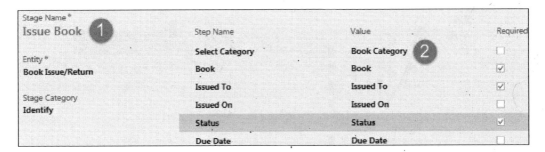

4. Click on the **Add branch link** and enter the following condition:

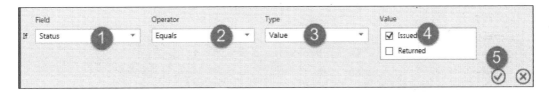

5. Set the **Return** stage based on the following screenshot:

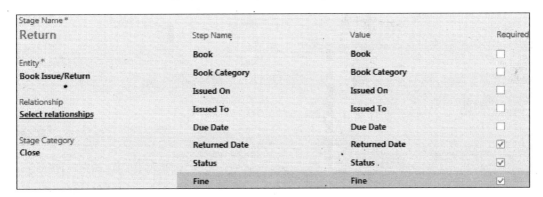

6. Click on the **Save** button and then the **Activate** button.

Now, when we try to create a book issue/return record, our form should look like the following screenshot:

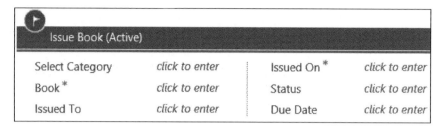

Understanding workflows

As discussed earlier, we can create two types of workflow: asynchronous and synchronous. Asynchronous workflows are best suited for long-running jobs such as sending bulk e-mails and long-running business logic whereas synchronous workflows are most applicable where we want to run our logic quickly.

The following screenshot shows the asynchronous workflow editor:

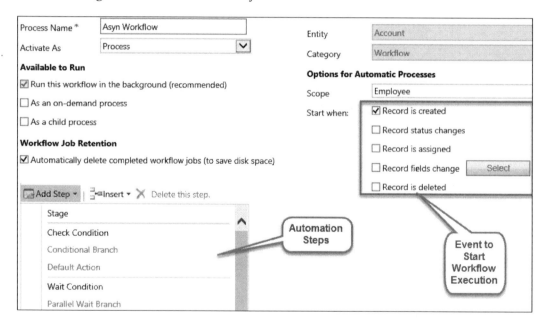

While creating workflows, we need to configure the different properties shown below that define workflow behavior.

Activating workflow

Workflows can be activated using the following two options:

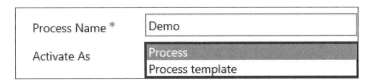

- **Process**: Used to activate workflows as a standard process
- **Process Template**: Used to activate workflows as templates. so that they can be reused to create similar workflows

Available to run

While creating a workflow we can define the workflow execution option. We can select the **Run this workflow in the background (recommended)** option if we want to create an asynchronous workflow. This option is deselected for synchronous workflows. Workflow can be initiated manually if the **As an on-demand process** option is selected. We can also call a workflow from another workflow if the **As a child process** option is selected.

Workflow job retention

This property is very important for cleaning all completed workflows jobs from the CRM database. We can select **Automatically delete completed workflow jobs (to save disk space)** to delete completed system jobs.

Automatic execution events

We have the following different events to start our workflow with automatically:

- **Record is created**: This event is used to execute the workflow when an entity record is created.
- **Record status change**: This event is used to execute the workflow as a record's status is changed—for example, active to inactive.
- **Record is assigned**: This event is initiated when an entity record is assigned a user or team.

- **Record fields change**: This option help us to execute workflows when selected fields are updated.

- **Record is deleted**: This event is used to execute workflow when an entity record is deleted.

Workflow scope

Workflow scope defines the target record set on which a workflow can be executed. Following are the scope options available for workflows:

- **User**: If set to this option only records owned by the user will be affected by the workflow

- **Business Unit**: If set to this option records owned by the user's business unit will be affected by the workflow

- **Parent Child Business Unit**: If set to this option records will be affected by workflows from the user's business unit as well as child business units

- **Organization**: If set to this option all organization records will be affected by the workflow

The preceding scopes are similar to the access level that we discussed in the **Entity Definition** topic while creating a custom entity.

Creating asynchronous workflows

Let's say we want to implement a simple book inventory update; when a book is issued, we need to decrease the quantity on hand field in the associated book record by 1 and when a book is returned we need to increase the quantity on hand by 1.

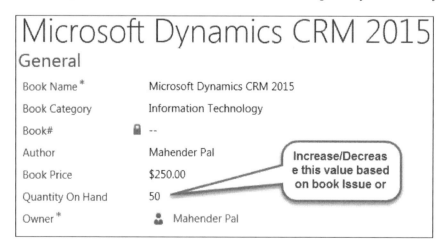

We can do this using a workflow, so perform the following steps to create one:

1. Navigate to **Components** | **Process** | **New**.

2. Enter the following properties and click on **OK**:

   Process name: **Update Book Inventory**

   Category: **Workflow**

   Entity: **Book Issue/Return**

   Keep **New blank process** option selected

   Keep **Run this workflow in background** option selected

3. Select the **Record is created** and **Record fields change** options, click on the **Select** button, and select the **him_status** field from available fields.

4. Click on the **Add Step** drop-down and select **Check Condition**, click on **Click to configure for the hyperlink**.

5. Add a condition such as the following by selecting the corresponding option from the select drop-down and click on **Save and Close**.

6. Click on **Select this row**, click **Add Step** line, and select **Update Record** under the **Add Step** drop-down. We need to select **Book** under the **Update** drop-down button and need to click on the **Set Properties** button.

7. Select the **Quantity On Hand** field and select the following properties from **Form Assistant**. Then click on **OK** and **Save and Close**:

   Operator: **Decrement by**

   Default value: **1**

8. Select the if condition block and select **Default Action** under **Add Step**, click on **Click to configure for the hyperlink**.

9. Follow step 5 to check the condition as follows:

10. Follow steps 6 and 7, with the following properties from the **Form Assistant**:

    Operator: **Increment by**
    Default value: **1**

After all these steps, our workflow should look like following screen:

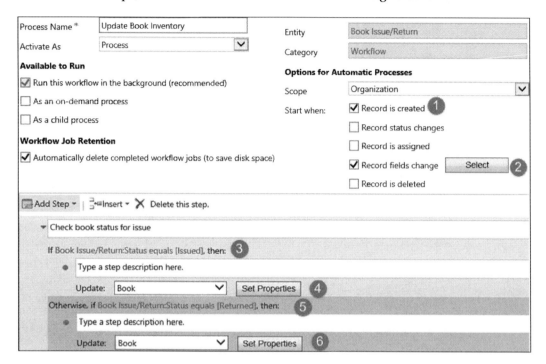

When the book is issued or returned, the preceding workflow will update the quantity on hand value accordingly.

Creating synchronous workflows

Real-time workflows were introduced in Microsoft Dynamics CRM 2013. They provide us with the flexibility to run our business logic before and after the core operation just like plug-ins. It also executes logic in transactions so, in the case of failure, all the modifications will be rolled back. They also introduced some new steps that are not available in asynchronous workflows.

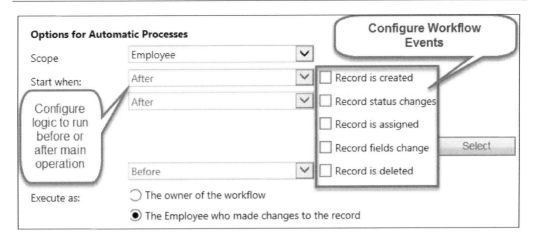

Let's take an example. We want to implement a business requirement where, before a book can be issued, we want to validate the book inventory. So we want to check if the quantity on hand is greater than 0; if it is equal to 0, we want to show an error message to the user. This requirement can't be implemented using asynchronous workflows because we need to show an error message to the user and also need to check the quantity on hand value quickly. To implement this requirement we need to create a real-time workflow. Perform the following steps to set up a real-time workflow:

1. Navigate to **Components | Process | New**.

2. Enter the following properties and click on **OK**:

   Process name: **Validate Book Inventory**

   Category: **Workflow**

   Entity: **Book Issue/Return**

   Keep **New blank process** option selected

   Deselect **Run this workflow in background** option

3. Select the **Record is created** option under **Start** when.

4. Click on **Add Step** and add two conditions such as the following:

5. Select the drop-down sign before both conditions one by one and click on the **Select Row** option from drop-down.

6. Click on the **Group OR button** once both conditions are selected.

7. Click on **Select this row**, click the **Add Step** line and select **Stop Workflow** under the **Add Step** drop-down.

8. Select the **Canceled** option under the drop-down, click on the **Set Properties** button, and enter "Book is not available. Please try another book" under the value text box. Click on **Save and Close**.

After following all the preceding steps our workflow should look like the following:

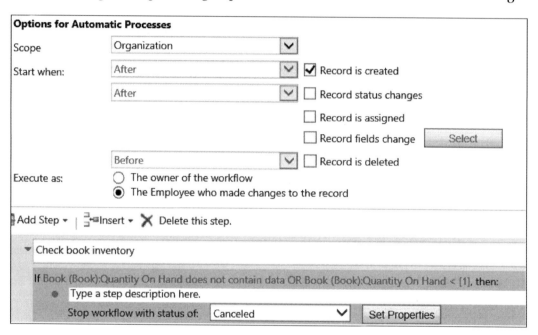

Now when we try to issue a book that is not available, it will show an error message like the following screen:

Generating Autoid using a real-time workflow

As synchronous workflows execute at that movement only, we can also use them to generate an auto ID for entity records. Let's say we want to use real-time workflows to generate an auto ID for our member, book, and book issue/return entities. Before creating the workflow we need to make sure our custom auto number configuration entity is created with a relationship with the preceding entities and we need to create a record for all three entities with a starting value. See the following screen:

Now perform the following steps to create a real-time workflow to generate an auto ID for our member entity when a new record is created for the member entity:

1. Navigate to **Components | Process | New**.

2. Enter the following properties and click on **OK**:

    Process name: MemberID

    Category: **Workflow**

    Entity: **Member**

    Keep **New blank process** option selected

    Deselect **Run this workflow in background** option

3. Select **Record** is created under the **Start** when option.

4. Add the update step from the **Add Step** drop-down button and select the **Member** entity from the drop-down.

5. Click on the **Set Properties** button and look for the **Autoid** lookup in the member form. We need to select our **Member** record under this lookup, to associate the member entity record with an existing auto number configuration record for the member. Click on **Save and Close**.

6. Add another update step from the **Add Step** drop-down button, again select the **Member** entity, and click on the **Set Properties** button.

7. Select the **Member ID** field and click on **OK** after setting the following properties in **Form Assistant**. Then select **Save and Close**:

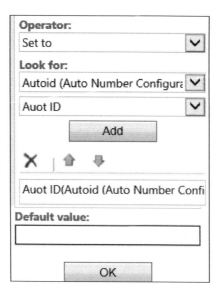

8. Add another update step and this time select the **Autoid (Auto Number Configuration)** option from the drop down and click on the **Set Properties** button.

9. Select the **Auto ID** field and click on **OK** in the **Form Assistant** after entering the following properties. Click on **Save and Close**:

    Operator: Increment by

    Default value: 1

After these steps our workflow should look like following:

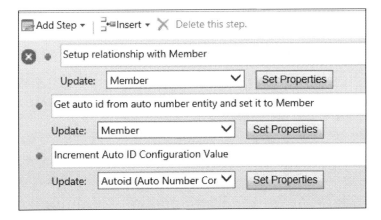

By following the preceding steps we can create another two real-time workflows for the book and book issue/return entities. But make sure you create an auto number configuration entity record with the initial start number first so that the records can be referenced in the workflow.

Understanding dialogs

If we have any requirement to design a user-interactive process we can use a dialog. Dialogs help us to design wizard-like processes, where we can design multiple screens called pages. We can interact with the user with the help of prompts and responses. We don't have the flexibility to customize dialog screens. Mostly, we use dialogs to help the user to complete some process; for example we can use them to design a process for a call center customer support representative to log a case for a customer after getting and verifying some details from the calling user.

Designing dialogs

We can design dialogs using the out-of-the-box process designer. We can navigate to **Settings | Process** and select **Dialog** under a category to design them.

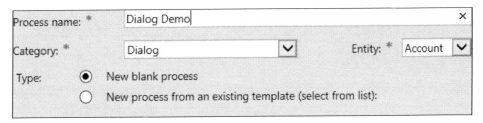

We can add single or multiple pages to a dialog, each of which represents a screen. A page can have one or more prompts and responses where we can get input from users and can store the response value. We can also query data from CRM using the **Query** step. For example, we can display a list of the books to a user based on the book category selected by the user.

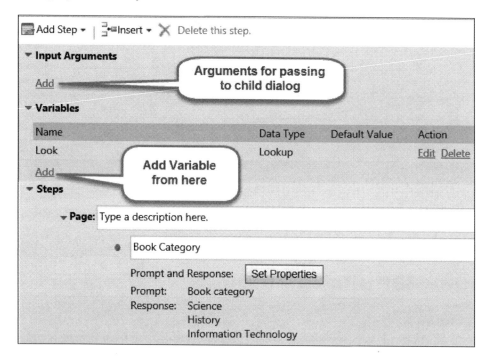

Responses capture from user can be stored into variables using **Assign** step available under **Add Step** drop-down or we can directly reference response in another dialogs step. While designing prompt and response, we can also define tips and call script, which can help CRM user to fill response fields

Calling Dialog

Dialogs are synchronous in nature and can't be started automatically. We need to manually execute dialogs by using the **Start Dialog** button under more commands (…) or we can call them using JavaScript. Also we can't customize dialog screens.

Understanding actions

Actions were introduced in CRM 2013; they allow us to design our custom messages like out-of-the-box events to execute our custom business logic. We can use actions to define our complex logic. Before actions there was no direct way to call server-side logic using client-side scripting. But actions allow us to define our own messages and call them using a SOAP request. We can't call them using OData end points. Once an action is defined, we can also register a plug-in on the action. We will discuss plug-ins in a later chapter.

Designing actions

Actions can be designed using the process designer; we can navigate to **Settings | Processes** to create a new action. Actions can be associated with a single entity or can be global, where they can be used with any entity. As soon as an action is created, CRM creates a corresponding synchronous workflow.

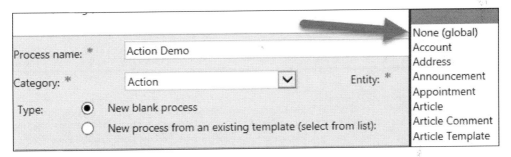

Action scopes

Actions always run under an organization scope, so we can't bind an action to run under other scopes such as user and business unit, and they always execute in the security context of the calling user.

Action arguments

Actions also allow us to use input and output arguments, so while designing we can configure an input or output argument that can used while calling actions.

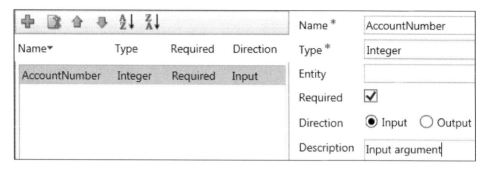

Calling actions

Once an action is designed we can call it in three ways:

- Using server-side code
- Using client-side code
- From a workflow

Calling actions from workflows is the new feature added in CRM 2015. Actions are synchronous and are executed under stage 30 of the execution pipeline. We will be discussing execution pipeline in greater detail in a later chapter, but if you want you can refer to https://msdn.microsoft.com/en-us/library/gg327941.aspx now.

We will be working with actions in more detail in a later chapter.

Business process flows versus workflows, dialogs, and actions

The following table will help us to understand the differences between all these processes.

	Business process flow	Workflow	Dialog	Actions
Business logic	Does not support complex logic	Supports complex logic	Supports complex logic	Supports complex logic

	Business process flow	**Workflow**	**Dialog**	**Actions**
Execution mode		Support for asynchronous or synchronous business logic	Supports synchronous business logic	Supports synchronous business logic
Trigger	Available as soon as entity record is opened	Can be associated with triggers or on demand	Always on demand	Can be associated with triggers or on demand
Interactive	Simple branching logic can be applied	Runs in background	Supports user interaction	Runs in background
SDK Support	Supports client-side logic	Provides SDK support	Provides SDK support	Supports SDK
Customization	Created from CRM application	Can be customized using Visual Studio	Can be customized only in CRM application	Can be customized in Visual Studio

Testing library management

Now our solution is ready for testing. We need to also do navigation changes by modifying the sitemap. Please refer to *Chapter 3, Client-side Logic with Microsoft Dynamics CRM 2015*, for how to modify sitemaps using **XrmToolBox**. We can modify it based the following screenshot:

We need to set up book records. We can create our book records or can import book records using the data import utility in Microsoft Dynamics CRM 2015.

 You can get details about data import from `https://msdn.microsoft.com/en-us/library/gg328321.aspx`.

Once book data is available we can test for book issue/return processes; we can also create one business rule to set the default value for due data, by adding five days to issued on data in the book issue/return entity.

As soon as the issue on date is completed, it will auto-populate the due date field.

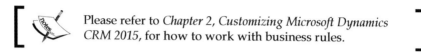

[Please refer to *Chapter 2, Customizing Microsoft Dynamics CRM 2015*, for how to work with business rules.]

When we try to create a record of the book issue/return entity, it will look like the following.

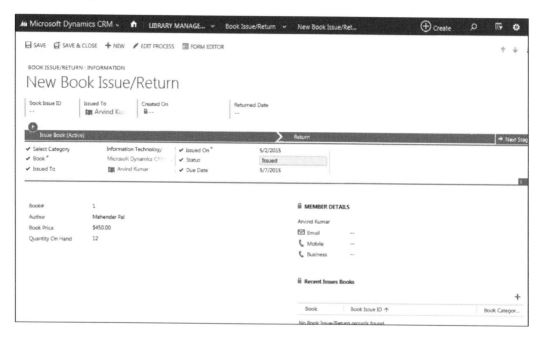

The corresponding workflow will update the book inventory based on the book status and the real-time workflow will generate an auto ID for us based on the auto number configuration records.

Summary

In this chapter we learned about Microsoft Dynamics CRM 2015 processes and their categories. We learned about creating custom entities and views. We also discussed the different access levels. We talked about creating business process flows and how we can create and use them. We worked with both asynchronous and synchronous flows for our library system solution. We will be updating our solution in a later chapter. In the next chapter, we will be working with Microsoft Dynamics CRM SDK.

Working with CRM SDK

5

In this chapter we are going to learn about using CRM extendibility architecture and its main components. We will discuss the CRM 2015 software development kit (SDK) and its resources. This chapter will help us to learn about CRM APIs and Web resources. We will be discussing different CRM Web services and their methods with examples. We will also write a console application using the CRM client API. We will also be discussing new enhancements for developers in CRM 2015. We will cover:

- Understanding CRM extendibility architecture
- Introduction to Microsoft Dynamics CRM SDK
- Knowing about CRM assemblies
- Understanding CRM web services
- Using client API for CRM connection
- Working with organization web service
- Working with discovery web service
- Fetching data from CRM database
- Top five new features in 2015 update 1 for developers
- Integrating CRM with other system

Understanding CRM extendibility architecture

Microsoft Dynamics CRM is a highly extendable business application, which means that we can always extend CRM using its APIs. It provides different component, that can be greatly extended to map with our custom business requirements. Although CRM provides a rich set of features that help us to execute different business operations without any modification, we still can extend its behavior and capabilities with supported customizations.

The following is the extendibility architecture of CRM 2015, where we can see how different components interact with each other and which components can be extended with the help of CRM APIs.

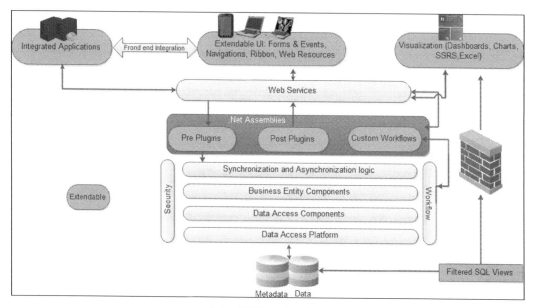

Extendibility architecture

Let's discuss these components one by one and possible extendibility options for them.

CRM databases

During installation of CRM, two databases (the organization and configuration databases) are created. The organization database is named **organization_MSCRM** and the configuration database is called **MSCRM_CONFIG**. The organization database contains the complete organization-related data stored on different entities. For every entity in CRM there is a corresponding table with the name of **Entityname+"Base"**. Although technically it is possible, direct data modification in these tables is not supported. Any changes to CRM data should be done by using CRM APIs only.

 Adding indexes to CRM databases is supported; you can refer to `https://msdn.microsoft.com/en-us/library/gg328350.aspx` for more details on supported customizations.

Apart from tables, CRM also creates special views for every entity called **Filtered+Entityname**. These views provide data based on the user security role so, for example, if you are a sales person you will only get data while querying the filtered view based on the sales person role. We use filtered views for writing custom reports for CRM. You can find more details on filtered views from `https://technet.microsoft.com/en-us/library/dn531182.aspx`.

 An entity relationship diagram for CRM 2015 can be downloaded from `https://msdn.microsoft.com/en-us/library/jj602918.aspx`.

Platform layers

Platform layers work as middleware between the CRM UI and database; it is responsible for executing inbuilt and custom business logic and moving data back and forth. When we browse CRM applications, the platform layer presents data that is available based on the current user security roles. We develop and deploy custom components on top of the platform layer.

Processes

We discussed the different process categories in an earlier chapter. A process is a way to implement automation in CRM. We can set up processes using the process designer and also develop custom assemblies to enhance the capability for the workflow designer and include custom steps.

CRM Web services

CRM provides the **Windows Communication Foundation (WCF)**-based Web service, which helps us to interact with organization data and metadata; thus, whenever we want to create or modify entity data or to customize CRM component metadata, we need to utilize these Web services. We can also develop custom Web services with the help of CRM Web services if required. We will be discussing CRM Web services in detail in a later topic.

Plug-ins

Plug-ins are another way to extend CRM capability. These are .NET assemblies that help us to implement our custom business logic in the CRM platform. They help us to execute our business logic before or after the main platform operation. We can also run our plug-in on transactions, similarly to SQL transactions, which means that, if any operation fails, all the changes will rollback. We can set up asynchronous and synchronous plug-ins. We will be discussing plug-in development in the next chapter.

Reporting

CRM provides rich reporting capabilities. We have many out-of-the-box reports for every module such as sales, marketing, and service. We can also create new reports and customize existing reports in Visual Studio. While working with reports we always utilize the entity-specific filtered view so that data can be exposed based on the user security role. We should never use CRM tables while writing reports. Custom reports can be developed using the out-of-the-box report wizard or using Visual Studio. The Report wizard helps us to create reports by following a couple of screens where we can select entity and filter criteria for our report with different rendering and formatting options. We can create two type of reports in Visual Studio: SSRS and FetchXML. Custom SSRS reports are supported on CRM on-premise deployments whereas CRM online only supports FetchXML.

 You can refer to `https://technet.microsoft.com/en-us/library/dn531183.aspx` for more details on report development.

Client extensions

We can also extend CRM applications from the Web and Outlook clients. We can also develop custom utility tools for these. Sitemap and Command bar editor add-ons are examples of such applications. We can modify different CRM components such as entity structure, Web resources, business rules, different type of Web resources, and other components. CRM Web services can be utilized to map custom requirements. We can do navigation changes from CRM clients by modifying sitemap and command bar definitions.

Integrated extensions

We can also develop custom extensions in terms of the custom utility and middle layer to interact with CRM using APIs. It can be a portal application or any .NET or non-.NET utility. CRM SDK comes with many tools that help us to develop these integrated applications. We will be discussing custom integration with CRM in a later topic.

An introduction to the Microsoft Dynamics CRM SDK

The Microsoft Dynamics CRM SDK contains resources that help us to develop code for CRM. It includes different CRM APIs and helpful resources such as sample code (both server-side and client-side) and a list of tools to facilitate CRM development. It provides complete documentation of API methods and their uses, so if you are a CRM developer, technical consultant, or solution architect, the first thing you need to do is download the latest CRM SDK.

 You can download the latest version of CRM SDK from http://www.microsoft.com/en-us/download/details.aspx?id=44567.

The following table provides different resources that come with CRM SDK:

Name	Descriptions
Bin	This folder contains all the assemblies of CRM.
Resources	This folder contains different resources such as data import maps, default entity ribbon XML definitions, and image icons of CRM applications.

Name	Descriptions
SampleCode	This folder contains all the server-side and client sample code that can help you to get started with CRM development. This folder also contains sample PowerShell commands.
Schemas	This folder contains XML schemas for CRM entities, command bars, and sitemaps. These schemas can be imported in Visual Studio while editing customization XML files manually.
Solutions	This folder contains a CRM 2015 solution compatibility chart and one portal solution.
Templates	This folder contains Visual Studio templates used to develop components for unified service desk and CRM package deployment.
Tools	This folder contains tools shipped with CRM SDK such as a metadata browser that can used to get CRM entity metadata, a plug-in registration tool, a Web resource utility, and others.
Walkthroughs	This folder contains console and Web portal applications.
CrmSdk2015	This is the .chm help file
EntityMetadata	This file contains entity metadata information.
Message-entity support for plug-ins	This is a very important file that will help you to understand events available for entities for writing custom business logic (plug-ins)

Knowing about CRM assemblies

CRM SDK ships with different assemblies under a `bin` folder that we can use to write CRM application extensions. We can utilize them to interact with CRM metadata and organization data. The following table provides details about the most common CRM assemblies:

Name	Details
Microsoft.Xrm.Sdk. Deployment	This assembly is used to work with CRM organizations. We can create, update, and delete organizations via these assembly methods.

Name	Details
`Microsoft.Xrm.Sdk`	This is a very important assembly as it contains the core methods and their details; this is a must-have assembly for every CRM extension. This assembly contains different namespaces for different functionality—for example, **query**, which contains different classes to query CRM DB; **metadata**, which helps us to interact with metadata of CRM applications; **discovery**, which helps us to interact with discovery services (we will be discussing discovery services in a later topic); and **messages**, which provides classes for all CURD operation requests and responses with metadata classes.
`Microsoft.Xrm.Sdk.Workflow`	This assembly help us to extend CRM workflow capability. It contains methods and types required for writing a custom workflow activity. This assembly contains the activities namespace, which is used by CRM workflow designer.
`Microsoft.Crm.Sdk.Proxy`	This assembly contains all non-core request and response messages.
`Microsoft.Xrm.Tooling`	This is a new assembly added in SDK. This assembly helps us to write Windows client applications for CRM.
`Microsoft.Xrm.Portal`	This assembly provides methods for portal development that include security management, cache management, and content management.
`Microsoft.Xrm.Client`	This is another assembly that is used in CRM client applications to communicate with CRM from the application. It contains connection classes that we can use to set up connection using different CRM authentication methods.

We will be working with these APIs in later topics.

Understanding CRM web services

Microsoft Dynamics CRM provides web service support that can be used to work with CRM data or metadata. CRM has the following web services:

Deployment service

Deployment service helps us to work with organizations, so using this web service we can create new organizations and delete or update existing organizations.

Discovery service

This is used to identify correct web service endpoints based on the user. Let's take an example where we have multiple CRM organizations, and we want to get a list of the organizations where current users have access; we can utilize the discovery service to find out the unique organization ID, endpoint URLs, and other details. We will be working with discovery service in a later topic.

Organization service

This is used to work with CRM organization data and metadata. It has CRUD (create, retrieve, update, and delete) methods and other request and response messages. For example, if we want to create or modify any existing entity record we can use organization service methods.

Organization data service

Organization data service is a RESTful service that we can use to get data from CRM. We can use this service's CRUD methods to work with data, but we can't use this service to work with CRM metadata.

To work with CRM web services, we can use the following two programming models:

- Late bound
- Early bound

Early bound

In early bound classes we use proxy classes generated by `CrmSvcUtil.exe`. This utility is included in CRM SDK under the `SDK\Bin` path. This utility generates classes for every entity available in the CRM system. In this programming model schema, names are used to refer to the entity and its attributes and it provides intelligence support, so we don't need to remember the entity and attribute name; as soon as we type the first letter of the entity name, it will show all entities with that name.

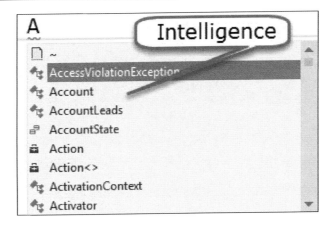

We can use the following syntax to generate proxy classes for CRM on-premise:

```
CrmSvcUtil.exe
/url:http://<ServerName>/<organizationName>/XRMServices/2011/
Organization.svc/out:proxyfilename.cs /username:<username>
/password:<password> /domain:<domainName>
/namespace:<outputNamespace>
/serviceContextName:<serviceContextName>
```

And the following code generate a proxy for CRM online:

```
CrmSvcUtil.exe
/url:https://orgname.api.crm.dynamics.com/XRMServices/2011/
Organization.svc /out:proxyfilename.cs
/username:"myname@myorg.onmicrosoft.com" /password:"myp@ssword!"
```

The `Organization` service URL can be obtained by navigating to **Settings | Customization | Developer Resources**. We are using CRM online for our demo, in case the CRM online `organization` service URL is dependent on the region where your organization is hosted. You can refer `https://msdn.microsoft.com/en-us/library/gg328127.aspx` to get details about different CRM online regions.

We can perform the following steps to generate a proxy class for CRM online:

1. Navigate to the **Developer Command Prompt** under **Visual Studio Tools** on the development machine where Visual Studio is installed.

2. Go to the `Bin` folder under CRM SDK and paste in the following command:

```
CrmSvcUtil.exe
/url:https://ORGName.api.crm5.dynamics.com/XRMServices/2011/
Organization.svc      /out:Xrm.cs
/username:"user@ORGName.onmicrosoft.com" /password:"password"
```

```
C:\         Bin>CrmSvcUtil.exe /url:https://         .
ervices/2011/Organization.svc      /out:Xrm.cs /username
t.com" /password:"        "
CrmSvcUtil : CRM Service Utility [Version 7.0.0000.305
c 2014 Microsoft Corporation.  All rights reserved.

Code written to            \Bin\Xrm.cs.
```

CrmSVCUtil

Once this file is generated we can add this file to our Visual Studio solution.

Late bound

In the late bound programming model, we use a generic `Entity` object to refer to our entities, which means that we can also refer to an entity that is not yet part of the CRM. In this programming model, we need to use the logical name to refer to an entity and its attribute. No support is available during code development in the case of late bound. Next is an example of using the `Entity` class:

```
Entity AccountObj = new Entity("account");
```

Using client APIs for CRM connections

CRM client APIs help us to connect with CRM easily from .NET applications. It simplifies setting up connections with CRM using a simplified connection string. We can use this connection string to create organization service objects.

Perform the following setup on the console application for demo purposes:

1. Connect to Visual Studio and select **File | New | Project**.

2. Select **Visual C# | Console Application** and enter CRMConnectiondemo in the **Name** textbox:

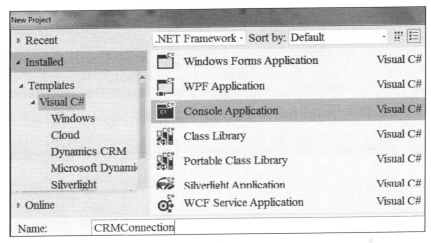

console app

 Make sure you have installed the .NET 4.5.2 and the NET 4.5.2 developer pack before creating the sample application.

3. Right-click on **References** and add the following CRM SDK:

   Microsoft.Xrm.SDK

   Microsoft.Xrm.Client

   We also need to add the following .NET assemblies:

   System.Runtime.Serialization

   System.Configuration

4. Make sure to add the `App.config` file if not available in the project. We need to right-click on the project name and select **Add Item**, and add the application configuration file as follows:

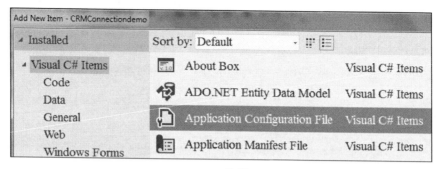

app.configfile

5. We need to add a connection string to our `app.config` file as follows. We are using CRM online for our demo application, so we will be using following connection string:

```xml
<?xml version="1.0" encoding="UTF-8"?>

<configuration>

    <connectionStrings>

        <add name="OrganizationService"
connectionString="Url=https://CRMOnlineServerURL;
Username=User@ORGNAME.onmicrosoft.com; Password=Password;" />

    </connectionStrings>

</configuration>
```

6. Right-click on the project, select **Add Existing File**, and browse our proxy file that we generated in an earlier step, to add it to our console application.

7. Now we can add two classes in our application—one early bound and another late bound—and let's name them `Earlybound.cs` and `Latebound.cs`

You can refer to `https://msdn.microsoft.com/en-us/library/jj602970.aspx` to access a connection string for other deployment types, if not using CRM online.

After adding the preceding classes our solution structure should look like the following:

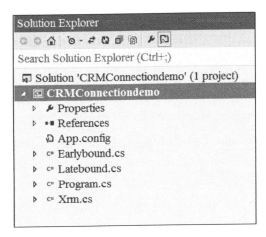

Working with organization web services

Whenever we need to interact with CRM SDK, we need to use CRM web services. Most of the time we will be working with the organization service to create and modify data. Organization services contains the following methods to interact with metadata and organization data; we will add these methods in our corresponding `Earlybound.cs` and `Latebound.cs` files in our console application.

Create

This method is used to create entity records: system or custom. We can use `create` method when we want to create an entity record using CRM SDK—for example, if we need to develop a utility for data importing we can use this method or if we want to create a lead record dynamically from a custom Web site. This methods takes the `entity` object as a parameter and returns the GUID of the record created. The following is an example of creating an account record, early and late bound, with different data types. We are setting some of the basic account entity fields in the following code:

- **Early bound**:

```
private void CreateAccount()
  {
    using (OrganizationService crmService = new
         OrganizationService("OrganizationService"))
```

```
        {
          Account accountObject = new Account
            {
              Name = "HIMBAP Early",
              Address1_City = "Delhi",
              CustomerTypeCode = new OptionSetValue(3),
              DoNotEMail = false,
              Revenue = new Money(5000),
              NumberOfEmployees = 50,
              LastUsedInCampaign = new DateTime(2015, 3, 2)
            };
          crmService.Create(accountObject);
        }
    }
```

- **Late bound**:

```
private void Create()
  {
    using (OrganizationService crmService = new
           OrganizationService("OrganizationService"))
      {
        Entity accountObj = new Entity("account");
        //setting string value
        accountObj["name"] = "HIMBAP";
        accountObj["address1_city"] = "Delhi";
        accountObj["accountnumber"] = "101";
        //setting optionsetvalue
        accountObj["customertypecode"] = new
                                    OptionSetValue(3);
        //setting boolean
        accountObj["donotemail"] = false;
        //setting money
        accountObj["revenue"] = new Money(5000);
        //setting entity reference/lookup
        accountObj["primarycontactid"] = new
                    EntityReference("contact", new Guid
            ("F6954457-6005-E511-80F4-C4346BADC5F4"));
        //setting integer
        accountObj["numberofemployees"] = 50;
```

```
//Date Time
accountObj["lastusedincampaign"] = new
                        DateTime(2015, 05, 13);
Guid AccountID = crmService.Create(accountObj);
    }
}
```

 You can get the GUID from CRM. Please refer to *Chapter 3, Client-side Logic with Microsoft Dynamics CRM 2015*, for how to get the GUID of an entity record.

We can also use the `create` method to create primary and related entities in a single call; for example, in the following call we are creating an account and a related contact record in a single call:

```
private void CreateRecordwithRelatedEntity()
    {
    using (OrganizationService crmService = new
            OrganizationService("OrganizationService"))
        {
        Entity accountEntity = new Entity("account");
        accountEntity["name"] = "HIMBAP Technology";
        Entity relatedContact = new Entity("contact");
        relatedContact["firstname"] = "Vikram";
        relatedContact["lastname"] = "Singh";
        EntityCollection Related = new EntityCollection();
        Related.Entities.Add(relatedContact);
        Relationship accountcontactRel = new
                    Relationship("contact_customer_accounts");
        accountEntity.RelatedEntities.Add(accountcontactRel,
                                Related);
        crmService.Create(accountEntity);
        }
    }
```

In the preceding code, first we created an `accountEntity` object and then created an object of the `relatedContact` entity and added it to the `Entity` collection. After that we added the related entity collection to the primary entity with an entity relationship name; in this case it is `contact_customer_accounts`.

After that we passed our account entity object to the `create` method to create the account and related contact record. We will run this code to create an account as follows:

relatedrecord

Update

This method is used to update existing record properties; for example we may want to change the account city or any other address information. This methods takes the entity object as a parameter, but we need to make sure to update the primary key field to update any records. The following are example of updating the account city and setting the state property:

- **Early bound**:

```
private void Update()
    {
        using (OrganizationService crmService = new
               OrganizationService("OrganizationService"))
        {
          Account accountUpdate = new Account
            {
                AccountId = new Guid("85A882EE-A500-E511-80F9-
                                     C4346BAC0E7C"),
                Address1_City = "Mandi",
                Address1_StateOrProvince = "Himachal Pradesh"
                };
            crmService.Update(accountUpdate);
        }
    }
```

- **Late bound**:

```
private void Update()
    {
        using (OrganizationService crmService = new
               OrganizationService("OrganizationService"))
```

```
        {
          Entity accountUpdate = new Entity("account");
          accountUpdate["accountid"] = new Guid("85A882EE-
                          A500-E511-80F9-C4346BAC0E7C");
          accountUpdate["address1_city"] = "Mandi";
          accountUpdate["address1_stateorprovince"] =
                                    "Himachal Pradesh";
          crmService.Update(accountUpdate);
        }
    }
```

Similarly, to create a method, we can also use the update method to update the primary entity and the related entity in a single call, as follows:

```
    private void Updateprimaryentitywithrelatedentity()
    {
      using (OrganizationService crmService = new
          OrganizationService("OrganizationService"))
      {
        Entity accountToUpdate = new Entity("account");
        accountToUpdate["name"] = "HIMBAP Technology";
        accountToUpdate["websiteurl"] = "www.himbap.com";
        accountToUpdate["accountid"] = new Guid("29FC3E74-B30B-
                          E511-80FC-C4346BAD26CC");
        Entity relatedContact = new Entity("contact");
        relatedContact["firstname"] = "Vikram";
        relatedContact["lastname"] = "Singh";
        relatedContact["jobtitle"] = "Sr Consultant";
        relatedContact["contactid"] = new Guid("2AFC3E74-B30B-
                          E511-80FC-C4346BAD26CC");
        EntityCollection Related = new EntityCollection();
        Related.Entities.Add(relatedContact);
        Relationship accountcontactRel = new
                    Relationship("contact_customer_accounts");
        accountToUpdate.RelatedEntities.Add(accountcontactRel,
                                    Related);
        crmService.Update(accountToUpdate);
      }
    }
```

Retrieve

This method is used to get data from the CRM based on the primary field, which means this will only return one record at a time. This method takes three parameters:

- **Entity**: We need to pass the logical name of the entity as the first parameter
- **ID**: We need to pass the primary id of the record that we want to query
- **Columnset**: We need to specify a list of the fields list that we want to fetch

The following are examples of using the `Retrieve` method

- **Early bound**:

```
private void Retrieve()
  {
    using (OrganizationService crmService = new
          OrganizationService("OrganizationService"))
      {
       Account retrievedAccount =
      (Account)crmService.Retrieve(Account.EntityLogicalName,
       new Guid("7D5E187C-9344-4267-9EAC-DD32A0AB1A30"), new
       ColumnSet(new string[] { "name" }));
      }
  }
```

- **Late bound**:

```
private void Retrieve()
  {
    using (OrganizationService crmService = new
          OrganizationService("OrganizationService"))
      {
       Entity retrievedAccount = (Entity)
       crmService.Retrieve ("account", new
       Guid("7D5E187C-9344-4267-9EAC-DD32A0AB1A30"), new
       ColumnSet(new string[] { "name"}));
      }

  }
```

RetrieveMultiple

The `RetrieveMultiple` method provides options to define our `query` object where we can define criteria to fetch records from the primary and related entity. This method takes the `query` object as a parameter and returns an entity collection as the response. The following are examples of using `RetrieveMulitple` with both early and late bound:

- **Late Bound**

```
private void RetrieveMultiple()
{
    using (OrganizationService crmService = new
           OrganizationService("OrganizationService"))
    {
        QueryExpression query = new QueryExpression
        {
            EntityName = "account",
            ColumnSet = new ColumnSet("name",
                                       "accountnumber"),
            Criteria =
            {
                FilterOperator = LogicalOperator.Or,
                Conditions =
                {
                    new ConditionExpression
                    {
                        AttributeName = "address1_city",
                        Operator = ConditionOperator.Equal,
                        Values={"Delhi"}
                    },
                    new ConditionExpression
                    {
                        AttributeName="accountnumber",
                        Operator=ConditionOperator.NotNull
                    }
                }
            }
        };
        EntityCollection entityCollection = crmService.RetrieveMultiple(query);
```

```
                        foreach (Entity result in entityCollection.
Entities)
                {
                    if (result.Contains("name"))
                    {
                        Console.WriteLine("name ->" + result.GetAt
tributeValue<string>("name").ToString());
                    }
                }
            }
```

- **Early Bound**:

```
private void RetrieveMultiple()
   {
     using (OrganizationService crmService = new OrganizationServic
e("OrganizationService"))
        {
            QueryExpression RetrieveAccountsQuery = new
                                        QueryExpression
            {
               EntityName = Account.EntityLogicalName,
               ColumnSet = new ColumnSet("name",
                                    "accountnumber"),
               Criteria = new FilterExpression
                 {
                   Conditions =
                   {
                      new ConditionExpression
                      {
                        AttributeName = "address1_city",
                        Operator = ConditionOperator.Equal,
                          Values = { "Delhi" }
                      }
                   }
                 }
            };
        EntityCollection entityCollection =
        crmService.RetrieveMultiple(RetrieveAccountsQuery);
        foreach (Entity result in entityCollection.Entities)
          {
            if (result.Contains("name"))
              {
                Console.WriteLine("name ->" +
                result.GetAttributeValue<string>
                ("name").ToString());
```

```
            }
        }
    }
}
```

Delete

This method is used to delete entity records from the CRM database. This method takes the entity name and primary ID fields as parameters:

```
public void Delete()
    {
        using (OrganizationService crmService = new
                OrganizationService("OrganizationService"))
        {
            crmService.Delete("account", new Guid("85A882EE-A500-E511-
                            80F9-C4346BAC0E7C"));
        }
    }
```

Associate

This method is used to set up a link between two related entities. It takes the following parameters:

- **Entity Name**: The logical name of the primary entity
- **Entity Id**: This is the primary entity records ID field.
- **Relationship**: Name of the relationship between two entities
- **Related Entities**: This is the correction of references

The following is an example of using this method with early bound.

```
public void Associate()
    {
        using (OrganizationService crmService = new
                OrganizationService("OrganizationService"))
        {
            EntityReferenceCollection referenceEntities = new
                                    EntityReferenceCollection();
            referenceEntities.Add(new EntityReference("account", new
                    Guid("38FC3E74-B30B-E511-80FC-C4346BAD26CC")));
            // Create an object that defines the relationship between
            the contact and account (we want to set up primary contact)
```

```
Relationship relationship = new
                Relationship("account_primary_contact");
//Associate the contact with the  accounts.
crmService.Associate("contact", new Guid("38FC3E74-B30B-
            E511-80FC-C4346BAD26CC "), relationship,
                                    referenceEntities);
    }
}
```

Disassociate

This method is the reverse of associate. It is used to remove links between two entity records. This method takes the same parameter setup as the associate method takes. The following is an example of disassociate account and contact records:

```
public void Disassociate()
  {
    using (OrganizationService crmService = new
          OrganizationService("OrganizationService"))
      {
        EntityReferenceCollection referenceEntities = new
                                EntityReferenceCollection();
        referenceEntities.Add(new EntityReference("account", new
              Guid("38FC3E74-B30B-E511-80FC-C4346BAD26CC ")));
        // Create an object that defines the relationship between
        the contact and account.
        Relationship relationship = new
                    Relationship("account_primary_contact");
        //Disassociate the records.
        crmService.Disassociate("contact", new Guid("15FC3E74-
              B30B-E511-80FC-C4346BAD26CC "), relationship,
                            referenceEntities);
      }
  }
```

Execute

Apart from the common methods that we discussed, the Execute method helps to execute requests that are not available as a direct method. This method takes a request as a parameter and returns a response as result. All the common methods that we used earlier can be also used as a request with the Execute method. The following is an example of working with metadata and creating a custom event entity using the Execute method:

```
public void Usingmetadata()
  {
```

```
using (OrganizationService crmService = new
        OrganizationService("OrganizationService"))
  {
    CreateEntityRequest createRequest = new CreateEntityRequest
      {
        Entity = new EntityMetadata
          {
            SchemaName = "him_event",
            DisplayName = new Label("Event", 1033),
            DisplayCollectionName = new Label("Events", 1033),
            Description = new Label("Custom entity demo", 1033),
            OwnershipType = OwnershipTypes.UserOwned,
            IsActivity = false,
          },
        PrimaryAttribute = new StringAttributeMetadata
          {
            SchemaName = "him_eventname",
            RequiredLevel = new
                        AttributeRequiredLevelManagedProperty
                        (AttributeRequiredLevel.None),
            MaxLength = 100,
            FormatName = StringFormatName.Text,
            DisplayName = new Label("Event Name", 1033),
            Description = new Label("Primary attribute demo",
1033)
          }
      };
        crmService.Execute(createRequest);
  }
}
```

In the preceding code we utilized the CreateEntityRequest class, which is used to create a custom entity. After executing the preceding code, we can check our entity and the default solution by navigating to **Settings** | **Customizations** | **Customize the System**.

 You can refer to https://msdn.microsoft.com/en-us/ library/gg309553.aspx to see other requests that we can use with the Execute method.

Testing the console application

After adding the preceding methods we can test our console application by writing a simple test method where we can all our CRUD methods. For the testing we have added the following method in our `Earlybound.cs` file:

```
public void EarlyboundTesting()
        {
                Console.WriteLine("Creating Account Record.....");
                CreateAccount();
                Console.WriteLine("Updating Account Record.....");
                Update();
                Console.WriteLine("Retriving Account Record.....");
                Retrieve();
                Console.WriteLine("Deleting Account Record.....");
                Delete();
        }
```

After that we can call this method in the `Main` method of the `Program.cs` file as follows:

```
static void Main(string[] args)
        {
                Earlybound obj = new Earlybound();
                Console.WriteLine("Testing Early bound");
                obj.EarlyboundTesting();
        }
```

Press *F5* to run our console application.

Working with discovery web service

Discovery web service helps us to get details of the organizations that belong to a user. To connect to the discovery server, we can set up another connection string, just like we did for organization services. We can navigate to **Settings | Customization | Developer Resources** to get the discovery URL and can add the following connection string in the `app.config` file:

```
<add name ="Discovery" connectionString ="Url=https://disco.crm5.
dynamics.com/XRMServices/2011/Discovery.svc;
        Username=mpal@himbapb5.onmicrosoft.com; Password=Himbap123;"/
>undefined</connectionStrings>
```

Similar to the organization service URL, the discovery service URL is also dependent on the region where your organization is hosted. For complete online region URLs, you can refer to: `https://msdn.microsoft.com/en-us/library/gg328127.aspx`.

The following is sample code to reads all organizations and organization service URLs:

```
private void WorkingWithDiscovery()
  {
    using (DiscoveryService discoveryService = new
         DiscoveryService("DiscoveryService"))
     {
       RetrieveOrganizationsRequest request = new
                              RetrieveOrganizationsRequest();
       RetrieveOrganizationsResponse response =
               (RetrieveOrganizationsResponse)discoveryService
               .Execute(request);
       foreach (OrganizationDetail orgDetail in response.Details)
         {
           Console.WriteLine("Your Organization Name is " +
                           orgDetail.FriendlyName);
           foreach (var endpoint in orgDetail.Endpoints)
            {
               Console.WriteLine("  Name: {0}", endpoint.Key);
               Console.WriteLine("  URL: {0}", endpoint.Value);
             }
           Console.ReadLine();
          }
       }
    }
```

After we have executed the preceding method, it should look like the following:

```
Your Organization Name is HIMBAP
  Name: WebApplication
  URL: https://        .crm4.dynamics.com/
  Name: OrganizationService
  URL: https://        .api.crm4.dynamics.com/XRMS
  Name: OrganizationDataService
  URL: https://        .api.crm4.dynamics.com/XRMS
```

Fetching data from the CRM database

As we discussed in an earlier topic, we have two direct methods available to get data from CRM: `Retrieve` and `RetrieveMultiple`. The `Retrieve` method only fetches a single record based on the primary key passed to it, but `RetrieveMultiple` can fetch one or more records based on the query passed to it. To write a query for the `RetrieveMultiple` method we can use the following different options:

- `QueryByAttribute`
- `QueryExpression`
- `FetchXML`

QueryByAttribute

`QueryByAttribute` is the simplest way to build your query to fetch data. But it does not provide options to define complex criteria to get data from the CRM. For example, the `QueryByAttribute` class can't be used to get data based on a conditional operator such as: fetch account where annual revenue > 50000, or something similar. It only checks for the equality operator and fetches data where the specified attribute/attributes match with the specified value/values. While using `QueryByAttribute`, we can use the following properties:

Name	Description	Example
EntityName	Entity name, which data we want to fetch	`QueryByAttribute query = new QueryByAttribute ("EntityName");` Use the entity's logical name in the case of late bound or use the entity schema name in the case of early bound

ColumnSet	List the column that we want to retrieve	`query.ColumnSet.AddColumns ("Firstfield1", "secondfield"...);`
		or
		`query.ColumnSet=new ColumnSet (new string[]{"fieldname"});`

Attributes	Conditional attribute	`query.Attributes. AddRange ("conditionfield");`
Values	Conditional attribute value	`query.Values.AddRange ("Valuetocheck");`
Orders	Sorting result set in Ascending/ order	`query.OrderType = OrderType.Descending;`

Name	Description	Example

PageInfo	Used to set number of pages and the number of records per page that we want to return from the query	`query.PageInfo = new PagingInfo();`
		`query.PageInfo.Count = 10;`
		`query.PageInfo.PageNumber = 1;`

 For more details on paging, you can refer to: `https://msdn.microsoft.com/en-us/library/gg327917.aspx`.

The following is an example of fetching account records based on the country India:

```
using (OrganizationService crmService = new
        OrganizationService("OrganizationService"))
{
    QueryByAttribute queryByAttribute = new
                                QueryByAttribute("account");
    queryByAttribute.ColumnSet = new ColumnSet("name",
                                    "address1_country");
    queryByAttribute.Attributes.AddRange("address1_country");
    queryByAttribute.Values.AddRange("US");
    EntityCollection retrieved =
                crmService.RetrieveMultiple(queryByAttribute);
    Console.WriteLine("Number of Clients from US is {0}",
                retrieved.Entities.Count);
}
```

 The query will only return non-null columns from the list of the columns defined under the column set property.

QueryExpression

The `QueryExpression` class is used to retrieve multiple data based on complex queries. It gives us the flexibility to define different options to filter our query. The following are the properties that we can use while building our `QueryExpression`:

Name	Description	Example

EntityName	Used to set the source entity that we want to query	`QueryExpression query = new QueryExpression("EntityName");`
		
		//use entity logical name in the case of late bound or use entity schema name in the case of early bound

ColumnSet	Used to define the set of attributes that we want to fetch	`query.ColumnSet.AddColumns("Firstfield1", "secondfield");`
		or
		`query.ColumnSet=new ColumnSet(new string[]{"fieldname"});`

Criteria	Used to define our conditions	`query.Criteria.AddCondition("Fieldname", ConditionOperator.Equal, "value");`
Distinct	Used to work with duplicate records	`Query.Distinct=true;`
LinKEntities	Used to work with related entities	`query.LinkEntities.Add(new LinkEntity("primary entity", "relatedentity", "lookupfieldonprimaryentity", "primarykeyofrelatedentity", JoinOperator.Inner));`
Order	Setting ordering options	`query.OrderType = OrderType.Descending;`

PageInfo	Used to set the number of the pages and the number of records	`query.PageInfo = new PagingInfo();`
		`query.PageInfo.Count = 10;`
		`query.PageInfo.PageNumber = 1;`

Now let's say we want to get all the accounts from CRM created in the last 30 minutes. The following sample code does this:

```
QueryExpression query = new QueryExpression
    {
        EntityName = "account",
```

```
        ColumnSet = new ColumnSet(new string[] { "name",
                                         "accountnumber" }),
        Criteria =
          {
            Conditions =
                {
                  new ConditionExpression
                  {
                    AttributeName = "createdon",
                    Operator = ConditionOperator.OnOrAfter,
                    Values={DateTime.UtcNow.AddMinutes(-30)}
                  },
                  }
          }
    };
    EntityCollection _Result = crmService.RetrieveMultiple(query);
      foreach (Entity Acc in _Result.Entities)
        {
          Console.WriteLine(Acc["name"].ToString());
        }
    }
```

If we want to fetch data using multiple conditions, we can use `FilterExpression` to combine multiple conditions, as follows:

```
using (OrganizationService crmService = new
        OrganizationService("OrganizationService"))
  {
    QueryExpression query = new QueryExpression
      {
        EntityName = "account",
        ColumnSet = new ColumnSet("name", "accountnumber"),
        Criteria =
          {
            FilterOperator = LogicalOperator.Or,
            Conditions =
              {
                new ConditionExpression
                  {
                    AttributeName = "address1_city",
                    Operator = ConditionOperator.Equal,
                    Values={"Delhi"}
                  },
```

```
                    new ConditionExpression
                      {
                          AttributeName="accountnumber",
                          Operator=ConditionOperator.NotNull
                      }
                  }
              };
          EntityCollection entityCollection =
                            crmService.RetrieveMultiple(query);
```

In the preceding example we have combined two conditions using `FilterExpression`; we are comparing these two conditions based on the `Or` logical operator, so it will return data where either the account city is equal to Delhi or the account number does contain data.

The following is an example of using the link entity in query expressions; in this code we are fetching account data based on the primary contact ID:

```
Guid _Contactid = new Guid("E8954457-6005-E511-80F4-
                 C4346BADC5F4");
//mention contact id which is used as primary contact in account
using(OrganizationService crmService=new
      OrganizationService("OrganizationService"))
  {
    QueryExpression _QueryLinkEntity = new QueryExpression();
    _QueryLinkEntity.EntityName = "account";
    QueryLinkEntity.ColumnSet = new ColumnSet(true);
    _QueryLinkEntity.LinkEntities.Add
        (
          new LinkEntity
            {
              LinkFromEntityName = "account",
              LinkToEntityName = "contact",
              LinkToAttributeName = "contactid",
              LinkFromAttributeName = "primarycontactid",
              LinkCriteria = new FilterExpression
                {
                  Conditions =
                    {
                new ConditionExpression
                ("contactid",ConditionOperator.Equal,_Contactid)
                    }
                }
            }
        );
```

```
EntityCollection _LinkResult =
                    crmService.RetrieveMultiple(_QueryLinkEntity);
foreach (Entity Acc in _LinkResult.Entities)
  {
    Console.WriteLine(Acc["name"].ToString());
  }
}
```

FetchXML

Another way of writing our query for `QueryExpression` is to use the FetchXML language. We can write our FetchXML query string, which is based on the FetchXML schema. All views in CRM internally use FetchXML to store a query for the view data source. All the properties in the `QueryExpression` class can be used with FetchXML as well. We can write out FetchXML query manually or get it from **Advanced Find**. Please refer to an earlier chapter for how to get queries from **Advanced Find**.

 We can also use add-ons available in the marketplace to write FetchXML queries—for example: `http://fxb.xrmtoolbox.com/`.

The following is an example of a FetchXML query to fetch all accounts where the city is Delhi:

```
string fetchxml = @"<fetch version='1.0' output-format='xml-
platform' mapping='logical' distinct='false' aggregate='true'>
<entity name='account'>
//<attribute name='address1_city' aggregate='COUNT' alias='Citycount'
/>
<filter type='and'>
<condition attribute='address1_city' operator='eq' value='Delhi' />
</filter>
</entity>
</fetch>";
using (OrganizationService crmService = new
                    OrganizationService("OrganizationService"))
      {
        EntityCollection results =
                            crmService.RetrieveMultiple
                            (new FetchExpression(fetchxml));
        if (results.Entities.Count > 0)
          {
            Entity result = results.Entities[0];
```

```
                AliasedValue Total =
                                (AliasedValue)result["Citycount"];
                Console.WriteLine("Total City Count=>"+Total.Value);
            }
        }
```

 Please refer to https://msdn.microsoft.com/en-us/ library/gg328117.aspx for more query samples.

LINQ

We can also use the LINQ query to fetch data from the CRM. LINQ allows us to write our query in SQL-like syntax; we can query different types of data using LINQ. If you are new to LINQ refer to https://msdn.microsoft.com/en-us/library/ bb397926.aspx to learn the basics of LINQ.

The following is the sample code:

```
using (OrganizationService crmService = new
     OrganizationService("OrganizationService"))
  {
    HIMBAPDev serviceContext = new HIMBAPDev(crmService);
    var accounts = (from a in serviceContext.AccountSet
    select new Account
    {  Name = a.Name });
    foreach (var account in accounts)
        {  Console.WriteLine(account.Name);}}
```

While generating early bound proxy classes, we used HIMBAPDev as the name of the service context, so in the preceding code we are passing an OrganizationService object to the service context and we can use that object to query CRM data.

 For more sample code for LINQ, please refer to: https://msdn. microsoft.com/en-us/library/gg328028.aspx.

Top five new features in 2015 Update 1 for developers

Microsoft Dynamics CRM 2015 Update 1 introduced new capabilities to the CRM SDK. The following are the new enhancements.

Update message improvement

CRM 2015 enhanced capability of update method not we can use the `Update` method to apply special operations for which we had separate requests earlier. For example, earlier we had to use a special request to perform assignment, status changes, and other special operations, but now we can set these properties in the update method only. The following is an example of using the `Update` method for assignment:

```
using (OrganizationService crmService = new OrganizationService("Organ
izationService"))
  {
    Entity accountToUpdate = new Entity("account");
    accountToUpdate["ownerid"] = new EntityReference("systemuser",
            new Guid("38FC3E74-B30B-E511-80FC-C4346BAD26CC "));
    crmService.Update(accountToUpdate);
  }
```

In the preceding code we are changing the owner of the record, which means we are assigning this record to another CRM user.

Executing multiple operations in a single transaction

New messages have been introduced to improve performance, where we can execute multiple options under a single transactions. This is very important when we are doing integration with another system (such as a financial management system) and performing multiple dependent changes, where we want to commit all of them or none. CRM 2015 Update 1 introduced `ExecuteTransactionRequest`, which helps us to combine multiple entity operations under one transaction; they will be executed based on the order in the collection. If any operation fails, it will rollback all the changes. `ExecuteTransactionFault` helps us to identify the operation that caused the fault. The following is an example of creating multiple account records:

```
using (OrganizationService crmService = new OrganizationService("Organ
izationService"))
{
  ExecuteTransactionRequest request = new ExecuteTransactionRequest()
    {
      Requests = new OrganizationRequestCollection()
    };
    for (int i = 1; i <= 10; i++)
      {
          Entity account = new Entity("account");
```

```
            account["name"] = string.Format("Account Transaction
                                             Demo {0}", i);
            CreateRequest createRequest = new CreateRequest() {
                                             Target = account };
            request.Requests.Add(createRequest);
        }
    ExecuteTransactionResponse response =
        (ExecuteTransactionResponse)crmService.Execute(request);
    }
```

In the preceding code we have created 10 account demo records in a single transaction; once this code is executed we can see 10 records created in the CRM:

accountlist

Alternate keys and upsert

Now we have the flexibility to define our own custom keys using the **Keys** option for our entities. This new feature helps us to uniquely identify our entity records using these key fields, which means that we now don't need to depend on the primary key attribute for record updates. On the basis of these custom keys, we update our entity record.

We can define alternate keys by following these steps:

1. Navigate to **Settings** | **Customization** | **Customize the System**.
2. Expand the **Entities** | **Account entity** and select **Keys** | **New**.
3. Complete **AccountID** under **Display Name** and select **Account Number** from the **Available Attributes** section. Click on the **Add>** button.
4. Click on **Publish All Customizations**.

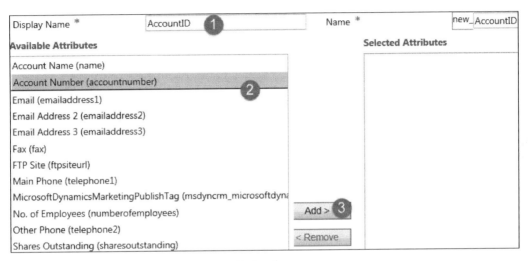

Custom keys

Upsert is another new enhancement that helps us to integrate CRM with other applications easily, especially if we are doing data synchronization between CRM and other applications. Sometimes we are not sure if a particular record exists in the CRM or not. The Upsert request helps us to create a record in the CRM database if it does not exist after validating the custom key; if the record exists, it will update with the latest values applied. The following is an example of executing Upsert over our member entity:

```
using (OrganizationService crmService = new
      OrganizationService("OrganizationService"))
  {
    Entity account = new Entity("account")
      {
        KeyAttributes = new KeyAttributeCollection
          {
            {"accountnumber", "1234" }
          }
      };
```

```
                account["name"] = "Upsert Example";
                UpsertRequest request = new UpsertRequest() { Target =
                                        account };
            UpsertResponse response =
            (UpsertResponse)crmService.Execute(request);
                }
```

This code will first check if there are any member records with the preceding member id value. If not, it will create a new member record with this value; otherwise, it will update the existing records.

Optimistic concurrency

The optimistic concurrency feature helps us to avoid any type of data inconsistency when many concurrent users are working. For example let's say that, once we have retrieved the entity record, we need to work on another calculation; then we need to update the same record. But if during that this time another user has updated that entity record it can lead to data inconsistency. To avoid this situation, now we can check the record's RowVersion and can apply the logic to update it is the same as before while updating the entity record.

 You can refer to https://msdn.microsoft.com/en-us/ library/dn707955.aspx for more detail on optimistic concurrency.

Tracing

If you are a developer, then most of the time you will be using tracing to troubleshoot development issues and for debugging your code. When exceptions are thrown by CRM or through the code, we can get tracing information by downloading the log file (it may be available under system jobs). We will discuss how to use tracing in our code in a later chapter.

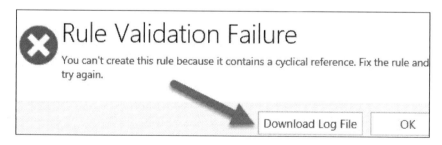

CRM 2015 Update 1 released a new plug-in tracing feature, where we can write our log in the `plugintracelog` entity so that later it can be viewed from the CRM UI.

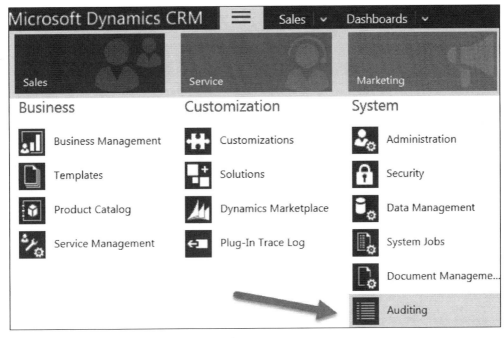

plug-In Trace

These logs will be written only when using the `ITracingService` service. By default this feature is disabled; we can enable it by navigating to **Settings | Administration | System Settings | Customization**.

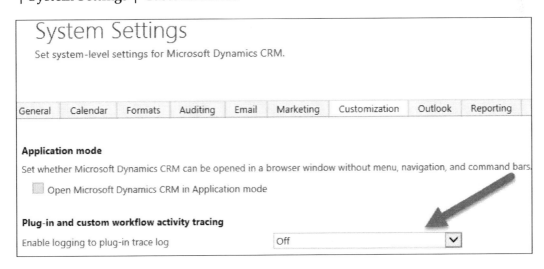

You can get details about ITracingService from: https://
msdn.microsoft.com/en-us/library/microsoft.xrm.
sdk.itracingservice.aspx.

Integrating CRM with other systems

Integrating CRM with other applications is a very common requirement nowadays.
Depending on the business model, every company requires some sort of application
to manage their accounting, financial, inventory, retail management, communication,
and other requirements. Although we can customize CRM to have these features, it
can't be built at the enterprise level. Then it becomes a requirement to integrate CRM
with another application system that provides these inbuilt features, such as Microsoft
Dynamics Great Plains (GP), Microsoft Dynamics Axapta (Ax), Microsoft Dynamics
Navision (NAV), and others. For example, we may want to process the send sales
order and line item details from CRM to Ax to maintain the inventory or we may
want to send invoices to GP so that payment and related taxes can be handled.

While talking about data integration, we move data back and forth between different
applications using two broad categories:

- On demand
- Batch processing

On demand

In the case of on demand integration, we want to bring or send data to other
applications once only; for example we may have one button to validate the
inventory while adding product on orders, or we may want to validate address
information using any third-party address verification tools, so the data moves
between the two applications synchronously. The most common way of
implementing these types of integration is using a plug-in in the CRM. Plug-ins are
server-side components associated with specific events and execute a particular
business logic when that event happens. We will be working with plug-ins in the
next chapter. In the case of CRM on-premise we can easily integrate plug-ins with
other applications, but in the case of online we need to keep security restrictions in
mind. You can refer to https://msdn.microsoft.com/en-us/library/gg334752.
aspx for more details on security.

Batch processing

In batch processing we integrate data between two systems in bulk, mostly asynchronously. Normally we develop jobs that are a combination of different options and are submitted to the queue manager responsible for their execution. These jobs can be executed after a specified time periodically. For these types of requirement, we can develop Windows services, asynchronous plug-ins, and custom workflows. We can also have a utility that can work with Windows scheduler.

We can implement integration between CRM and other systems by using connectors/add-ons available on the market or can write our own custom connector utilities. For example if we want to connect to other Microsoft Dynamics products we can utilize the Dynamics connector released by Microsoft on customer source.

> The following are the URLs for downloading the connector from customer source:
>
> - `https://mbs.microsoft.com/customersource/`
>   `northamerica/AX/downloads/service-packs/mdax_`
>   `dynamicsconnector`
> - `https://mbs.microsoft.com/customersource/`
>   `northamerica/GP/downloads/service-packs/mdgp_`
>   `dynamicsconnector`
> - `https://mbs.microsoft.com/customersource/`
>   `northamerica/NAV/downloads/service-packs/mdnav_`
>   `dynamicsconnector`
> - `https://mbs.microsoft.com/customersource/`
>   `northamerica/SL/downloads/service-packs/mdsl_`
>   `dynamicsconnector`

These connectors provide default data mapping between the source and target systems. For example, the following screenshot shows the default mapping between Microsoft Dynamics Ax and CRM:

Microsoft Dynamics ERP	Integration Direction	Microsoft Dynamics CRM
Customer	→	Account
Contact	⇔	Contact
Currency	→	Currency
BOM	→	Product
Item	→	Product
Sales Invoice	→	Invoice
Sales Order	⇔	Order
Employee	→	ERP System User
Unit and Unit Conversions	→	Unit Group / Unit
Enumerated Values	→	Picklists

connectorAxtoCRM

Apart from the preceding connector, there are other third-party connectors available. Apart from these connectors, we have other options such as scribe (`http://www.scribesoft.com/microsoft_dynamics_crm`) and Kingsway's SSIS connector (`http://www.kingswaysoft.com/products/ssis-integration-toolkit-for-microsoft-dynamics-crm`). We can also check for different connectors in Microsoft Pinpoint (`https://pinpoint.microsoft.com/en-ae`).

Summary

In this chapter, we learned about the Microsoft Dynamics CRM 2015 SDK feature. We discussed various tools that come with the CRM SDK. We learned about the different CRM APIs and their uses. We learned about different programming models in CRM to work with the CRM SDK, using different methods in CRM web services. We also discussed new enhancements for developers in CRM 2015 update 1. In this chapter we created a console application using a client API. Finally, we discussed various options for integrating CRM with other ERPs and custom web sites. In the next chapter, we will learn about creating plug-ins and custom workflows.

6

Extending Microsoft Dynamics CRM 2015

In this chapter, we are going to extend the CRM's capabilities by writing custom plug-ins, workflows, and actions. We will learn the complete details of plug-in development with code samples. We will also be discussing how to create custom workflow assemblies and using input and output arguments to pass data to custom workflows. Finally, we will be creating custom messages using actions and we will learn how to use actions in workflows and plug-ins.

In this chapter, we will cover the following topics:

- Introduction to plug-ins
- Synchronous versus asynchronous plug-ins
- Understanding plug-in event execution pipelines
- Writing sample plug-ins
- Understanding plug-in registration
- Understanding `iPlug-inExecutionContext`
- Applying validation using plug-ins
- Passing parameters to plug-ins
- Troubleshooting plug-ins
- Working with custom workflows
- Working with actions

Introduction to plug-ins

Plug-ins are an essential component of CRM applications and help us to write our custom logic and bind it to specific events for execution. Although we do have other ways to implement our business logic, the flexibility of using CRM SDK and the association with the events that plug-ins provide are not provided by other components. If you are a .NET developer or know .NET development, you can easily start working with plug-ins. A plug-in is basically a .NET assembly developed using CRM SDK, which we discussed in an earlier chapter.

Synchronous versus a synchronous plug-ins

We can write two types of plug-in: synchronous and asynchronous. Synchronous plug-ins are most suited where you need to execute your business logic immediately — for example, implementing any calculation logic or integration with another system where you may want to bring an output parameter once data is integrated. Synchronous plug-ins keep the CRM platform busy until executed completely. Synchronous plug-ins also support transactions, which means that, if you are doing multiple actions in your plug-in, everything will either be committed successfully or rolled back in the event of an error:

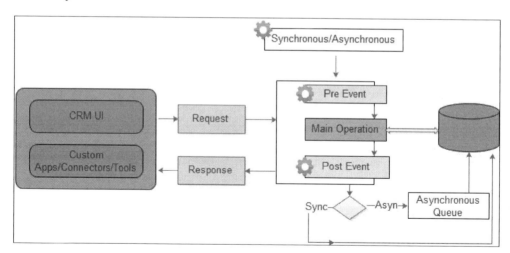

The plug-in execution

Asynchronous plug-ins are well suited for any logic that can be executed in the background and is not required to show output immediately—for example, updating an entity based on another entity in background, sending e-mails, integrating data to another system where you don't need any output parameters, such as sending syncing billing information to ERP from CRM. Asynchronous plug-ins are executed by the asynchronous queue manager, so all the asynchronous plug-ins are queued under an asynchronous queue and executed one by one, or in parallel if multi-threaded.

But, while developing both synchronous and asynchronous plug-ins, we need to make sure we write code that executes faster. It should not take more than two minutes of execution time, which is the execution limit of plug-ins, otherwise the CRM execution platform will throw a time-out error.

Understanding plug-in event execution pipelines

Every plug-in that we register is dependent on the event execution pipeline. Event plug-ins are divided into the following four stages, where each stage has its own significance.

Stage 10: Pre-validation

This is the first stage where we can register our plug-in. In this stage our business logic runs before the system main operation which means that, up to this point, there is no validation done for the user who is responsible for code execution; for example no security checks are done for the user if he has the privileges to perform the action that he is trying to do through the plug-in. Plug-ins at this stage fire only once if a compound operation is involved; for example we have the business logic to set up a related contact record when an account is created:

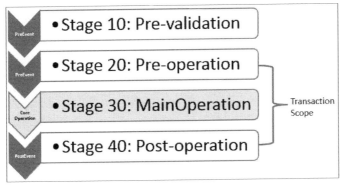

Plug-in pipeline

Stage 20: Pre-operation

This is the second stage where we can register our plug-in. Up to this stage, all validation and security checks for the user are done. They also execute before the main system operation. At this stage our business logic runs under the database transaction, so any business logic that we want to execute before the main system operation (such as auto-generation of unique IDs, financial calculations, and so on) should be registered at this stage.

Stage 30: Main-operation

This is the stage where the main core operations are executed by the CRM platform. So all the operations such as create, update, delete, and so on, are appended at this stage. There aren't any options to register our business logic at this stage.

Stage 40: Post-operation

This is the last stage where we can register our custom code. Plug-ins registered at this stage run after the main system operation, so any logic that we want to run after the main system operation can be registered here—for example, if we want to pass information from the CRM system to the ERP system once the operation is completed in the CRM, we can utilize this stage to do so.

Plug-in events

A plug-in is always bound to a specific event. Any plug-in registered under an event will be executed if the corresponding request is sent to the CRM platform using the CRM UI or any other server-side utility. For example, let's say we have an account where a create plug-in is registered; this plug-in will fire every time an organization service create request is executed from the CRM UI, such as a `create` and `import` operation or any other Web service call.

Microsoft Dynamics CRM SDK comes with a file of a complete list of possible plug-in events that can be used for registering custom logic. This file can be found in `SDK\ Message-entity support for plug-ins` in CRM 2015 SDK.

Writing your first sample plug-in

As we said, a plug-in is basically a .NET assembly, so we need Visual Studio to write one. We need Microsoft Visual Studio 2012 or 2013 or later with .NET Framework 4.5.2 to use the CRM SDK for writing plug-ins. While writing plug-ins, we need to add references to the CRM SDK. While writing plug-ins we inherit the `IPlug-in` interface, which is available in the `Microsoft.Xrm.Sdk` namespace. This interface exposes only one `Execute` method that we need to implement while writing plug-ins. Our plug-in execution starts from this method.

Let's write our first sample plug-in by performing the following instructions:

1. Open Visual Studio and navigate to **File | New | Project**.
2. Select **New Project** with the following settings:

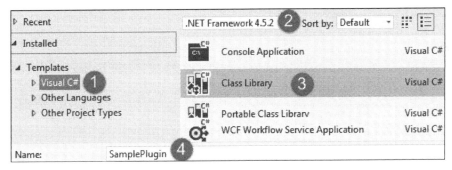

SampleVS

3. Right-click on **Reference | Add Reference** and select the following assemblies:
     ○ **Microsoft.Xrm.Sdk**
     ○ **System.Runtime.Serialization**
     ○ **System.ServiceModel**
4. Right-click on **SamplePlugin** and select **Properties | Signing**.
5. Click on the **Sign assembly** checkbox and select **New** from the drop-down.
6. Enter a value in the **Key file name** textbox and uncheck **Protect my key file with a password**.
7. Click on **Ok** and close the **Properties** dialog box.

8. Double-click on **Class1.cs** and enter the following code:

```
using Microsoft.Xrm.Sdk;
namespace SamplePlugin
{
  public class Class1:IPlugin
  {
    public void Execute(IServiceProvider serviceProvider)
    {
      throw new InvalidPluginExecutionException("Welcome to
        Plugin");
    }
  }
}
```

9. Navigate to the **Build** menu and select **Build Solution**.

Now our sample code is ready. As you can see in the preceding code, we have implemented the Execute methods of IPlugin, which have one argument of the IServiceProvider type and provide useful service information about the execution of the plug-in. In this plug-in we are throwing a plug-in execution exception, using the InvalidPluginExecutionException method and passing a string parameter. Now this plug-in can be deployed to CRM.

 Make sure to sign your assembly otherwise you will get an **Error registering plug-ins and/or workflows. Public Assembly must have public key** error while trying to register an unsigned assembly.

Understanding plug-in registration

Once our code is ready, we need to register it to the CRM platform, so that it can execute on corresponding events. We can register our plug-in using SDK or we can use the plug-in registration tool that comes with CRM SDK. We can find this registration tool under the \SDK\Tools\PluginRegistration location. We can run the PluginRegistration.exe file to register our plug-in.

Perform the following steps to set up a connection with the CRM server:

1. Double-click on the **PluginRegistration.exe** file and click on the **+ Create New Connection** button.

2. Select **Deployment Type** (for our demo we are connecting to CRM **Online**):

Login				
Deployment Type:	○ On-premises	○ Online	● Office 365	
Online Region	Asia Pacific Area		∨	
User Name	mpal@ ████ onmicrosoft.com			
Password	••••••••			
☐ Display list of available organizations				
Login	Cancel			

Plug-in connect

> We need to specify region information while connecting to CRM Online. If you don't have any idea about your organization region, you can select the **Don't Know** option under **Online Region**; then you will find organizations in all regions.

3. Click on the **Login** button to connect to the CRM server.

Once is it connected it will display the already registered assembly list, if any. Now we can register our plug-in. To register the plug-in we need to understand the concepts discussed in the following sections.

Plug-in mode

While registering a plug-in we have the option to register our plug-in in isolation mode, also known as sandbox mode, or none. Plug-ins registered in isolation mode run with limited resource access; they can't access file systems, the registry, certain protocols, and event log information. CRM Online only allows us to register plug-ins and custom workflows in isolation mode, so any plug-in or custom workflow registered on CRM Online can't use the preceding resources. But if required, we can use plug-ins and custom workflows for the integration. We can use custom Web services, deployed on a standard secured port (80 or 443), or on Microsoft Azure. Plug-ins registered in non-isolation mode don't have such restrictions and they make full use of resources.

Assembly storage

During the plug-in registration we also need to specify assembly storage; we have three options for plug-in storage: Database, Disk, and GAC.

Database

This is the recommended option for storing plug-in assembly. There are positive reasons for storing plug-ins in a database, such as recovery assembly; if the source code is damaged, we can get the assembly from the database. The benefit of storing assemblies in a database is that, when we are working on a multi server deployment, we don't need to keep our assembly in all the servers.

 You can refer to `http://nishantrana.me/2011/01/17/get-the-plugin-assembly-stored-in-database-in-crm/for` for more on how to get plug-in assemblies from the CRM database.

Disk

If you select the disk option for plug-in storage, you need to keep your assembly in the bin folder under CRM installation path: `\Server\bin` in CRM server. So if you are using multi server deployment, then you need to keep this in every CRM server.

GAC

If you select the GAC option, plug-in assembly should be registered in the Global Assembly Cache (GAC) of every CRM server.

Let's register our sample code using the following options:

1. Click on the **Register** drop-down and select **Register New Assembly**.
2. Click on the ellipse (...) under **Step 1:** and browse the sample plug-in assembly.
3. Keep the other options at their defaults and click on the **Register Selected Plugins** button.

4. Verify our assembly is available under the registered assemblies list:

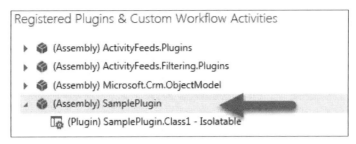

Registered plug-in

Registering plug-in steps

Now our plug-in is registered in the CRM platform, the next thing we need to do is to bind our plug-in with a specific event. We need to register new steps, so let's first understand the options available for step registration.

Message

Messages are the events that we need to use to trigger our plug-in—for example, `create`, `update`, `delete`, `retrieve`, `retrievemultiple`, and so on. As soon as you start typing the initial character it will show you the possible events available for plug-in registration. We will get all system events provided by the CRM platform and custom events that we can create using actions. We will be working on custom actions in a later topic.

Primary entity

Primary entity defines the source entity, if we want to trigger our plug-in on a specific entity on a specific message. So, for example, if we want to execute our business logic on an account entity record creation then our primary entity will be the account and the message will be create. But if you want to execute your business logic for all the entities, you can leave this field blank, so your message will trigger for all the entities. For example, if we register our plug-in on a retrieve message and don't specify the primary entity, it will run when any entity record is opened, but these types of scenario should be avoided because they can lead to performance issues.

Secondary entity

This option is not used normally; we complete the secondary entity only when two entities are required for any message—for example, the SetRelated and RemoveRelated messages. The following is a list of the primary and secondary entities supported for SetRelated:

Message Name	Primary Entity	Secondary Entity
SetRelated	Invoice	Contact
SetRelated	Lead	Account
SetRelated	Lead	Contact
SetRelated	Opportunity	Account
SetRelated	Opportunity	Contact
SetRelated	Opportunity	Competitor
SetRelated	Product	Lead
SetRelated	Product	Competitor
SetRelated	Quote	Contact
SetRelated	SalesLiterature	Competitor
SetRelated	SalesLiterature	Product
SetRelated	SalesOrder	Contact

Filtering attribute

The Filtering Attribute is very useful to avoid running our business logic on unnecessary changes. Let's say we need to run some custom business logic when the annual revenue of the account is changed, then we need to register the updated plug-in on the account entity. If during the registering plug-in step **All Attributes** is selected, our plug-in will first update any account entity fields, but if we just select the annual revenue field under the filtering attribute, our plug-in will only update those specific fields. This option is also useful for avoiding infinite loops in update plug-ins.

Run in user's context

This options allows us to set an impersonation option for our plug-in during registration. By default, plug-ins will be executing the security context of the calling user (who is responsible for the plug-in's execution), but we can impersonate our plug-in by selecting another user from this drop-down.

Execution order

Every plug-in runs in a specific order. This option is used to specify the order of execution for the plug-in if we have multiple plug-ins registered on the same event.

Event

In the event execution pipeline, we select the **Pre-validation**, **Pre-operation**, or **Post-operation** options. Please refer the earlier topic for the plug-in execution pipeline.

Execution Mode

This option allows us to configure whether our plug-in will work asynchronously or synchronously.

Deployment

This option allows us to configure if we want to run our plug-in on the server or if we also want to configure it to run for the Outlook offline client. We can select one or both options depending on our requirements.

Delete AsyncOperation if StatusCode = Successful

This option allows us to delete the record of the system job if our asynchronous plug-in is completed successfully.

> The system job entity is used to store information about asynchronous plug-ins, workflows, and other asynchronous operations by the CRM. You can get more details here: https://msdn.microsoft.com/en-us/library/gg328118.aspx.

Secured/Unsecured Configuration

This option is used to pass configuration information to plug-ins; we will be working on this in later topics.

So let's register our plug-in in line with the following screen:

1. Right-click on our sample plug-in and select **Register New Step**.
2. Enter the following information:

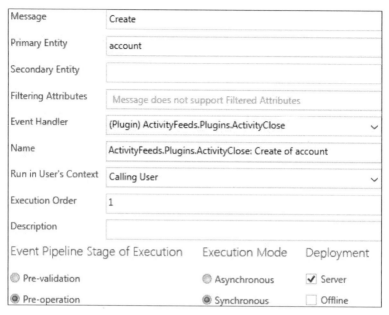

The sample plug-in step

3. Now our sample plug-in is ready for testing. When we try to create the account entity record, we should see the following message:

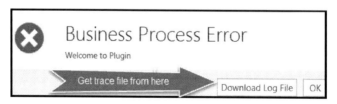

Exception

Understanding IPluginExecutionContext

IPluginExecutionContext can be considered the heart of a plug-in assembly because it supplies all the required information to the plug-in. It contains all the CRM context information, such as the entity the plug-in is executing, the user who is responsible for plug-in execution, and various input and output parameters with other related information. We can get IPluginExectuionCotext from IServiceProvider, as follows:

```
public void Execute(IServiceProvider serviceProvider)
{
  // Obtain the execution context
  IPluginExecutionContext context = (IPluginExecutionContext)
  serviceProvider.GetService(typeof(IPluginExecutionContext));
}
```

It contains many members that help us to get information for our plug-in. The following are the most used members of IPluginExecutionContext:

Name	Details
BusinessUnitId	Get business unit of the current user who is running the plug-in
CorrelationId	Used to track plug-in or custom workflow
Depth	Provides information about the call-stage depth; this is very useful to avoid infinite loop
InitiatingUserId	User who has initiated the plug-in execution
InputParameters	All the input parameters supplied by the user — for example, all dirty fields over the entity form
IsExecutingOffline	To check if the plug-in is executing from the offline Outlook client
IsInTransaction	To check if the plug-in is part of the transaction or not
IsOfflinePlayback	To check if the plug-in is fired because of the synchronization from offline to online
IsolationMode	Is the plug-in working in sandbox mode?
MessageName	Provides details about the message name of the plug-in: create, update, delete, and so on
Mode	Provides details about the plug-in execution mode
OrganizationId	Provides the current organization GUID
OrganizationName	Provides the name of the current organization
OutputParameters	Lists the parameters returned by the CRM platform, such as the record GUID after the record is created
PostEntityImages	A snapshot of the entity data after changes (need to register it separately under the plug-in step)

Name	Details
PreEntityImages	Snapshot of the entity data before any changes (need to register it separately under plug-in step)
PrimaryEntityId	Provides the primary entity record ID
PrimaryEntityName	Provides details about the primary entity on which the plug-in is executing
SecondaryEntityName	Provides the name of the secondary entity if used while registering
SharedVariables	Lists variables shared between two plug-ins
Stage	The plug-in execution pipeline where the plug-in is registered
UserId	Provides the current user ID

You can refer to https://msdn.microsoft.com/en-us/library/microsoft.xrm.sdk.ipluginexecutioncontext_members.aspx for more details on IPluginExecutionContext members.

Getting organization service

In order to perform operations on data and metadata we need to get organization services. We can get the organization service object from IServiceProvider using the following code:

```
IOrganizationServiceFactory serviceFactory =
    (IOrganizationServiceFactory)serviceProvider.GetService(
        typeof(IOrganizationServiceFactory));

IOrganizationService service =
    serviceFactory.CreateOrganizationService(context.UserId);
```

In the preceding code, we are getting the IOganizationService object by passing the current user ID, but if we pass a null value to the CreateOrganizationService method then the IOgranizationService object is created using the system user account, which has all privileges.

We can also impersonate the user using the code instead of the plug-in registration tool that we discussed earlier. To impersonate the user we can simply use the following code, after creating the organization service object. After using the following statement, the CRM will be reacting on the entire request based on the current user ID instead of the user used for authentication:

```
serviceProxy.CallerId = new Guid("GUID of the user");
```

But keep in mind that impersonation is only possible if the user has the **Act on Behalf of Another User** privilege; by default this privilege is configured in the **Delegate** security role, so in our case the authenticated user should have this security role assigned or should have the **Act on Behalf of Another User** privilege configured in their role.

 You can also refer to: `https://www.develop1.NET/public/post/User-Impersonation-in-Plugins-Workflow-and-Dialogs.aspx` to get more information about impersonation.

Getting input and output arguments

The input argument collections store all the data modified by the user and other entity information. Input argument collection is available by using context; we can get it using the following line of code:

```
context.InputParameters["Key"]
```

But every message has its own input and output parameters; what information is available on the input parameter and how we can get it are completely dependent on the plug-in message. So, for example, in the case of the create plug-in on the account entity, we will get Target as a key, so we can use the following to get the entity object:

```
if (context.InputParameters.Contains("Target") &&
  context.InputParameters["Target"] is Entity)
{
  Entity entity = (Entity)context.InputParameters["Target"];
}
```

 You can refer to a list of input and output parameters here: `http://www.patrickverbeeten.com/Blog/2008/01/25/CRM-40-Plug-in-message-input-parameters`. Although CRM 4.0 is referenced here, it's the same for CRM 2015.

It is always recommended that you first check the availability of the key using the Contains method and throwing an error if it's not available under the property beg instead of directly accessing it. After that we can get the entity object as earlier. If we have a requirement to write a plug-in on the setstage message we won't get Target as a key; instead we will get EntityReference as follows:

```
if (context.InputParameters.Contains("Target") && context.
InputParameters["Target"] is EntityReference)
```

```
{
  EntityReference entityReference =
    (EntityReference)context.InputParameters["Target"];
  string entityName = entityReference.LogicalName;
}
```

Similarly, output operations can be obtained from context depending on the message used; for example in the case of create, we can get the record ID from the output parameters as follows:

```
if (context.OutputParameters.Contains("id"))
{
  Guid AccountId = context.OutputParameters["id"];
}
```

Understanding shared variables

Sometimes, while working on business logic we may need to share variables between plug-ins because we don't want to store these values in the CRM database; instead we can store them in an entity and can read from that entity. We have the option available to share data between plug-ins using shared variables. Shared variables are basically collections of key-value pairs that can be added in one plug-in and can be collected from another plug-in:

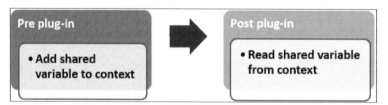

The shared variables

Let's take an example where we have pre- and post-plug-ins on the account entity, and we have some logic to check if approval is required for the account. So we can use the following code to add shared variables in our pre-create account plug-in:

```
context.SharedVariables.Add("ApprovalRequired", true);
```

Now in our post plug-in we can simply check if any shared variable exists under context; if yes, we can get it as follows:

```
if (context.SharedVariables.ContainsKey("ApprovalRequired"))
{
  bool isApprovalRequired = (bool)context.SharedVariables[
    "ApprovalRequired"];
}
```

Understanding plug-in images

Plug-in images allow us to capture specific or all fields of an entity on some events. They help us to get the entity field value before or after changes. We can register pre and post images in our plug-in. Which image we can use in our plug-in depends on the message. For example we can't register pre images on create messages and similarly we can't use post images for delete messages, but in update message we can use both pre and post images. So, for example, it may be that we want to keep a copy of the data before an update event and want to compare it with the data available after the update event. So we can register both pre and post images and do a data comparison between them. It is recommended that you get data from plug-in images instead of making service calls and getting it from the CRM database.

Plug-in images are registered after registering the step using **Register New Image**. We can store all entity fields under plug-in images, but it is recommended that you store only required fields to improve plug-in performance. We can select fields by clicking on the ellipse (**...**) next to the **Parameters** textbox:

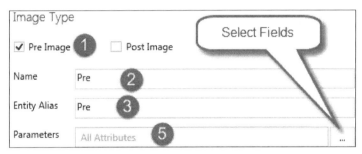

Plug-in image

Once the image is registered, we can access it using the input property beg as in the following code:

```
if (context.PreEntityImages.Contains("Pre")) //name of the
                                             //Entity Alias used
{
  Entity preImage = (Entity)context.PreEntityImages["Pre"];
}
```

Now we can get fields from the **preImage** object just like we can get them from the entity object, as in the following code:

```
if(preImage.Contains("address1_city"))
{
  string city = preImage.GetAttributeValue<string>(
    "address1_city");
}
```

Applying validation using plug-ins

Let's say we want to implement a business scenario for a member entity in our library management system. When any CRM admin tries to delete the member entity record, we will be validating whether a book has been issued to this member or not; if yes, we won't allow them to delete the record.

We need to register our plug-in on the pre delete event and we will be using a pre image to get the attribute of the entity. Perform the following steps to implement our requirement:

1. Set up a new assembly project and the required assemblies as we did in our sample plug-in.

2. Right-click on **Class1** and rename it to **ValidateMember**.

3. Inherit **IPlugin** and implement the **Execute** method.

First, we need to get context from the service provider and the organization service object. Since we are going to register the pre image, we will get our entity object from the pre image as follows:

```
public void Execute(IServiceProvider serviceProvider)
{
  try
  {   //get context
    IPluginExecutionContext context = (IPluginExecutionContext)
    serviceProvider.GetService(typeof(IPluginExecutionContext));
    //create service factory object
    IOrganizationServiceFactory serviceFactory =
      (IOrganizationServiceFactory)serviceProvider.GetService(
      typeof(IOrganizationServiceFactory));
      //get service object from service factory
      IOrganizationService service =
        serviceFactory.CreateOrganizationService(context.UserId);

    if (context.PreEntityImages.Contains("preImage"))
    {
      Entity prememberEntity =
        (Entity)context.PreEntityImages["preImage"];
      if (BookIssueValidation(prememberEntity.Id, service))
      {
        throw new InvalidPluginExecutionException("This is book
          issued for this Member, so it can't be deleted");
      }
    }
  }
}
```

```
    catch (FaultException<OrganizationServiceFault> ex)
    {
      throw new InvalidPluginExecutionException("An error occurred
        in the validtion plug-in.", ex);
    }
  }
}
```

After that, we need to pass the member ID and service object to another function to validate if there are any books issued to this user; it use return `true` else return `false`:

```
private bool BookIssueValidation(Guid MemberId,
  IOrganizationService service)
{
  //query bookissue entity based on member id
  QueryExpression query = new QueryExpression
  {
    EntityName = "him_bookissue",
    ColumnSet = new ColumnSet(true),
    Criteria = new FilterExpression
    {
      Conditions =
      {
        new ConditionExpression
        {
          AttributeName = "him_issuedto",
          Operator = ConditionOperator.Equal,
          Values = { MemberId }
        },
        new ConditionExpression
        {
          AttributeName = "him_status",
          Operator = ConditionOperator.Equal,
          Values = { 1 }
        }
      }
    }
  };
  return (service.RetrieveMultiple(query).Entities.Count > 0 ?
    true : false);
}
```

Passing parameters to plug-ins

While working with plug-ins, sometimes we need additional information; it may be related to another entity or some form of configuration data. If we need to read information from any other entity, we can simply use organization service methods to fetch data from the CRM. In the case of configuration, we can also create a configuration entity in the CRM and store data there, which can be read easily in plug-ins. Apart from that, we could also create XML Web resources to store this data and read it into the plug-in.

Another option available in plug-ins to pass configuration data is to use secured configurations and unsecured configurations. A secured configuration is only accessible by the CRM Administrator, other users can't read this information in plug-ins, whereas an unsecured configuration is available to every user. Apart from that, a secure configuration is not available in new environments if a plug-in having a plug-in step with a secure configuration is imported as part of a managed solution; but an unsecure configuration will be available in the new environment. We can pass our configuration data while registering plug-in steps in terms of an XML string. We can be read by plug-in constructors as follows:

```
public class SamplePlugin : IPlugin
{
  string FirstName = string.Empty;
  string LastName = string.Empty;
  public SamplePlugin(string unsecureConfig, string secureConfig)
  {
    FirstName = !string.IsNullOrEmpty(unsecureConfig) ?
      unsecureConfig : string.Empty;
    LastName = !string.IsNullOrEmpty(secureConfig) ?
      secureConfig : string.Empty;
  }
}
```

These configurations can be defined in the **Unsecure Configuration** and **Secure Configuration** sections under the plug-in step as follows:

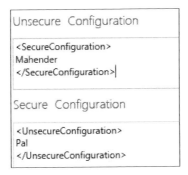

Plug-in step configuration

Troubleshooting plug-ins

During plug-in development, we need to troubleshoot our plug-in code for different errors that we may face during execution of the code. It is always a good practice to have your code well documented with proper exception handling. We can troubleshoot plug-in code in three ways:

1. Using the `ITracingService` service.
2. Using debugging.
3. Writing logs to text files.

`ITracingService` helps us to generate logging information that we may want to do at different steps. This is especially useful when we don't have debugging tools available and need logging information to troubleshoot our code. We can get `ITracingService` from the service provider object as follows:

```
//Extract the tracing service for use in debugging sandboxed plug-ins.
ITracingService tracingService =
  (ITracingService)serviceProvider.GetService(typeof(
    ITracingService));
```

`ITracingService` has one method `Trace` that we can use to create logs as follows:

```
//adding log information
tracingService.Trace("Logging Message");
```

All the tracing information generated in plug-ins can be accessed in the following ways:

- Using the **Download Log File** button in the **Business Process Error** dialog
- Using the **Plug-in Trace log** available under **Settings | Plug-In Trace Log**
- Using log files generated in the CRM installation path:
  `\ Microsoft Dynamics CRM\Trace`

Plug-in tracing in CRM applications is not enabled by default; we need to enable it from the **Customization** tab by navigating to **Settings | System Settings**. Once this setting is enabled we can see tracing information in the CRM as follows:

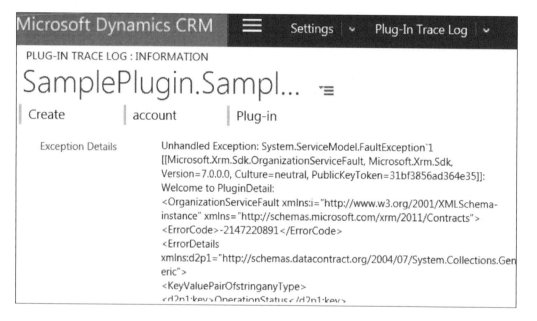

We can also get tracing information into log files at the server level if tracing is enabled in the CRM server. To enable tracing in the CRM server you can refer to: `https://technet.microsoft.com/en-us/library/hh699694.aspx#BKMKserver_level_tracing`.

Debugging plug-ins

Debugging is the process where we execute our code line by line in order to identify runtime errors and fix them. We can debug both non-isolation and isolation plug-ins; in the case of non-isolation plug-ins, we need to copy the PDB and DLL files to the `server\bin\assembly` folder on the CRM server and we need to attach the service process based on the plug-in type in Visual Studio. The following table presents the different services that we need to attach:

Plug-in Type	Process Name
Online	`w3wp`
Offline	`microsoft.crm.application.hoster`
Asynchronous plug-in and workflow	`Crmasyncservice`

You need to perform the following steps to debug your on-premise plug-in, where Visual Studio is installed on the CRM server:

1. Build your code and keep the PDB and DLL files in `server\bin\assembly`.

2. Register the updated code to the CRM.

3. Attach the **w3wp** process in Visual Studio (make sure you are logged in with admin rights).

4. Add a breakpoint in your source code.

5. Execute your event in the CRM.

>
> If Visual Studio is not installed on the CRM server then we need to use remote debugging. You can refer to `https://community.dynamics.com/crm/b/zhongchenzhoustipstricksandportaldevelopment/archive/2012/05/16/dynamics-crm-remote-debugging-step-by-step` for the steps required for remote debugging.

In the case of sandbox plug-ins, we need to copy the PDB and DLL files under `server\bin\assembly` folder on the server running the sandbox worker process (the Sandbox Processing Service role server). In the case of the sandbox server, we need to attach `Microsoft.Crm.Sandbox.WorkerProcess` for debugging.

We can also debug our plug-in using the plug-in registration tool; this is especially useful when you are working with CRM Online deployment. Please refer to: `http://nishantrana.me/2014/07/02/debugging-online-plugin-in-crm-2013/`.

Working with custom workflows

We can extend the CRM process capability by writing custom .NET assemblies known as custom workflows. Similar to plug-ins, we can also write custom workflows using Visual Studio and register them in the CRM platform; then our assembly will be available as a custom step in workflow designer. In the case of workflows, we can only register our custom assembly; we cannot register our steps and images just like plug-ins. We need to use our custom functionality with the existing steps in workflow designer. We can create custom workflows similarly using Visual Studio and use the CRM SDK just like a plug-in.

Using parameters in custom workflows

In custom workflows, we can use input and output parameters. We can use the input parameter to pass information to a workflow that can be used in the code for our custom logic. The following is an example of declaring the input type parameter:

```
[Input("Name of Parameter")]
[Default("Default value")]
public InArgument<Datatype> NameofinputProperty { get; set; }
```

The following code declares the integer type of parameter:

```
[Input("Total Value")]
[Default("500")]
public InArgument<int> IntotalvalueParameter { get; set; }
```

Similarly, we can define an output parameter that will be available in the form assistant in the workflow designer. The following is an example of an integer output variable:

```
[Output("Account Name")]
[Default("Primary Account")]
public OutArgument<string> PrimaryAccountName { get; set; }
```

We can also define properties for both in and out arguments, as follows:

```
[Input("Total Value Input")]
[Output("Total Value Output")]
[Default("500")]
public InOutArgument<int> InOutParameter { get; set; }
```

In some of the properties, we need to provide some additional reference information. For example, the following is the code for declaring the reference and option set type of parameters:

```
[Input("EntityReference input")]
[ReferenceTarget("account")]
public InArgument<EntityReference> AccountName { get; set; }


[Input("Custom Category")]
[AttributeTarget("account", "customertypecode >")]
public InArgument<OptionSetValue> CustomerCategoryCode{ get; set; }
```

Adding custom workflows in library management systems

We have a requirement to create a marketing list to promote the new books added in a library management system. We need to provide members with the option to select whether they are interested in book promotions. If a member is interested, we need to add the member to the marketing list automatically. Let's implement this requirement using a custom workflow.

First, we need to set up a marketing list in the CRM. Currently, we don't have access to the marketing list entity because we modified the sitemap to hide everything other than the required entity links, so we need to add a new link for the marketing list. Perform the following steps to add a new link for the marketing list:

1. Connect to XrmToolBox.
2. Click on the **Load SiteMap** button, right-click on **Group (Extensions)**, and select **Add New Sub Area**.
3. Select the **Marketing list** entity by clicking on the **Select entity** button.

4. Click on **Save** and then click on **Update SiteMap**:

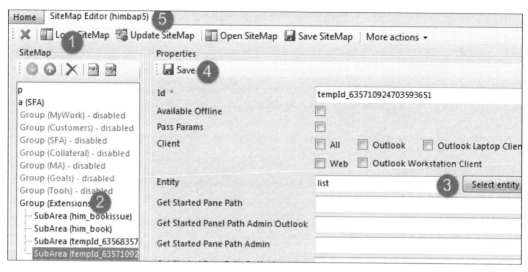

The marketing list

Now we need to create the marketing list for the book promotion. Perform the following steps:

1. Connect to the **Library Management System** application and click on the **Main** area.

2. Select **Marketing Lists** and click on the **+ New** button:

The Marketing Lists icon

3. Enter the following information and click on the **Save and Close** button:

   Name: New Book Promotion

   List Type: Static

   Targeted At: Contact

Now let's write our workflow by performing the following steps:

1. Start **Microsoft Visual Studio** and navigate to **File | New | Project**.
2. Select **Visual C#** and **Workflow | Activity Library** in the **Installed Templates** pane.
3. Specify a name and location for the solution, and then click on **OK**.
4. Make sure **.NET Framework 4.5.2** is selected as the target framework.
5. Right-click on the project name and add a reference to the following assemblies:

   Microsoft.Xrm.Sdk.dll

   Microsoft.Xrm.Workflow.dll

   Microsoft.Crm.Sdk.Proxy

6. Delete the **Activity1.xaml** file in the project; right-click on the project and add a new class to it.
7. Open the class file and add the following using directives:

   ```
   using System.Activities;
   using Microsoft.Xrm.Sdk;
   using Microsoft.Xrm.Sdk.Workflow;
   using Microsoft.Crm.Sdk.Messages;
   using Microsoft.Xrm.Sdk.Query
   ```

8. Now we need to inherit **CodeActivity** and declare an input argument to accept the name of the marketing list, as follows:

   ```
   class AddmemberToMarketingList:CodeActivity
   {
     [Input("Marketing List")]
     [ReferenceTarget("list")]
     public InArgument<EntityReference> MarketingList
       {get;set;}
   ```

We need to add a new two-option set field in our member entity to get this member's preferences on book promotion. So we have added a two-option set field called `him_interestedinbookpromotions` in the member entity, where they can select the **Yes** or **No** option.

In the workflow, we override the `Execute` method available under the `CodeActivity` class, as follows. This will provide access to the workflow execution context and organization service access:

```
protected override void Execute(CodeActivityContext executionContext)
{
  //Create the tracing service
  ITracingService tracingService = executionContext.GetExtension
    <ITracingService>();
  try
  {
    //Create the context
    IWorkflowContext context = executionContext.GetExtension
      <IWorkflowContext>();
    IOrganizationServiceFactory serviceFactory =
      xecutionContext.GetExtension<IOrganizationServiceFactory>();
    IOrganizationService service =
      serviceFactory.CreateOrganizationService(context.UserId);
    //get entity id and query interested in book promotion
    tracingService.Trace("Reading data from member entity");
    Entity member = service.Retrieve("contact",
      context.PrimaryEntityId, new ColumnSet(
        "him_interestedinbookpromotions"));
    //updating tracing
    tracingService.Trace("Validating if member is interested in
      book promotions");
    if (member.Contains("him_interestedinbookpromotions") &&
      member.GetAttributeValue<bool>(
        "him_interestedinbookpromotions"))
    {
      //add member to promolist
      AddToMarktingList(member.Id, service, executionContext);
    }
    tracingService.Trace("Execution Completed");
  }
  catch (Exception Ex)
  {
```

```
        tracingService.Trace("There is any error in adding member to
          marketing list" + Ex.Message);
        throw new InvalidPluginExecutionException(Ex.Message);
    }
}
```

In the workflow, the entity object is not available under the workflow execution context, so we are getting the primary entity ID and retrieving the contact entity attribute `him_interestedinbookpromitions`; we are validating whether the user has selected this option.

To add a member to our marketing list we need to use `AddMemberListRequest`, which we will be passing to the `Execute` method of the organization service; this request has two parameters: the record ID and the ID of the list record:

```
private void AddToMarktingList(Guid Memberid, IOrganizationService
    service, CodeActivityContext contxt)
{
    AddMemberListRequest req = new AddMemberListRequest();
    req.EntityId = Memberid;
    req.ListId = MarketingList.Get<EntityReference>(contxt).Id;
    AddMemberListResponse resp =
        (AddMemberListResponse)service.Execute(req);
}
```

Now our workflow is ready, build the solution by navigating to **Build Solution** under the **BUILD** menu. Now we can connect to the plug-in registration tool and can register our workflow assembly just like we registered our plug-in in earlier topics. After the workflow is registered, we can set the workflow group and step name, using properties in the plug-in registration tool as follows. Now our custom steps will be available under the **Custom Workflow** group in workflow designer:

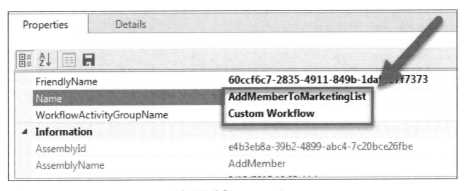

The Workflow properties

Using custom workflows

Now let's use our custom workflow. Perform the following steps to create a book promotion workflow:

1. Navigate to **Components | Processes** and click on **New** from the right-hand process toolbar in the **LibraryManagement** solution that we created earlier.

2. Enter the following details and click on **Ok**:

   Process Name: Add Member to Book Promotion

   Entity: Member

   Category: Workflow

   Run this workflow in the background (recommended): Selected

3. Select **Record is created** and **Record fields change** and click on the **Select** button to select v**Interestedinbookpromotions** field in the field list under **Start When**.

4. Click on **Add Step** and select our custom assembly:

Custom workflow step

> Assemblies are cached by the CRM so you may have to restart the CRM website to see the new or updated deployed assembly.

5. Click on **Set Properties** and select our marketing list record as follows:

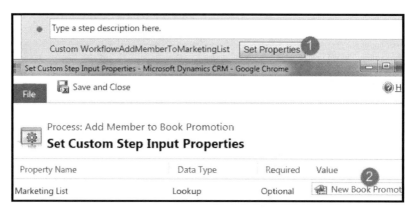

Selecting the Marketing List option

6. Click on **Activate** and then close the workflow dialog.

Now when we create our update, a new member with **Interested in book Promotions select members** will automatically be added to the marketing list as follows:

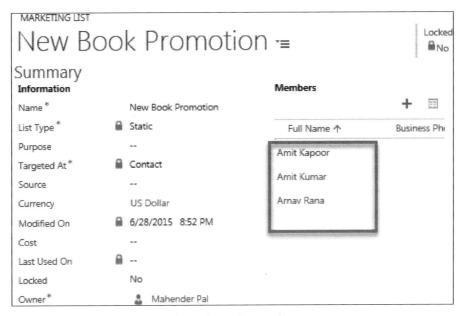

The marketing list members

For CRM development using Visual Studio, we can also use the Developer toolkit. At the time of writing, the CRM 2015 Developer toolkit has not been released, but the CRM 2013 Developer toolkit can be also used for CRM 2015. Refer to: `https://msdn.microsoft.com/en-us/library/hh547400(v=crm.6).aspx` for details on using the CRM 2013 Developer toolkit.

Understanding actions

Have you ever thought of creating your own events just like we have out-of-the-box events available in organization services? If yes, then actions can help you. Actions were released in CRM 2013 initially, to allow us to define our own custom messages that can be called using server-side code or client-side code. If you are working with 2013 you can just access actions using SDK calls alone, but with the new enhancements in CRM 2015, we can call actions through workflows and dialogs as well.

Actions can be created for a particular entity or can be global; they are always synchronous and run on the current user security context. Thus, similar to synchronous plug-ins, actions are also transactional. Once an action is activated, it is available like messages and we can register plug-ins on them.

Designing actions

Let's take an example where we want to set up a custom message to calculate the fine on a book issued if it is submitted after five days. We will create an action that will take the issue date, return the date as an input argument, and will calculate the output based on the date difference. To implement this requirement, first we will design our action so it just holds the definition of our custom message and then we will register a plug-in on our action to calculate the fine. Perform the following steps to create actions:

1. Navigate to **Components** | **Process** and click on the **New** button from the process toolbar.

2. Enter the following properties and click on **Ok**:

   Process Name: Fine Calculation

   Category: **Action**

   Entity: Book Issue or Return

3. Click on the + sign to add a new argument and change the properties of the argument as follows:

   Name: IssueDate

   Type: DateTime

   Required: Selected

   Direction: Input

4. Repeat Step 3 to add two other arguments using the following properties:

Name	Type	Required	Direction
ReturnDate	DateTime	Selected	Input
Fine	Integer	Unselected	Output

5. After adding all the arguments, you should see:

Name▼	Type	Required	Direction
IssueDate	DateTime	Required	Input
ReturnDate	DateTime	Required	Input
Fine	Integer	Optional	Output

The action arguments

6. Click on **Activate** and then the **Close** button.

Our action is ready; as soon as it is activated, it is available as a custom message, which can be called from SDK and can be used for plug-in registration. Now let's develop our fine calculation plug-in that we will be registering in our custom action. Perform the following steps:

1. Add a **New Class Library** project that is similar to earlier examples that we did for custom workflows.

2. Rename **class1** to **CalculateFineAmt**, add a **Microsoft.Xrm.Sdk** assembly to the project, and sign the assembly like we did earlier.

3. Add the following code to the `CalculateFineAmt.cs` file:

```
public void Execute(IServiceProvider serviceProvider)
{
  // Obtain the execution context IPluginExecutionContext
    context = (IPluginExecutionContext)
  serviceProvider.GetService(typeof(
    IPluginExecutionContext));
  if (context.InputParameters.Contains("IssuedDate") &&
    context.InputParameters.Contains("ReturnDate"))
  {
    //read input arguments
    DateTime issueDate = (DateTime)context.InputParameters
      ["IssuedDate"];
    DateTime ReturnDate = (DateTime)context.InputParameters
      ["ReturnDate"];
    //calcuate date
    double TotalDays = (ReturnDate - issueDate).TotalDays;
    if (TotalDays > 5)
    {
```

```
        //set output argument
        context.OutputParameters["Fine"] =
          Convert.ToInt32((TotalDays - 5) * 5);
    }
  }
}
```

In the preceding code, first we are reading action input arguments, they will be accessible by the input argument, and then we are calculating the difference between the start and end date; if it is greater than five days, we calculate the fine by multiplying by five:

1. Build the assembly and connect to the plug-in registration tool.

2. Register our assembly just like we did for the plug-in example.

3. Register **New Step** and select our custom message for the `him_bookissue` entity (as for the **Post** operation) as follows:

Now we have our custom message available with the fine calculation logic, we can simply use it by creating a real-time workflow and passing the required input arguments as follows:

1. Create a real-time workflow using the following properties:

   Name: Calling Custom Calculation Action

   Category: **Workflow**

   Entity: **Book Issue/Return**

   Run this workflow in background (recommended): Unselected

2. Configure it to start when Record is created and when Return date is changed (select the return date field under the Selection option for the Record field changes).

3. Click on **Add Step | Perform Action** and select our action name from the drop-down button.

4. Click on the **Set Properties** button and set action arguments as follows using **Form Assistant** available on the right hand side:

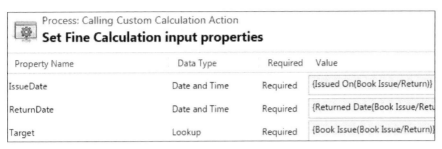

The custom action values

5. Add the update step and click on the **Set Properties** button to set the fine field as follows:

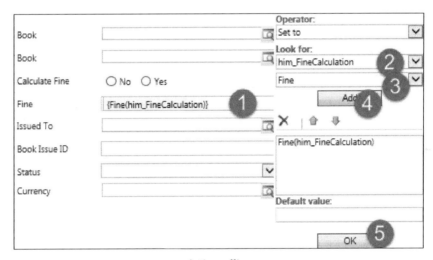

Action calling

6. Save and activate the workflow.

Now let's test our actions. Open any book issue or return entity record, where the book is issued, and complete **Return Date**. Once we save the book issue or return record, it will calculate the fine using our custom action as follows:

 We can also call actions using server-side and client-side calls. You can refer to: http://a33ik.blogspot.ae/2013/10/custom-actions-walkthrough-for-net-and.html for information on using actions with server-side and client-side code.

Summary

In this chapter we learned about extending the CRM using plug-ins, custom workflows, and actions. We discussed all the options available in plug-ins and workflows. In this chapter we enhanced our library management system by adding new plug-in validation. We developed a custom workflow to add members to the book promotion marketing list. We learned how can we design actions and call them using workflows. We also discussed how we can register plug-ins on custom messages created using actions. In the next chapter, we are going to build an application tracking system.

7
Creating a Project Tracking Application

In this chapter, we will be creating a sample project tracking application utilizing different Microsoft Dynamics CRM features. We will be setting up custom entities for our application and will learn how to use rollup fields to show aggregations from child entities. We will also see how we can use calculated field for performing calculations using formulas. We will learn about the activity feed feature in CRM 2015 and will learn about configuring activity feeds for entities and activity feed rules as follows.

- Creating a project tracking application
- Project tracking application design
- Customizing CRM 2015 for the project tracking application
- Using rollup fields for aggregation
- Understanding activity feeds
- Configuring activity feeds
- Setting up teams
- Creating charts and dashboards

In this chapter we are going to develop a custom solution for a project tracking application. In this solution, we are going to develop features required by project management software. Project tracking applications are used by companies to create the main project life cycle. A traditional project tracking application provides the following features:

- Ability to maintain project catalogs
- Maintain a list of the project user stories and project tasks

- Ensure visibility of the project task status
- Manage project timesheet entries
- Clear view of project issues submitted and resolved
- Maintain project teams
- Ability to maintain project-related documents
- Ability to schedule project meetings
- Data visualization for the projects status

All the preceding features can be implemented using CRM 2015's out-of-the-box capabilities; we will be customizing CRM 2015 to achieve all the preceding requirements for our custom solution. We will be using the CRM 2015 online trial for this application. You can set up the CRM 2015 online trial using the `http://www.microsoft.com/en-sg/dynamics/Default.aspx` link.

Project tracking application design

To map our application requirements, we will be using some out-of-the-box entities and creating some custom entities to capture project-related information. The following table provides information about the entities that we will be using:

Name	Type	Description
Account	System	Account entity is used to store client information
Project	Custom	A custom entity to store project details
User stories	Custom	Custom entities used to store user store/use cases of the project
Project tasks	Custom	This entity is used to store the project task details
Issue	Custom	This entity is used to store project issue details
User	System	To store project team members
Team	System	To store project team details
Activity entities	System	We will be using activity entities such as tasks, e-mails, and appointment for maintaining different activities

We need to set up a parent child relationship for the preceding entities; for example one account can have any number of projects, and similarly one project can have any number of project tasks and user stories. So we need to set up a 1: N relationship between these entities.

The following diagram represents the relationship between these entities:

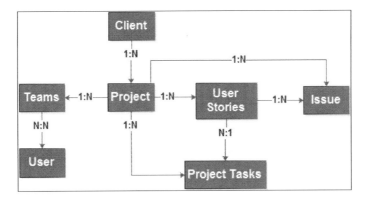

Customizing CRM for the project tracking application

In order to customize CRM 2015 for our application, let's first set up our custom solution like we did in earlier chapters. We have created a custom publisher with the name of **HIMBAP** for our solution and we will be using this publisher for our solution. Refer to *Chapter 2, Customizing Microsoft Dynamics CRM 2015,* to create a new solution with the name of ProjectTrackingSystem as follows:

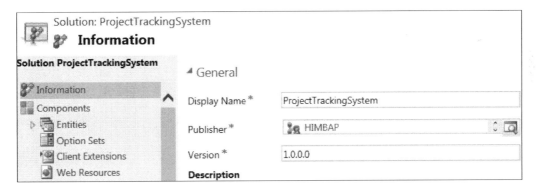

Adding existing entities to the solution

First we will be adding our existing entities to the solution so that we can customize their look and feel based on our application requirements. Perform the following steps to add existing entities:

1. Navigate to **Components** | **Entities** and click on the **Add Existing** button from the right-hand side command bar.

2. Select the following entities from the list to add them to our solution:

    - **Account**
    - **Appointment**
    - **Email**
    - **Task**
    - **User**
    - **Team**

3. Select **No** in the **Missing Dependency** dialog.

Customizing the account entity

Now we have an account entity as part of our solution so let's quickly customize it. We will use existing fields in the account entity for our application and will add one field to assign the account manager to the account. Perform the following steps to customize the account entity:

1. Expand **Entities** | **Account**, select **Fields** | **New**, and create the following field using the following settings (keep the other settings at their defaults):

Property	Description
Display name	Account Manager
Name	him_accountmanager
Data type	Lookup
Target record type	User

2. Open the **Account** main form and rearrange the body field, header fields, and sections based on the following screenshot:

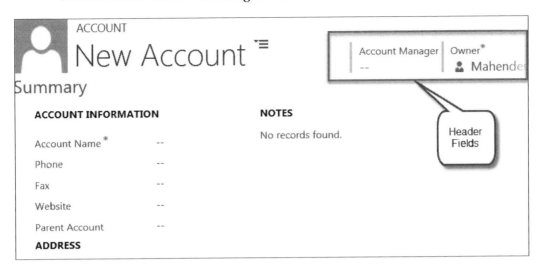

3. Rearrange the **Details** tab as follows and remove all other fields and sections.

Details

COMPANY PROFILE		CONTACT PREFERENCES		BILLING	
Industry	--	Contact Method	Any	Currency	US Dollar
Ownership	--	Email	Allow	Credit Limit	--
		Bulk Email	Allow	Credit Hold	No
		Phone	Allow	Payment Terms	--
Description		Fax	Allow		
--		Mail	Allow		

4. Click on **Save and Close**.

Setting up the project entity

We will create a standard custom entity to store project-related information. This entity will act as the parent entity for other entities such as user stories, project tasks, issues, and timesheets. At this point we will just create the project entity so that it can be used to define relationships in child entities. Use the following configuration to set up the project entity:

1. Navigate to **Components | Entities** under our solution and click on the **New** button to create the entity.

2. Enter the following properties:

    Display Name: Project

    Plural Name: Projects

    Name: him_project

    Ownership: User or Team

    Areas that display this entity: Sales

    Notes: Selected

    Duplicate Detection: Selected

    Activities: Selected

3. Deselect all other option and click on the **Save** button.

We will be updating this entity with some additional rollup fields that we are going to set up in later topics. You can refer to *Chapter 1 , Getting Started with Microsoft Dynamics CRM 2015* for rollup fields.

Setting up a user story entity

Every project is divided into multiple user stories or use cases. So we will set up a custom entity for the user story and the entity will store project user stories/use cases name and descriptions with other details like parent project.

Perform the following steps to set up a project task entity:

1. Navigate to **Components | Entities** under our solution and click on the **New** button to create an entity.

2. Enter the following properties:

    Display Name: User Story

    Plural Name: User Stories

    Name: him_userstory

Ownership: User or Team

Areas that display this entity: Sales

Notes: Selected

Duplicate Detection: Selected

3. Deselect all other option and click on the **Save** button.

Once the entity is created we need to set up its data structure; please refer to *Appendix A, Data Model for Client Entities* and create fields for the project task entity by navigating to **User Story | Fields** or from the main form. Once the field is created we need to place it over main user story form as in the following screen:

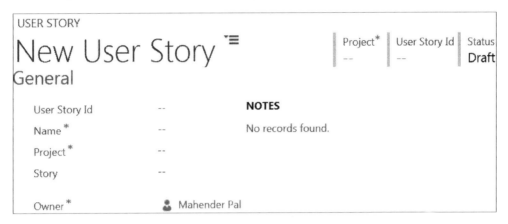

Now let's add our custom fields to the default **Active UserStories** view. Perform the following steps to do this:

1. Navigate to **User Story | Views**.

2. Double-click on the **Active UserStories** view to open it.

3. Click on **Add Columns** under **Common Tasks** and add the following field to the view:

4. Click on **Save and Close**.

Setting up a project tasks entity

We will create another custom entity to store project task details. This entity will contain information about the parent project and user story with other task-related details such as the start date, end date status, and assigned to.

Perform the following steps to set up the project task entity:

1. Navigate to **Entities** under our solution and click on the **New** button to create the entity.

2. Enter the following properties:

   Display Name: Project Task

   Plural Name: Project Tasks

   Name: him_projecttask

   Ownership: User or Team

   Areas that display this entity: Sales

   Notes: Selected

   Duplicate Detection: Selected

3. Deselect all other option and click on the **Save** button.

Now we need to set up the data structure for our project task entity; please refer to *Appendix A*, *Data Model for Client Entities* and create fields for the project task entity by navigating to **Project Task | Fields** or from the main form. Once the field is created we need to place it over the main project task form as in the following screen:

New Project Task		Assigned To	Project Id*	Task Status
General		--	--	--

Task Id	--	**NOTES**
Task Name *	--	No records found
Project *	--	
User Story	--	
Assigned To	--	
Start Date	--	
End Date	--	
Description	--	

Using filtered lookups

The filtered lookup feature was initially introduced in CRM 2011 and allows us to filter lookups based on other lookup values using a simple configuration and using JavaScript. So for example, we just want to show **User Story** related to the project selected in the **Project** lookup. Perform the following steps to implement this requirement:

1. Double-click on the **User Story** lookup field to open the field property window.

2. Set up the **Related Records Filtering** section as follows and click **OK**.

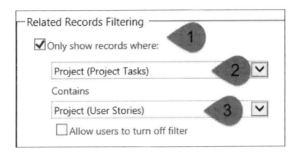

Apart from the simple lookup filtering configuration we can also use the SDK for complex lookup filtering.

> Please refer to *Chapter 3, Client-side Logic with Microsoft Dynamics CRM 2015*, to filter lookups using JavaScript.

Now we need to set up views for the project task entity just like we did for the user story entity. Let's first modify the **Active Project Tasks** view based on the following information:

View Name	Customization	Fields
Active project tasks	Add/remove column	Task name, Assigned to, Start date, End date, Task ID

Once the preceding changes are done we can set up another view where we need similar fields; let's setup another view for completed project tasks using the following steps:

1. Double-click on the **Active Project Tasks** view to open it.

2. Click on the **Save As** command button on the view command bar and name it **Completed Project Tasks**. Click on **OK**.

3. Click on **Edit Filter Criteria** under the **Common Tasks** area and add criteria as follows:

4. Click on **OK** and **Save and Close** the view definition.

Setting up a timesheet entity

We want to also keep track of the time used to work on project activities so we will create one custom entity to store timesheet details related to the project. This entity will store information about how much time the user spends on project tasks. This entity will contain information about the parent project and user story and project tasks with other timesheet-related details such as start date, end date status, and total hours.

Perform the following steps to set up the project task entity:

1. Navigate to **Entities** under our solution and click on **New** to create the entity.

2. Enter the following properties:

   Display Name: Timesheet

   Plural Name: Timesheets

   Name: him_timesheet

   Ownership: **User or Team**

   Areas that display this entity: **Sales**

   Notes: Selected

   Duplicate Detection: Selected

3. Deselect all other options and click on **Save**.

Now we need to set up the data structure for our timesheet entity; please refer to *Appendix A, Data Model for Client Entities* and create fields for the project task entity by navigating to **Timesheet | Fields** or from the main form.

Using calculated fields

Another exciting feature added in CRM 2015 is support for calculated fields, which we discussed in *Chapter 1, Getting Started with Microsoft Dynamics CRM 2015*. Calculated fields allow us to automate calculation by simply defining its property. Calculation is done in real time and we can also refer to other data type fields in the formulas of calculated fields but we can't refer to them in their own formula.

 We can only reference current entity fields in calculated fields; there is no way to reference related entity fields under calculated fields.

We are going to use calculated fields in our timesheet entity to calculate the total hours used to complete project tasks. Perform the following steps to create a calculated field:

1. Navigate to **Timesheet | Fields | New**.

2. Enter the following information in the field property window:

    Display Name: Total Hours

    Name: him_totalhours

    Data Type: Whole Number

    Field Type: Calculated

3. Click on the **Edit** button next to **Field Type**.

4. Click on **ACTION** and configure it as follows. Click on **Save and Close**:

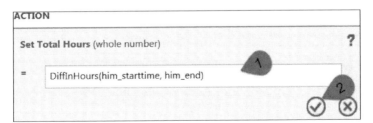

You can find more details about calculated fields at `https://technet.microsoft.com/en-us/library/dn832103.aspx`.

Once fields are created we need to place them over the main timesheet form like the following screen:

New Timesheet

Timesheet Code	Owner*	Total Hours
--	Mahender	--

General

Timesheet Code	--
Project	--
User Story	--
Task	--
Start	--
End	--
Name*	--
Description	--
Total Hours	--
Owner*	Mahender Pal

Now we can set up lookup filtering in **User Story** and **Task** like we did in an earlier step. First we need to filter **User Story** based on **Project** and then we can do the configuration to filter **Task** based on the **User Story**, based on the following information:

Filtering User Story Based on Project	
Only show records where:	Project (Timesheets)
Contains	Project (User Stories)
Filtering Task Based on User Story	
Only show records where:	User Story (Timesheets)
Contains	User Story (User Stories)

We also need to customize the default **Active Timesheets** view like we did in an earlier step based on the following information:

View Name	Customization	Fields
Active Timesheets	Add/Remove column	Name, Project, Task, Start, End, Total hours, Created on

Setting up issue entity

We need to set up another entity that will be storing issues related to project tasks. In this entity we will store information such as submitted by, assigned to, parent project, parent task and so on.

Perform the following steps to set up a project issue entity:

1. Navigate to **Entities** under our solution and click on **New** to create the entity.

2. Enter the following properties:

   Display Name: Issue

   Plural Name: Issues

   Name: him_issue

   Ownership: **User or Team**

   Areas that display this entity: **Sales**

   Notes: Selected

   Duplicate Detection: Selected

3. Deselect all other options and click on **Save**.

After the issue entity is created we need to set up the data structure for it; please refer to *Appendix A, Data Model for Client Entities* and create fields for the project task entity by navigating to **Issue | Fields** or from the main form. Once the field is created we need to place it over the main issue form like the following screen:

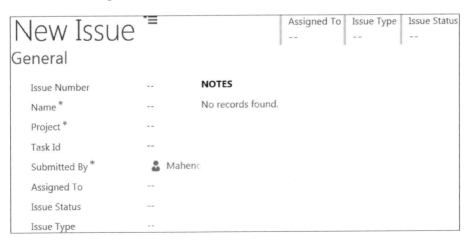

We can set up lookup filtering for Task ID based on the project like we did in an earlier step. Use the following information to set up a filter lookup:

Filtering Task ID based on Project	
Only show records where:	Project (Issues)
Contains	Project (Project tasks)

We also need to customize the default **Active Issues** view like we did in an earlier step based on the following information:

View Name	Customization	Fields
Active issues	Add/Remove column	Name, Submitted on, Assigned to, Issue status, Issue type, Submitted by, Task ID

We also need to add additional criteria to the active issues view to show issues where the status is open or reopen, so add another criterion as follows using the **Edit Filter Criteria** option under **Common Tasks**:

We can also set up another view by using the **Save As** option like we did in an earlier steps to create another view to show fixed tasks, where we need to check for **Issue Status Equals** to **Fixed**.

Using rollup fields for aggregation

Microsoft Dynamics CRM 2015 introduced rollup fields. We discussed these features in *Chapter 1, Getting Started with Microsoft Dynamics CRM 2015*. We use rollup fields for aggregation basically. For example, if we want to count child entity records or show the total of any money field available in the child entity in the parent entity form, we can use rollup fields. All these aggregations are done by recurring asynchronous system jobs, which by default run 12 hours after a field is created or updated.

If you are a System Administrator, you can modify rollup system job behavior. You can navigate to **Settings | System Jobs** and can select **Recurring System Jobs** to display all the recurring rollup jobs. We can select a job and can select an action from the **More Actions** drop-down as follows:

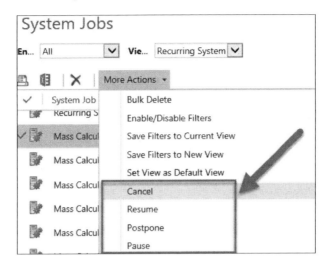

Now let's use rollup fields in our project tracking application. In our application the project entity will act like a parent and we want to show aggregation of the related project tasks, issues, user stories, and timesheets.

We will be showing the following rollup fields in the project entity:

Name	Description
Total User Stories	Total count of the user stories for current project
Total Project Tasks	Total count of project tasks
Total Completed Tasks	This field will show how many project tasks are completed
Total Issues	This field will count total issues reported for particular project
Solved Issues	This field will count total issues fixed for project
Total Time Entered	This field will sum all the hours entered for project

This information will help us to know the updated project status. So let's first add aggregation details about the user stories in the project entity.

Perform the following steps to add rollup fields in the project entity to show the total count of the project user stories:

1. Navigate to **Entities | Project | Fields** in our solution and click on **New** under the field's command bar.

2. Enter the following information under the field definition window:

   Display Name: Total User Stories

   Name: him_totaluserstories

   Data Type: Whole Number

   Field Type: Rollup

3. Click on the **Edit** button next to **Field Type**.

4. Select **User Stories (Project)** under the **Related** drop-down.

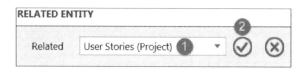

5. Select **COUNT** under **Aggregate Function** and **Project Task** under the **Aggregated Related Entity Field**. Click on the tick mark sign.

After we have completed all the steps, our rollup field definition should look as follows:

6. Click on **Save and Close** in both the windows.

 The rollup field is calculated based on the system job called **Mass Calculate Rollup Fields**; by default it runs after 12 hours. If required you can run it before 12 hours by using **More Actions** | **Postpone** after selecting this system job under **Settings** | **System Jobs**.

Now let's add a similar type of field to display the total count of the project tasks:

1. Click on **New** under the field's command bar.

2. Enter the following information under the field definition window:

   Display Name: Total Project Tasks

   Name: him_totaltasks

   Data Type: **Whole Number**

   Field Type: **Rollup**

3. Click on the **Edit** button next to **Field Type**.

4. Select **Project Tasks (Project Id)** under **Related** drop-down and click on the tick mark sign.

5. Select **COUNT** under **Aggregate Function** and **Project Task** under **Aggregated Related Entity Field** and click on the tick mark sign.

When completed, it should look as follows:

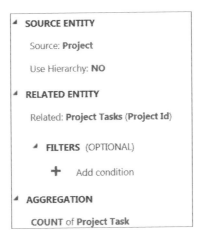

6. Click on **Save and Close** in both dialogs to close the field definition window.

Apart from the total project tasks that it will show, we also want to show the total completed project tasks to know how many project tasks are completed. Perform the following steps to create another field to show the total completed tasks count:

1. Click on **New** under the field's command bar.

2. Enter the following information under the field definition window:

   Display Name: Total completed Tasks

   Name: him_totalcompletedtasks

   Data Type: Whole Number

   Field Type: Rollup

3. Click on **Edit** next to **Field Type**.

4. Select **Project Tasks (Project Id)** under the **Related** drop-down and click on the tick mark sign.

5. Click on the **Add Condition** link and add a filter as follows:

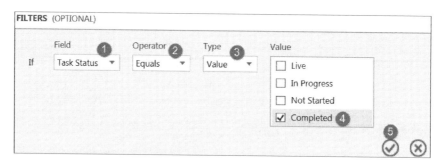

6. Select **COUNT** under **Aggregate Function** and **Project Task** under **Aggregated Related Entity Field** and click on the tick mark sign.

7. Click on **Save and Close** in both dialogs to close the field definition window.

Now we need to add a rollup field for the total time entered for project tasks; perform the following steps to do this:

1. Click on **New** under the field's command bar.

2. Enter the following information under the field definition window:

   Display Name: Total Time Entered

   Name: him_totaltimeentered

   Data Type: Whole Number

   Field Type: Rollup

3. Click on the **Edit** button next to **Field Type**.

4. Select **Timesheets (Project)** under the **Related** drop-down and click on the tick mark sign.

5. Click on the **AGGREGATION** link and add selected details as follows:

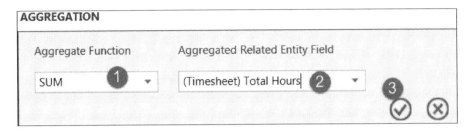

6. Click on **Save and Close** in both dialogs to close the field definition window.

Similarly, we need to set up another two rollup fields for project issues. Use the following information to set up these fields, like we did for project tasks:

Display Name	Entity	Name	Data Type	Field Type	Rollup Definition
Total issues	Project	him_totalissues	Whole number	Rollup	• **Related Entity: Issues (Project)** • **Aggregate Function: COUNT** • **Aggregated Related Entity Field: Issue**
Solved issues	Project	him_solvedissues	Whole Number	Rollup	• **Related Entity: Issues (Project)** • **FILTERS** • **Field: Issue Status** • **Operator: Equals** • **Type: Value** • **Value: Fixed** • **Aggregate Function: COUNT** • **Aggregated Related Entity Field: Issue**

Display Name	Entity	Name	Data Type	Field Type	Rollup Definition
Total project	Account	`him_totalproject`	Whole number	Rollup	• **Related: Projects (Client)** • **Aggregate Function: COUNT** • **Aggregated Related Entity Field: Project**

We need to place the **Total Project** rollup field in the **Account** header section.

Completing the project entity design

After adding all the rollup fields we need to add other simple lookup field to the project entity. Please refer to *Appendix A, Data model for Client Entities* and create fields for the project entity by navigating to **Project | Fields** or from the main project form. Once the field is created we need to put it in the project entity form. We also need to add sub-grids for the related entities. Perform the following steps to add a user story entity sub-grid:

1. Select on the **INSERT** tab and click on **Sub-Grid**.

2. Enter the details as follows in the **Sub-Grid** property dialog (keep all other details at their defaults) and click on the **Set** button:

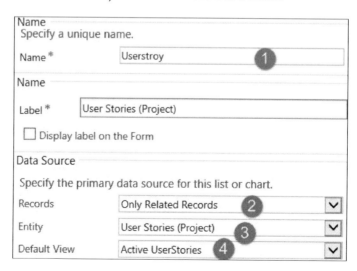

Similarly to this we need to add sub-grids for other entities using the following information and keep the other details at their default:

Name	Records	Entity	Default View
Issuesdetails	Only Related Records	Issues (Project)	Active Issues
Tasks	Only Related Records	Project Tasks (Project Id)	Active Project Tasks

Now let's rearrange project **General** tab and **Header** section of main entity form design like following screen:

We need to rearrange the **Details** tab like the following screen:

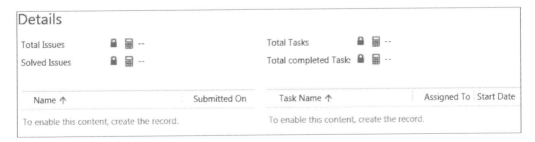

Understanding activity feeds

Microsoft Dynamics CRM has a very cool **activity feed** feature that was introduced in CRM 2011. This feature is similar to getting updates in social media tools such as Facebook, LinkedIn, and Yammer. We can also follow records and like/unlike posts as we do in social media. In our project tracking application we are going to use this feature so that the entire internal project team members can be up-to-date about the project status.

 You can refer to `https://technet.microsoft.com/en-us/library/dn659847.aspx` for details on social media integration

Most business entities are enabled for activity feeds; we can see activity feeds on **What's New** dashboards and in the **Social Pane** in the respective entity. For example, in the following screen we can see posts related to account and related entity updates:

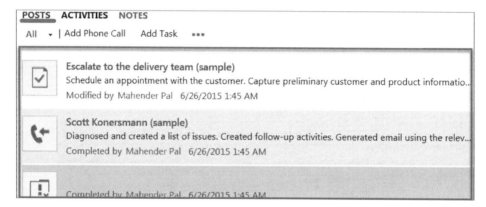

 POSTS can be selected as the default tab from the **Social Page** property by selecting **Default Tab** as **Post** under **Display tab**.

Activity feeds are available in entity records, personal walls in social panes, or in **What's New** dashboards. We can see two types of post in the wall:

- **User**: This post is basically created by the user, if the user wants to provide some updates on the record or any other information. In our case, let's say the testing team just tested a critical showstopper issue and want to convey a message that this issue is fixed; they can simply post this message over the project record.

- **Auto Post**: Auto posts are generated by the CRM based on the predefined auto post rules. So, for example, there can be an auto post rule to post a message over the project record wall that a new issue is submitted. While posting messages, we can post the entity record information as well.

Activity feeds are not available for all entities, whereas the entity posts we can see depend on two configurations, basically:

- **Activity Feed Configuration**: We can access this configuration by navigating to **Settings | Activity Feed Configuration**. This is the place where activity feeds for the entities are enabled. This view will show all the entities that can be enabled for activity feeds; only some of the system entities are available for this. A record of the configuration is created by the CRM. When we create a custom entity, the CRM generates a record for the activity feed configuration for those entities; for example, the following screenshot shows a list of the entities that we created for our solution:

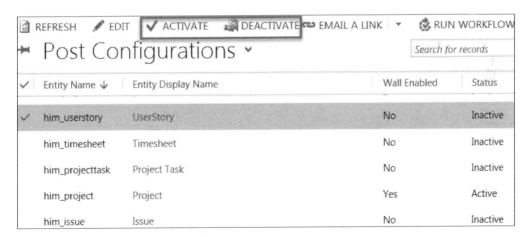

We can select a record and click on the **ACTIVATE** and **DEACTIVATE** buttons to enable or disable activity feed configuration. To enable the **Wall Enabled** option we need to open the record and select the **Wall Enabled** checkbox.

- **Activity Feed Rules**: We can access this configuration by navigating to **Settings | Activity Feed Rules**. Activity feed rules defines when activity feeds will be generated for the activity feed-enabled entities. There are pre-defined rules for the system entities for some events such as account create, opportunity won or lost, and so on. But there are no activity feed rules for custom entities, so if we want to enable activity feeds for a custom entity first we need to enable the `etc` activity feed configuration record for our custom entity and then we need to set up a workflow to create post records on the wall.

You can refer to `https://msdn.microsoft.com/en-us/library/hh547452.aspx` for more detail on activity feeds

Utilizing activity feeds

We want to utilize activity feeds for our project tracking application and want to ensure that every member of the project team is up-to-date with the project status. To enable activity feeds for the project entity we will enable the activity feed configuration record for the project entity and then we will set up a workflow to auto post on the corresponding project record wall about the child entity's status. Perform the following steps to enable this configuration:

1. Navigate **to Settings | Activity Feed Configuration**.
2. Select the **him_project** record and click on the **ACTIVATE** button to enable it.

3. Double-click on the same record and open it.

4. Select the **Enable walls for this** option, click on the **Save** button, and close the record.

Setting the auto post rule

We can directly write user posts on the wall but unfortunately there is no direct way to create an auto post rule for activity feeds. As a workaround we can set up a workflow for auto post. So let's say we want to post messages on the project wall as soon as a project issue is submitted. Perform the following steps to set up this workflow:

1. Navigate to **Settings | Process | New**.

2. Enter the following details and click on **OK**:

   Process Name: AutoIssuePost

   Activity As: **Process**

   Entity: **Issue**

   Category: **Workflow**

3. Set the workflow scope to **Organization** and select **Record is created** under **Start when**.

4. Click on the **Add Step | Create Record** option and select **Post** under the **Create** drop-down. Click on **Set Properties**.

5. Click on **Text Field** and write A new Issue. Select **Record URL(Dynamic)** and click on **Add** and then **OK** as follows:

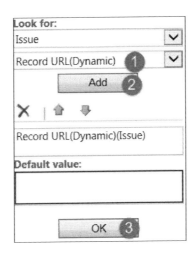

6. Similarly, use other dynamic fields from **Look For** and complete the post message as follows:

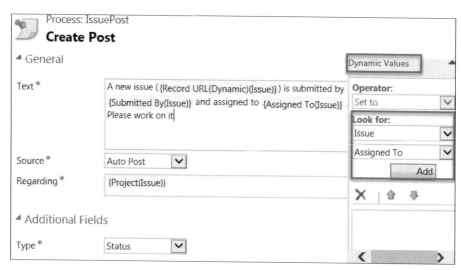

7. Click on **Save and Close** and activate the workflow.

We need to set up another workflow to post when the issue is resolved. Perform the following steps to set it up:

1. Navigate to **Components | Processes | New** under our solution.

2. Enter the following details and click on **OK**:

   Process Name: AutoPostIssueFixed

   Activity As: **Process**

   Entity: **Issue**

   Category: **Workflow**

3. Set the workflow scope to **Organization** and select **Record fields change** under **Start when**.

4. Click on the **Select** button next to **Record fields change** and select the **Issue Status** field. Click on **OK**.

5. Click on **Add Step | Check Condition** and click on the condition to check if the issue status is equal to fixed.

6. Select the row under condition and select **Add Step | Create Record**. We need to select **Post** under the **Create** drop-down and click on **Set Properties**.

7. Click on **Text field** and write a message, using dynamic values from **Look For** under **Form Assistant**.

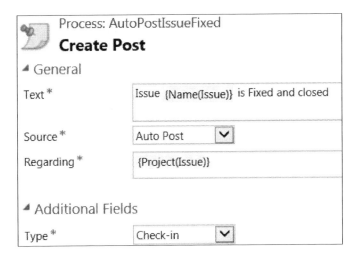

8. Click on **Save and Close** and activate the workflow.

Similarly, we can set up other workflows to do posts for other related entities such as project tasks—for example, when a project task is completed, a time sheet entered, and so on.

Getting updates

By default activity feeds are available on the entity record and the **What's New** wall, but if we want to get updates on a personal wall, we need to follow that record using the **FOLLOW** button on activity-feed enabled entities. The following screenshot shows the other available buttons apart from the **FOLLOW** button:

Once we start following records, we will be able to get all the updates for the followed records in our personal wall as follows:

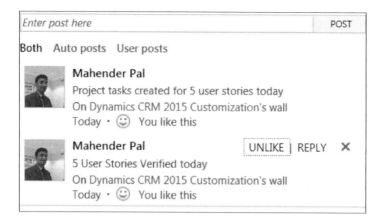

When any entity is enabled for activity feeds, new views are created by the system to display records listed as followed by us. We can also query these records using **Advanced Find**.

Setting up teams

As in CRM, users can access data based on security roles, so it may be that in our development team some user will have a user level security role so they won't be able to access entity records created by others unless they are shared with them or assigned to them. Teams provide the best option to share records with a group instead of sharing records with individual members of the team.

CRM 2015 provides us with the functionality to define access teams and owner teams. Access teams are considered lightweight teams as they don't require security role assignments; thus, they can't own entity records. In the case of access teams, individual entity records are shared with team members so individual record access is provided to team members using different access rights such as Delete, Write, Assign, Append, Append To, Share, and Read. To use access teams first we need to define an access team template based on the entity. We can only a create an access team template for an entity if the **Access Teams** option is checked under the entity definition.

Communication & Collaboration

- ☑ Notes (includes attachments) †
- ☑ Activities †
- ☑ Connections †
- ☐ Sending email (If an email field does not exist, one will be created) †
- ☑ Mail merge
- ☐ Document management
- ☑ Access Teams ⬅
- ☐ Queues †

Once it is done we can define access teams by navigating to **Settings | Security | Access Team Templates**. After that we use the access team template in our entity by adding a sub-grid for the user entity.

 You can find more details on how to create and use access teams from: `http://www.microsoft.com/en-us/dynamics/crm-customer-center/create-a-team-template-and-add-to-an-entity-form.aspx`.

As the name suggests, owner teams can own entity records and so require security role assignment. While creating owner teams, we need to assign a security role to the team and all the team members will automatically inherit this security role. The team members will be able to access data based on the team security role even if a less privileged security role is assigned to them.

In our application we need to set up two owner teams to work on the project. We are going to set up a development team. This team will include different technical and function consultants, with developers and team leads. We need another team that will be responsible for the QA testing and deployment; this team will include members who will be testing the project and will be responsible for the deployment from one server to another.

Let's set up our two teams. Perform the following steps:

1. Navigate to **Settings | Security | Teams**.
2. Click on the **New** command button and use the following information to set up a development team:

   Team Name: CRM Dev Team

   Business Unit: Keep as default

Administrator: Select the user who we want to make admin of the teams

Team Type: **Owner**

3. Click on the **Save** button to save the team. Once the team is saved we can click the **+** sign under the **Team members** sub-grid to add a member to our team.

Similarly we need to set up our **QA team** and the members in it.

Sharing records with a team

Now our team is ready, so let's implement this requirement. As soon as any team is added to the project, we want to share that project with all the team members, so that they will have access to the project. There is no out-of-the-box way to share entity records with teams, but we could implement this requirement with the help of a custom development. Instead of developing this solution, we are going to use a free solution, **Dynamics CRM 2015 Workflow Tools**, which is available in CodePlex. This utility was developed by my colleague MVP Demian Adolfo Raschkovan.

Perform the following steps to use this utility:

1. Download the utility from: `https://msdyncrmworkflowtools.codeplex.com/releases/view/612295`.

2. Import it to our CRM application by navigating to the **Settings | Solution | Import** option.

3. Navigate to **Settings | Processes** and click on the **New** button to create a new workflow.

4. Enter the following details:

   Process Name: `Share Project`

   Category: **Workflow**

   Entity: **Project**

   Keep other setting as default and click on **OK**.

5. Select **Record is Created** and **Record fields change** (select the **Development Team** field using the **Select** button).

6. Click on **Add Step** and select the **msdyncrmWorkflowTools. ShareRecordWithTeam** option under **msdyncrmWorkflowTools custom group** as follows:

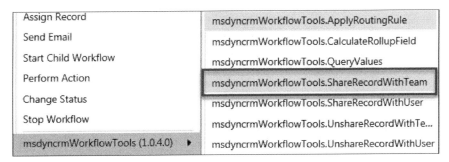

7. Click on the **Set Properties** button and set the input arguments as follows:

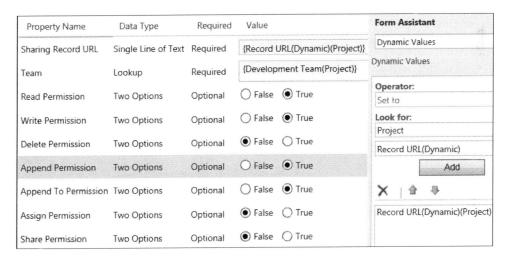

8. **Save and Close**. Now activate our workflow.

We need to set up a similar workflow for the QA team as well. This workflow will share the record with the Development and QA teams when a project record will be created or updated with these team lookup filled. We can set up our custom security roles where we can provide user level access to our custom entities. Then we can assign that security role to our development and QA team.

Preparing data visualization

Now our entities are ready for our solution so let's set up a couple of charts that we can use for the application dashboard. CRM 2015 has rich out-of-the-box data visualization tools; we can utilize out-of-the-box charts or can create our own custom charts to represent different types of information. Similarly, we can use the out-of-the-box dashboard or we can create our own custom dashboards for data visualization. The out-of-the-box entity contains some charts but for our custom entities we need to create a chart. Both charts and dashboards can be of two types: user and system. User charts and dashboards are only available to the user who has created them unless they are shared with other members. But system charts and dashboards are available to every user and are created using solutions.

 You can get more information on data visualization from:
https://msdn.microsoft.com/en-us/library/gg328110.aspx.

For our application we will be setting up the following charts:

- **Estimated Revenue by Technology**: This chart will help us to provide the total estimated revenue based on the different technology project we are using

- **Total Time Entered versus Total Estimation/hrs**: This chart will provide us with details about the total project estimation versus the total time for the project so far

- **Issue Type versus Issue Status**: To see total issues based on their type

Perform the following steps to create the earlier charts in the project entity:

1. Navigate to **Entities | Project | Charts | New**.
2. Select **Active Projects** under the **View used for chart preview** drop-down.
3. Call the chart **Estimated Revenue by Technology**.
4. Click on the drop-down under the **Bar** chart and select the **Bar** option.

5. Select **Series** and **Category** as follows:

6. Click on **Save and Close**.

Similarly, design other charts using the following steps:

1. Navigate to **Charts | New**.
2. Select **Active Projects** under the **View used for chart preview** drop-down.
3. Call the chart **Total Time Entered versus Total Estimation/hrs**.
4. Click on the drop-down under the **Column** chart and select the **Column** option.
5. Select **Series** and **Category** as follows:

We can also set up another chart to see issue details by following the following steps:

1. Navigate to **Issue | Charts | New**.
2. Select **Active Issues** under the **View used for chart preview** drop-down.
3. Call the chart **Issue Type versus Issue Status**.

4. Click on the **Pie** chart and select **Series** and **Category** as follows:

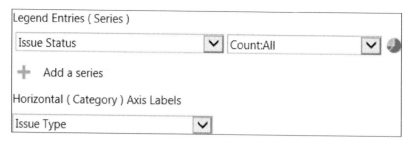

Creating dashboard

Microsoft Dynamics CRM 2015 contains many dashboards for every module and it allows us to create dashboards using out-of-the-box tools, so let's set up a new dashboard for our application. Perform the following steps to create the dashboard:

1. Navigate to **Components | Dashboard | New**.

2. Select **2-Column Regular Dashboard** under the layout options and click on **Create**.

3. Click on the **Insert Chart** option available under the first section and select options as follows:

    Record Type: Issue

    View: Active Issues

    Chart: Issue Type Vs Issue Status

Similarly, add another two charts that we created for the project entity and in the last section add an active timesheet view. Click on **Publish** to publish our changes. After refreshing the CRM browser window we should be able to access our project tracking application dashboard from the dashboard drop-down as follows:

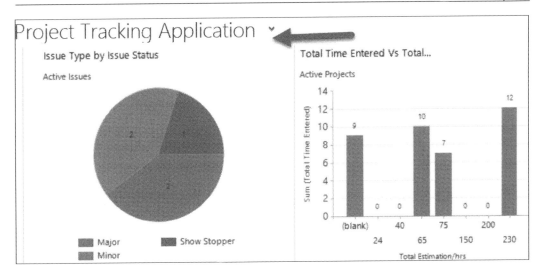

Further, we can customize the navigation of our application like we did in earlier chapters and remove the unwanted areas from the CRM navigation. Real-time workflows can be set up for generating auto IDs for the entities used in the application.

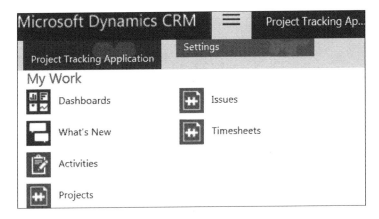

We can utilize the out-of-the-box note attachment functionality in CRM 2015 to attach documents related to the project and we could also enable out-of-the-box SharePoint integration to further use the full document management potential in SharePoint.

Apart from that we can also use the out-of-the-box appointment tool to set up status calls and other meetings.

Summary

In this chapter we learned about creating a complete solution for our project tracking application. We utilized different Microsoft Dynamics CRM 2015 features to set up the various functionality required for the project tracking application. We learned about how to use calculated fields and rollup fields. We also learned about the activity feed feature in CRM 2015 and learned how to create activity feed rules using workflows.

In next chapter we are going to discuss the Microsoft CRM 2015 mobile client and will learn to set up trial for Microsoft Dynamics Marketing.

8
Introduction to Mobile Client and Microsoft Dynamics Marketing

In this chapter, we are going to learn about the mobility options for Microsoft Dynamics CRM 2015 and **Microsoft Dynamics Marketing (MDM)**. We will be discussing the free mobile, tablet, and paid clients available on the market from other vendors. This chapter will also help you to understand the MDM tool used for additional marketing features not present in the out-of-the-box CRM marketing module. We will learn to set up a trial account for MDM.

The following topics will be discussed in this chapter:

- Microsoft Dynamics CRM Mobility Introduction
- Accessing CRM using mobiles
- Access CRM using tablets
- Entities available over mobiles
- Customization for mobile clients
- New enhancements for MOCA
- Other mobile clients
- Introduction to Microsoft Dynamics Marketing
- Setting up Microsoft Dynamics Marketing trial
- Integration with CRM

Introduction to Microsoft Dynamics CRM mobility

We are living in an era where the number of mobile users is increasing rapidly. Now we are more interested in accessing every application from mobile devices instead of using desktops or laptops. In the following diagram we can see the number of mobile users increasing every year.

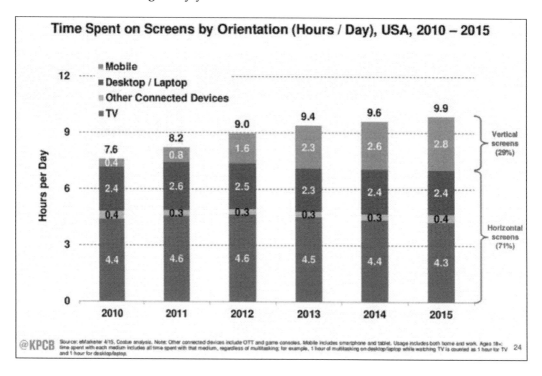

This screenshot was taken from: `http://www.smartinsights.com/mobile-marketing/mobile-marketing-analytics/mobile-marketing-statistics/`.

So we can say that accessing business applications using mobile devices is becoming a key requirement nowadays for a wide category of business users, such as sales persons who want to quickly view sales-related information from CRM systems or maybe an executive who wants to see the sales performance for this month. Keeping these requirements in mind, Microsoft has provided support for mobile and tablet devices to access the CRM application. Just like Web clients and the Outlook client, Microsoft Dynamics CRM 2015 can also be accessed using mobile and tablet devices.

Accessing CRM using mobiles

We have different options to access the CRM application based on the deployment model. To access the CRM application from mobile devices our CRM should be accessible from the extranet; so for example if we are working with CRM Online, we can access our organization using mobile devices without any configuration. We have different options; for example, we can directly browse CRM URLs from mobile browsers or can download native apps but, if we are using CRM on-premise or in a hosted deployment, we need to set up IFD (Internet Facing Deployment) to access our CRM application from mobiles first and then we can access it in the same way as in CRM Online.

> You can get information about setting up IFD for CRM 2015 from `https://technet.microsoft.com/en-us/library/dn609803.aspx`.

So we can say that we have basically two ways to access the CRM application using mobile devices:

- Using mobiles apps
- Using mobile browsers

There are multiple mobile apps available depending on the mobile device that can be used to access CRM 2015; the following table lists download links for the different mobile types:

Device Type	Download Link
iPhone	`https://itunes.apple.com/us/app/microsoft-dynamics-crm-for/id723891307?mt=8`
Android	`https://play.google.com/store/apps/details?id=com.microsoft.crm.crmhost`
Windows	`https://www.microsoft.com/en-us/store/apps/dynamics-crm-for-phones-express/9wzdncrdtbnx`

With the release of CRM 2015 Update 1, a new CRM phone app was introduced called CRM for Phones, but if you are using CRM 2013 and CRM 2015, you can still use the older CRM app called now CRM for Phones Express. This is the same app that was present earlier as Mobile Express and can be used for earlier clients. CRM for Phones can only be used with CRM 2015 Online Update 1; we can't use this app with the older CRM Online and on-premise versions. The new app provides a similar experience to the CRM for Tablet Clients in CRM for Phones. We can use this app for phone and tablet devices.

Now when we try to search for the phone app in the corresponding phone app store we will see two apps as follows:

We can perform the following steps to connect to CRM using the mobile app:

1. Download Dynamics CRM for Phone.
2. Select the CRM app under the available apps list in our mobile.
3. Enter the CRM organization server URL.
4. Enter user credentials when prompted.
5. Let it configure the app completely, and you should get the following screen once the configuration has completed:

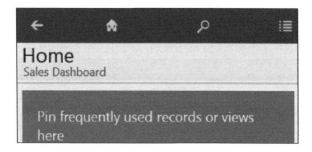

6. Click on the menu and select an individual sub area for navigation, as shown in the following screenshot:

We can click on the ellipse icon to pin any individual item to the home page as follows:

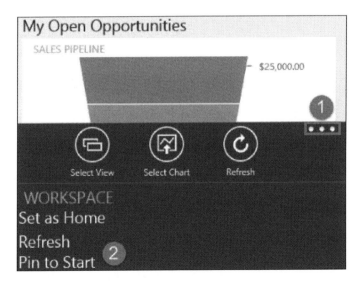

In addition to using mobile apps, we can also access CRM 2015 via mobile browsers. We can also test CRM for Phones Express from our desktop or laptop using the `https://Orgname.crm5.dynamics.com/m` URL for CRM Online. As you can see in the URL we have appended `/m`, which will instruct CRM to render its UI like a phone client. The following screenshot is an example of accessing CRM for Phones Express using a Web browser:

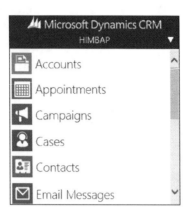

 Please note that the CRM Online organization's URL is dependent on the data center where it is hosted. Please refer to: `https://msdn.microsoft.com/en-us/library/gg328127.aspx` to see the CRM Online URL for your region.

In order to access the CRM application from mobile devices, the user should have the required permissions. You can enable/disable these permissions from the user security roles by navigating to **Settings | Security | Security Role | Business Management**.

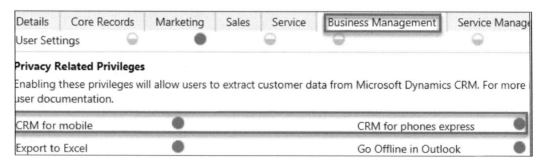

 You can refer to `https://technet.microsoft.com/en-us/library/dn832105.aspx` for more details on setting up mobile clients.

Accessing CRM on tablets

CRM 2015 can also use tablet devices, with a similar experience. It can also connect to both CRM Online organizations and CRM on-premises deployments. Just like earlier versions, it displays the same main form in the tablet client with a different rendering, so we don't need to set up or customize another form for tablet clients.

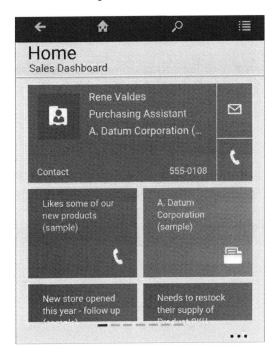

CRM for tablet clients presents elements of the main application in an optimized way for tablets. So tabs in CRM forms are arranged horizontally. And all the related entities are displayed in the left section of the form instead of the top navigation bar.

 In the case of multiple forms, users will get the first form in the form order based on his security role.

CRM for tablet clients only renders the first five tabs or the first 75 fields on entity forms. We can also display up to 10 sub-grids in tablet clients.

Entities available over mobiles

Not all the system entities are enabled for mobile and tablet phones. We can navigate to **Settings** | **Customization** | **Customize the system** | **Components** | **Entities** and can select an entity name to verify if the entity is enabled for mobile phones or not, as shown:

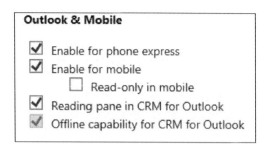

But we can enable this feature for all of our custom entities. Following is a list of the system entities that are enabled for Phone Express and mobile; we can enable or disable these entities using the earlier options: Account, Activity, Appointment, Attachment, Case, Competitor, Connection, Contact, Email, Entitlement, Knowledge Base, Lead, Note, Opportunity, Opportunity Product, Phone Call, Product, Queue, Queue Item, Social Activity, Social Profile, SLA, Task, Team, User, and Web Resource.

Customizing mobile clients

We don't need to do additional customization for CRM for Phones and tablet clients because they share the same updated entity form like the Web and Outlook client. We need to select which fields we want to show for Phone Express. We can add the required fields through the Mobile-express form. We can open the Mobile-express form and can add fields under **Selected Attributes** using the **Add** button. Fields are present in the same order as they appear in the **Selected Attributes** section. We can use the **Move Up** and **Move Down** buttons to rearrange the field order. We can also make fields read-only using the **Read Only** button.

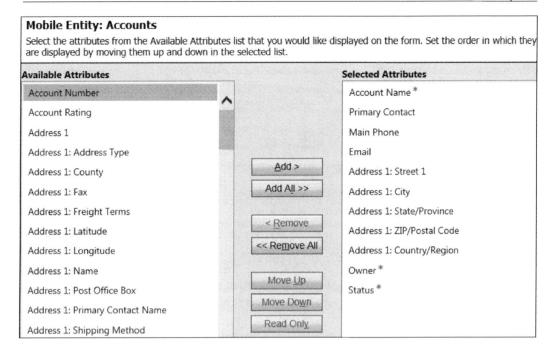

Once fields are added we can save and publish our changes. We can create more than one **Mobile-express** form just like other entity form types. Following is a screenshot of the access account record using Mobile Express:

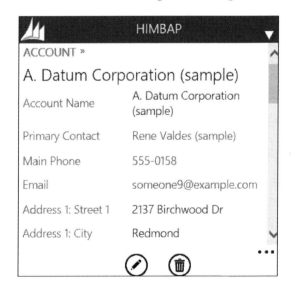

We can also use JavaScript for mobile clients although the Mobile-express client does not support JavaScript; however, CRM for Phones and CRM for tablets clients support JavaScript. There are some methods that do not support CRM for tablets clients; you can find more details about using JavaScript for CRM for tablets clients here: https://msdn.microsoft.com/en-us/library/dn481572.aspx.

New enhancements for MOCA

Windows Mobile Client Application (MOCA) is a native tablet client for CRM. Initially it was released for CRM 2013, but with the release of CRM 2015 there are some enhancements for the MOCA client. In the following sections we will discuss a few of these.

Offline drafts

One new feature in the MOCA client allows us to access and edit records in offline mode created while offline. We can create and update entity records in draft mode while offline; these will be synchronized to the server when we connect. All the records created or updated in draft mode are available in the **Draft Records** area.

We can access all the draft records and can do further changes if required.

Please note that all draft records will be deleted when the user signs out of MOCA.

Multiple dashboards

Another enhancement in MOCA allows us to add any number of dashboards from the system or personal category. Previously, only the sales dashboard was exposed, but now we can add any type of dashboard whether personal or system. We can also pin dashboards to the home page.

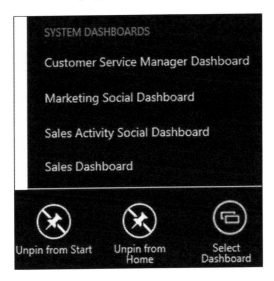

To make any dashboard available for mobile and tablet clients, we can edit its property and can set **Availability** options as in the following screen.

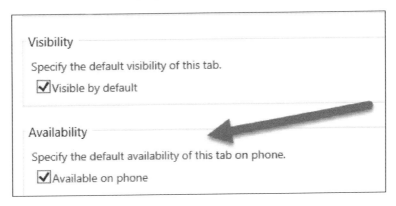

Other mobile clients

Apart from CRM for Phones and CRM for Phone Express, there are other vendors who have created mobile clients for CRM. These mobile clients provide some additional features.

Resco Mobile CRM

Resco.net is a leading mobile software development company that provides a mobile client for Microsoft Dynamics CRM. This client supports different CRM versions such as 4.0/2011/2013/2015 and also provides support for all CRM deployments.

 You can get more information on the Resco mobile client from its website: http://www.resco.net/mobilecrm/.

This application can be downloaded from different online stores depending on the type of mobile device being used, such as Android, iPhone, or Windows. We can download a trial version for this client. Following are some of the features provided by the Resco Mobile CRM:

- Accessing the CRM application from offline
- Adding signatures
- Camera support

- Barcode support
- Attachments to entity records
- SharePoint integration
- Reporting
- Support for color themes
- Support for custom views
- Support for SMS integration
- Reminder support

 You can refer to `http://blog.resco.net/2013/11/12/` `microsoft-vs-resco/` for a comparison between Resco and CRM Phone for mobiles.

CWR Mobile CRM for Microsoft Dynamics CRM

Another mobile client called CWR Mobile CRM is available from CWR Mobility. This client supports all types of device such as Android, BlackBerry, iPhone, iPad, and Windows phones with all the CRM deployment models.

We can get a trial version from the CWR Mobility site at: `http://www.cwrmobility.` `com/#footer` URL. It provides a configure section to customize CWR Mobility according to our requirements. We can navigate to the configuration section via **Settings | CWR Mobile CRM.** This client also supports creating user profiles, which allows us to select forms and views based on user profiles.

Following are some of the features in the CWR Mobile client:

- Offline data access support
- Dashboard support

- Support for background synchronization
- Support for accessing SharePoint and other applications within the app
- Multi-device access support for users
- Mapping and navigation
- Background synchronization.
- Multi Device Access
- Easy deployment

 You can get more information on CWR from their website: `http://www.cwrmobility.com/`.

Introduction to MDM

Microsoft Dynamics Marketing is a marketing tool from Microsoft that can be used with CRM 2015 to enhance its marketing capabilities. It is actually an enhanced version of the Marketing Pilot product that Microsoft acquired back in 2012 and it is a separate application. MDM is available only in the cloud model but can be integrated with both cloud and on-premise CRM deployments. Although the out-of-the-box CRM marketing module provides the functionality to design and execute our campaign effectively, MDM provides more features to analyze our campaign with additional options for automation, collaboration, and social media integration.

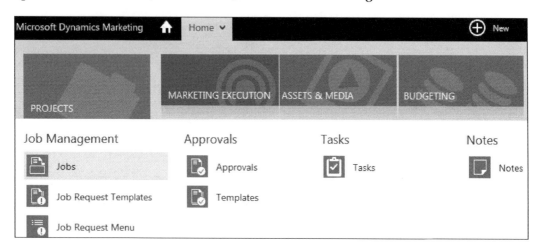

MDM's functionalities are mainly in the areas discussed in the following sections.

Projects

This section is about how organizations can handle different projects internally. This area mainly provides the functionality to maintain jobs and their approval, check job status, and work with the tasks and notes. Apart from this there are different reports to analyze information for different jobs.

Marketing execution

This area provides MDM core features such as managing customers, marketing lists, designing campaigns, landing pages, and forms. This area also provides options to create and manage events and manage social media, websites, and calendars.

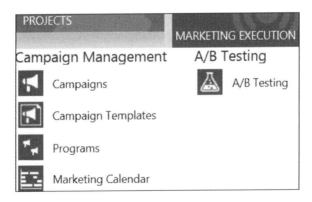

We can use the management console to design our campaigns easily by drag-and-drop campaign activities. With the release of CRM 2015, the campaign management console is enhanced; now it supports multi-condition triggers, and embedded cross-campaign offers. The new email editor enables the MDM user to use existing templates or design new emails using a drag-and-drop build process or an advanced editor for the CSS and HTML experts.

Assets and media

As the name suggests, this area provides options for resource management and media planning. Under the **Files** area, we can upload documents to MDM records, just like using SharePoint integration in CRM. It provides the same sort of file management features as Share Point.

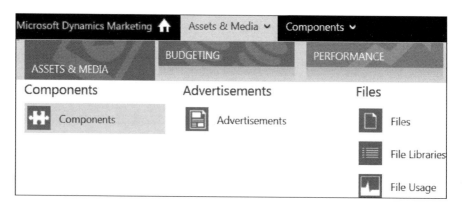

Apart from that, we can use the media section to maintain media-related requirements such as serving media outlets, placing ads, and maintaining rate card details.

Budgeting

Budgeting is the key factor while working on marketing functionality, so this section provides different financial tools to maintain expenses, orders, payments, and invoices.

Performance

This area provides access to the reporting capability of MDM; using this area we can track the performance of the different marketing activities. We can track our project's performance and review the marketing results and campaign performance; this information can be also downloaded into Excel files using the **Export to Excel** option.

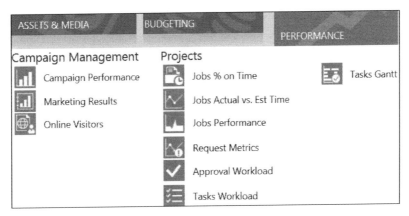

Setting up the Microsoft Dynamics Marketing trial

Microsoft allows us to set up a trial MDM online account, based on the user role selected; it is valid for 30 days, so we can perform the following steps to set up the MDM trial:

1. Navigate to the following URL for the trial account: `https://www.microsoft.com/en-us/dynamics/crm-test-drive-start.aspx`.

2. Select your role and click on the **Start Test Drive** button.

3. Once the test drive is completed, click on the **Start Free Trial** button.

4. Enter your location and company details and click on the **Next** button.

5. Enter your user name and password.

6. Enter your valid phone number and, once the unique id has been received on your mobile, enter it to complete the free trial.

7. Click on the **Office 365** link and the link is ready. We can check if the MDM setup is complete or not by navigating to the menu as follows:

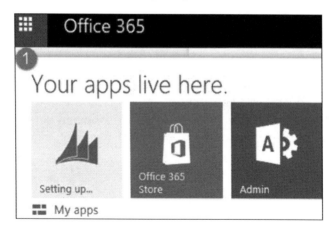

8. Once the MDM setup has been completed, the icon should change to **Marketing** as follows:

Once our trial is set up, we can navigate to MDM and can start entering our customer data and using it for different marketing activities.

Integration with CRM

MDM provides out-of-the-box integration options with CRM. We can configure integration by navigating to **Settings | Administration | Integration Options**. Afterwards, the integration option data can be synchronized between CRM and MDM. We can set up this connector for both online and on-premise deployment. Some of the objects can be synchronized back and forth, whereas some objects can be synchronized only in one way. The following table lists the object synchronization mapping between MDM and CRM 2015:

MDM	CRM	Synchronization Option
Companies	Accounts	Both Side
Contacts	Contacts	Both Side
Marketing List	Marketing List	Both Side
Leads	Leads	MDM to CRM
Opportunity	Opportunity	CRM to MDM
Campaigns	Campaigns	MDM to CRM
Notes	Notes	Both Side
Tasks	Task	MDM to CRM

Perform the following high-level steps to set up integration between CRM and MDM:

1. Download and install the MDM connector from: `https://www.microsoft.com/en-us/download/details.aspx?id=43108`.

2. Start the CRM application, from which we want to synchronize data to MDM.

3. Navigate to **Settings | Customizations | Solutions** and click on the **Import** button on the ribbon command bar.

4. Browse to `Program Files (x86)\Microsoft Dynamics Marketing\Connector for Microsoft Dynamics CRM\Solutions` and import the `DynamicsMarketingConnector_for_CRM2015_managed.zip` solution to CRM.

5. Start the MDM application and navigate to **Settings | Administration | Integration Options**.

6. Navigate to the CRM Service Section and click on the button to enable the CRM service.

7. Navigate to the **CRM Endpoint** section and click on the following button to configure CRM service endpoints:

8. To connect to our CRM Online instance use the following:

9. Click on the **Submit** button.

Refer to `http://blogs.technet.com/b/lystavlen/` `archive/2014/07/02/connecting-dynamics-` `marketing-to-dynamics-crm.aspx` for more detailed information on configuring integration.

Once the connector is set up, data synchronization will happen between CRM and MDM based on the pre-defined mapping. If required, we can disable a specific mapping. We can get more details about integration connector mapping at: `https://www.microsoft.com/en-us/dynamics/marketing-customer-center/` `configure-the-sdk-and-dynamics-crm-connector.aspx`.

Summary

In this chapter we learned about the Microsoft CRM 2015 mobile client and apps available for mobile phones and tablet clients. We discussed the different features available on different apps. We also discussed the Microsoft Dynamics Marketing tool and its features. We discussed how we can set up a trial for MDM and set integration with Microsoft Dynamics CRM.

A
Data Model for Client Entities

The following table provides fields that we are using in our client entity form. We have not created any custom fields:

Logical Name	Display Name	Type	Custom?	Additional data
emailaddress1	Email	String	False	Format: Email Max length: 100
modifiedon	Modified On	DateTime	False	Format: DateAndTime
websiteurl	Website	String	False	Format: Url Max length: 200
donotpostalmail	Do not allow Mails	Boolean	False	True: Do Not Allow False: Allow Default Value: False
paymenttermscode	Billing Cycle	Picklist	False	Options: 1: Weekly 2: Monthly 3: Quarterly 4: Yearly Default: 1
creditlimit	Credit Limit	Money	False	Minimum value: 0 Maximum value: 10,00,00,00,00,00,000 Precision: 2
numberofemployees	No. of Employees	Integer	False	Minimum value: 0 Maximum value: 1,00,00,00,000
name	Client Name	String	False	Format: Text Max length: 160

Logical Name	Display Name	Type	Custom?	Additional data
revenue	**Annual Revenue**	Money	False	**Minimum value: 0** **Maximum value: 10,00,00,00,00,00,000** **Precision: 2**
primarycontactid	**Primary Contact**	Lookup	False	**Targets: contact**
parentaccountid	**Parent Client**	Lookup	False	**Targets: account**
createdon	**Created On**	DateTime	False	**Format: DateAndTime**
donotbulkemail	**Do not allow Bulk Emails**	Boolean	False	**True: Do Not Allow** **False: Allow** **Default Value: False**
donotfax	**Do not allow Faxes**	Boolean	False	**True: Do Not Allow** **False: Allow** **Default Value: False**
address1_composite	**Address 1**	Memo	False	**Format: TextArea** **Max length: 1000**
ownershipcode	**Ownership**	Picklist	False	**Options:** **1: Public** **2: Private** **3: Subsidiary** **4: Other** **Default: 1**
description	**Description**	Memo	False	**Format: TextArea** **Max length: 2,000**
donotemail	**Do not allow Emails**	Boolean	False	**True: Do Not Allow** **False: Allow** **Default Value: False**

Logical Name	Display Name	Type	Custom?	Additional data
industrycode	**Industry**	Picklist	False	**Options:** **1: Clienting** **2: Agriculture and Non-petrol Natural Resource Extraction** **3: Broadcasting, Printing, and Publishing** **4: Brokers** **5: Building Supply Retail** **6: Business Services** **7: Consulting** **8: Consumer Services** **9: Design, Direction, and Creative Management** **10: Distributors, Dispatchers, and Processors** **11: Doctors' Offices and Clinics** **12: Durable Manufacturing** **13: Eating and Drinking Places** **14: Entertainment Retail** **15: Equipment Rental and Leasing** **16: Financial** **17: Food and Tobacco Processing** **18: Inbound Capital Intensive Processing** **19: Inbound Repair and Services** **20: Insurance** **21: Legal Services** **22: Non-Durable Merchandise Retail** **23: Outbound Consumer Service** **24: Petrochemical Extraction and Distribution** **25: Service Retail** **26: SIG Affiliations** **27: Social Services** **28: Special Outbound Trade Contractors** **29: Specialty Realty** **30: Transportation** **31: Utility Creation and Distribution** **32: Vehicle Retail** **33: Wholesale** **Default: 1**

Logical Name	Display Name	Type	Custom?	Additional data
transactioncurrencyid	Currency	Lookup	False	Targets: transactioncurrency
fax	Fax	String	False	Format: Text Max length: 50
ownerid	Owner	Owner	False	
accountnumber	Client Number	String	False	Format: Text Max length: 20
donotphone	Do not allow Phone Calls	Boolean	False	True: Do Not Allow False: Allow Default Value: False
createdby	Created By	Lookup	False	Targets: systemuser
preferredcontact methodcode	Preferred Method of Contact	Picklist	False	Options: 1: Any 2: Email 3: Phone 4: Fax 5: Mail Default: 1
telephone2	Other Phone	String	False	Format: Text Max length: 50

Data model for contact entities

The following table provides fields that we are using for our contact entity. Most of the fields are out-of-the-box fields only, we just need to rearrange them on a form based on the design:

Logical Name	Display Name	Type	Custom?	Additional data
emailaddress1	Email	String	False	Format: Email Max length: 100
donotpostalmail	Do not allow Mails	Boolean	False	True: Do Not Allow False: Allow Default Value: False

Logical Name	Display Name	Type	Custom?	Additional data
gendercode	**Gender**	Picklist	False	**Options:** **1: Male** **2: Female** **Default: 1**
mobilephone	**Mobile Phone**	String	False	**Format: Text** **Max length: 50**
birthdate	**Birthday**	DateTime	False	**Format: DateOnly**
telephone1	**Business Phone**	String	False	**Format: Text** **Max length: 50**
preferredcontact methodcode	**Preferred Method of Contact**	Picklist	False	**Options:** **1: Any** **2: Email** **3: Phone** **4: Fax** **5: Mail** **Default: 1**
donotbulkemail	**Do not allow Bulk Emails**	Boolean	False	**True: Do Not Allow** **False: Allow** **Default Value: False**
donotfax	**Do not allow Faxes**	Boolean	False	**True: Do Not Allow** **False: Allow** **Default Value: False**
address1_composite	**Address 1**	Memo	False	**Format: TextArea** **Max length: 1,000**
description	**Description**	Memo	False	**Format: TextArea** **Max length: 2,000**
donotemail	**Do not allow Emails**	Boolean	False	**True: Do Not Allow** **False: Allow** **Default Value: False**

Logical Name	Display Name	Type	Custom?	Additional data
him_contacttype	**Contact Type**	Picklist	True	**Options:** **10,00,00,000: Employee** **10,00,00,001: Trainer** **10,00,00,002: Client Contact** **100000003: Vendor** **Default: -1**
donotphon	**Do not allow Phone Calls**	Boolean	False	**True: Do Not Allow** **False: Allow** **Default Value: False**
jobtitle	**Job Title**	String	False	**Format: Text** **Max length: 100**
fax	**Fax**	String	False	**Format: Text** **Max length: 50**
ownerid	**Owner**	Owner	False	
parentcustomerid	**Company Name**	Customer	False	
anniversary	**Anniversary**	DateTime	False	**Format: DateOnly**
familystatuscode	**Marital Status**	Picklist	False	**Options:** **1: Single** **2: Married** **3: Divorced** **4: Widowed** **Default: 1**
fullname	**Full Name**	String	False	**Format: Text** **Max length: 160**

Data model for proposal entities

We are using the following fields for the proposal entity. Most of the fields are out-of-the-box only. We just need to create the field where the Custom column is True.

Logical Name	Display Name	Type	Custom?	Additional data
isrevenuesystem calculated	**Revenue**	Boolean	False	**True: System Calculated** **False: User Provided** **Default Value: False**
freightamount	**Freight Amount**	Money	False	**Minimum value: 0** **Maximum value: 10,00,00,00,00,000** **Precision: 2**
parentcontactid	**Contact**	Lookup	False	**Targets:** **contact**
statuscode	**Status Reason**	Status	False	**States:** **1: In Progress** **2: On Hold** **3: Won** **4: Canceled** **5: Out-Sold**
estimatedclosedate	**Est. Close Date**	DateTime	False	**Format: DateOnly**
parentaccountid	**Client**	Lookup	False	**Targets:** **account**
pricelevelid	**Price List**	Lookup	False	**Targets:** **pricelevel**
description	**Description**	Memo	False	**Format: TextArea** **Max length: 2000**
estimatedvalue	**Est. Revenue**	Money	False	**Minimum value: 10,00,00,00,00,000** **Maximum value: 10,00,00,00,00,000** **Precision: 2**
totalamountless freight	**Total Pre-Freight Amount**	Money	False	**Minimum value: -92,23,37,20,36,85,477** **Maximum value: 92,23,37,20,36,85,477** **Precision: 2**
customerid	**Potential Customer**	Customer	False	

Logical Name	Display Name	Type	Custom?	Additional data
totallineitema mount	**Total Detail Amount**	Money	False	**Minimum value: 922337203685477** **Maximum value: 922337203685477** **Precision: 2**
transaction currencyid	**Currency**	Lookup	False	**Targets:** **transactioncurrency**
customerneed	**Specific Topics**	Memo	False	**Format: TextArea** **Max length: 2000**
ownerid	**Owner**	Owner	False	
discountpercentage	**Proposal Discount (%)**	Decimal	False	**Minimum value: 0** **Maximum value: 100** **Precision: 2**
him_trainer	**Trainer**	Lookup	True	**Targets:** **contact**
purchasetimeframe	**Purchase Timeframe**	Picklist	False	**Options:** **0: Immediate** **1: This Quarter** **2: Next Quarter** **3: This Year** **4: Unknown** **Default: 1**
budgetamount	**Budget Amount**	Money	False	**Minimum value: 0** **Maximum value: 10,00,00,00,00,000** **Precision: 2**
name	**Topic**	String	False	**Format: Text** **Max length: 300**
totalamount	**Total Amount**	Money	False	**Minimum value: 92,23,37,20,36,85,477** **Maximum value: 92,23,37,20,36,85,477** **Precision: 2**
totaltax	**Total Tax**	Money	False	**Minimum value: 92,23,37,20,36,85,477** **Maximum value: 92,23,37,20,36,85,477** **Precision: 2**

Logical Name	Display Name	Type	Custom?	Additional data
him_technology	**Technology**	Picklist	True	**Options:** **1: .Net** **2: ASP.Net** **3: SQL Server** **4: SharePoint** **5: Microsoft Dynamics CRM** **6: Microsoft Dynamics Ax** **7: Microsoft Dynamics GP** **8: Automated Testing** **Default: 1**
discountamount	**Proposal Discount Amount**	Money	False	**Minimum value: 0** **Maximum value: 10,00,00,00,00,000** **Precision: 2**
purchaseprocess	**Purchase Process**	Picklist	False	**Options:** **0: Individual** **1: Committee** **2: Unknown** **Default: 1**
currentsituation	**More Details**	Memo	False	**Format: TextArea** **Max length: 2000**

Data model for training request entities

We are using the following fields for the training request entity. Most of the fields are out-of-the-box only. We just need to create a field where the Custom column is True.

Logical Name	Display Name	Type	Custom Attribute	Additional data
emailaddress1	**Email**	String	False	**Format: Email** **Max length: 100**
websiteurl	**Website**	String	False	**Format: Url** **Max length: 200**
him_isstudymaterial required	**Study Material Required**	Boolean	True	**True: Yes** **False: No** **Default Value: False**

Logical Name	Display Name	Type	Custom Attribute	Additional data
mobilephone	Mobile Phone	String	False	Format: Text Max length: 20
numberofemployees	No. of Attendee	Integer	False	Minimum value: 0 Maximum value: 10,00,000
him_proposedend	Proposed End	DateTime	True	Format: DateOnly
companyname	Client Name	String	False	Format: Text Max length: 100
createdon	Created On	DateTime	False	Format: DateAndTime
him_proposedtrainer	Proposed Trainer	Lookup	True	Targets: contact
address1_composite	Training Address	Memo	False	Format: TextArea Max length: 1000
evaluatefit	Evaluation Required	Boolean	False	True: No False: Yes Default Value: False
qualification comments	Specific Topics	Memo	False	Format: TextArea Max length: 2000
description	More Details	Memo	False	Format: TextArea Max length: 2000
modifiedby	Modified By	Lookup	False	Targets: systemuser
him_proposedstart	Proposed Start	DateTime	True	Format: DateOnly
subject	Description	String	False	Format: Text Max length: 300

Logical Name	Display Name	Type	Custom Attribute	Additional data
industrycode	**Industry**	Picklist	False	**Options:** **1: Clienting** **2: Agriculture and Non-petrol Natural Resource Extraction** **3: Broadcasting Printing and Publishing** **4: Brokers** **5: Building Supply Retail** **6: Business Services** **7: Consulting** **8: Consumer Services** **9: Design, Direction, and Creative Management** **10: Distributors, Dispatchers, and Processors** **11: Doctors' Offices and Clinics** **12: Durable Manufacturing** **13: Eating and Drinking Places** **14: Entertainment Retail** **15: Equipment Rental and Leasing** **16: Financial** **17: Food and Tobacco Processing** **18: Inbound Capital Intensive Processing** **19: Inbound Repair and Services** **20: Insurance** **21: Legal Services** **22: Non-Durable Merchandise Retail** **23: Outbound Consumer Service** **24: Petrochemical Extraction and Distribution** **25: Service Retail** **26: SIG Affiliations** **27: Social Services** **28: Special Outbound Trade Contractors** **29: Specialty Realty** **30: Transportation** **31: Utility Creation and Distribution** **32: Vehicle Retail** **33: Wholesale** **Default: 1**
schedulefollowup _qualify	**Evaluation Date**	DateTime	False	**Format: DateAndTime**

Logical Name	Display Name	Type	Custom Attribute	Additional data
jobtitle	**Version**	String	False	**Format: Text** **Max length: 10**
transaction currencyid	**Currency**	Lookup	False	**Targets:** **transactioncurrency**
him_technology	**Technology**	Picklist	True	**Options:** **1: .Net** **2: ASP.Net** **3: SQL Server** **4: SharePoint** **5: Microsoft Dynamics CRM** **6: Microsoft Dynamics Ax** **7: Microsoft Dynamics GP** **8: Automated Testing** **Default: 1**
budgetamount	**Budget Amount**	Money	False	**Minimum value: 0** **Maximum value: 10,00,00,00,00,000** **Precision: 2**
createdby	**Created By**	Lookup	False	**Targets:** **systemuser**
him_traininglevel	**Training Level**	Picklist	True	**Options:** **1: Level 1** **2: Level 2** **3: Level 3** **Default: 1**
telephone1	**Business Phone**	String	False	**Format: Text** **Max length: 50**
fullname	**Vendor**	String	False	**Format: Text** **Max length: 160**

B
Data Model for
Account Entities

The following table provides fields that we are using on account entity form:

Logical Name	Display Name	Type	Custom?	Additional data
emailaddress1	Email	String	False	Format: Email Max length: 100
websiteurl	Website	String	False	Format: Url Max length: 200
donotpostalmail	Do not allow Mail	Boolean	False	True: Do Not Allow False: Allow Default Value: False
creditonhold	Credit Hold	Boolean	False	True: Yes False: No Default Value: False
paymenttermscode	Payment Terms	Picklist	False	Options: 1: Net 30 2: 2% 10, Net 30 3: Net 45 4: Net 60 Default: 1
creditlimit	Credit Limit	Money	False	Minimum value: 0 Maximum value: 10,00,00,00,00,00,000 Precision: 2
name	Account Name	String	False	Format: Text Max length: 160

Logical Name	Display Name	Type	Custom?	Additional data
him_accountmanager	**Account Manager**	Lookup	True	**Targets:** systemuser
primarycontactid	**Primary Contact**	Lookup	False	**Targets:** contact
parentaccountid	**Parent Account**	Lookup	False	**Targets:** account
donotbulkemail	**Do not allow Bulk Emails**	Boolean	False	**True: Do Not Allow** **False: Allow** **Default Value: False**
donotfax	**Do not allow Faxes**	Boolean	False	**True: Do Not Allow** **False: Allow** **Default Value: False**
address1_composite	**Address 1**	Memo	False	**Format: TextArea** **Max length: 1,000**
ownershipcode	**Ownership**	Picklist	False	**Options:** **1: Public** **2: Private** **3: Subsidiary** **4: Other** **Default: 1**
description	**Description**	Memo	False	**Format: TextArea** **Max length: 2,000**
donotemail	**Do not allow Emails**	Boolean	False	**True: Do Not Allow** **False: Allow** **Default Value: False**

Logical Name	Display Name	Type	Custom?	Additional data
industrycode	**Industry**	Picklist	False	**Options:** **1: Accounting** **2: Agriculture and Non-petrol Natural Resource Extraction** **3: Broadcasting, Printing, and Publishing** **4: Brokers** **5: Building Supply Retail** **6: Business Services** **7: Consulting** **8: Consumer Services** **9: Design, Direction, and Creative Management** **10: Distributors, Dispatchers, and Processors** **11: Doctors' Offices and Clinics** **12: Durable Manufacturing** **13: Eating and Drinking Places** **14: Entertainment Retail** **15: Equipment Rental and Leasing** **16: Financial** **17: Food and Tobacco Processing** **18: Inbound Capital Intensive Processing** **19: Inbound Repair and Services** **20: Insurance** **21: Legal Services** **22: Non-Durable Merchandise Retail** **23: Outbound Consumer Service** **24: Petrochemical Extraction and Distribution** **25: Service Retail** **26: SIG Affiliations** **27: Social Services** **28: Special Outbound Trade Contractors** **29: Specialty Realty** **30: Transportation** **31: Utility Creation and Distribution** **32: Vehicle Retail** **33: Wholesale** **Default: 1**

Logical Name	Display Name	Type	Custom?	Additional data
transactioncurrency id	**Currency**	Lookup	False	**Targets: transactioncurrency**
fax	**Fax**	String	False	**Format: Text** **Max length: 50**
ownerid	**Owner**	Owner	False	
accountnumber	**Account Number**	String	False	**Format: Text** **Max length: 20**
donotphone	**Do not allow Phone Calls**	Boolean	False	**True: Do Not Allow** **False: Allow** **Default Value: False**
him_totalproject	**Total Project**	Integer	True	**Minimum value: 2,14,74,83,648** **Maximum value: 2,14,74,83,647**
preferredcontact methodcode	**Preferred Method of Contact**	Picklist	False	**Options:** **1: Any** **2: Email** **3: Phone** **4: Fax** **5: Mail** **Default: 1**
telephone2	**Other Phone**	String	False	**Format: Text** **Max length: 50**
telephone1	**Main Phone**	String	False	**Format: Text** **Max length: 50**

Data model for project entity

The following are the list of fields which is used for project entity:

Logical Name	Display Name	Type	Custom?	Additional data
him_totalcompleted tasks	**Total completed Tasks**	Integer	True	**Minimum value: 2,14,74,83,648** **Maximum value: 2,14,74,83,647**
him_proposedstart	**Proposed Start**	DateTime	True	**Format: DateOnly**
him_name	**Project Name**	String	True	**Format: Text** **Max length: 100**

Logical Name	Display Name	Type	Custom?	Additional data
him_totalissues	**Total Issues**	Integer	True	**Minimum value:** 2,14,74,83,648 **Maximum value:** 2,14,74,83,647
him_accountmanager	**Account Manager**	Lookup	True	**Targets:** systemuser
him_enddate	**End Date**	DateTime	True	**Format: DateOnly**
him_proposedend	**Proposed End**	DateTime	True	**Format: DateOnly**
him_developmentteam	**Development Team**	Lookup	True	**Targets:** team
him_estimatedrevenue	**Estimated Revenue**	Money	True	**Minimum value: 0** **Maximum value:** 92,23,37,20,36,85,477 **Precision: 4**
him_totalestimation	**Total Estimation/ hrs**	Integer	True	**Minimum value: 0** **Maximum value:** 2,14,74,83,647
him_startdate	**Start Date**	DateTime	True	**Format: DateOnly**
ownerid	**Owner**	Owner	False	
him_projectcode	**Project Code**	Integer	True	**Minimum value: 0** **Maximum value:** 2,14,74,83,647
him_qateam	**QA Team**	Lookup	True	**Targets:** team
him_solvedissues	**Solved Issues**	Integer	True	**Minimum value:** 2,14,74,83,648 **Maximum value:** 2,14,74,83,647
him_client	**Client**	Lookup	True	**Targets:** account
him_projectstatus	**Project Status**	Picklist	True	**Options:** **4: Live** **1: In Progress** **3: Not Started** **2: Completed** **Default: 1**
transactioncurrencyid	**Currency**	Lookup	False	**Targets:** transactioncurrency

Logical Name	Display Name	Type	Custom?	Additional data
him_totaluserstories	**Total User Stories**	Integer	True	**Minimum value: 2,14,74,83,648** **Maximum value: 2,14,74,83,647**
him_totaltasks	**Total Tasks**	Integer	True	**Minimum value: 2,14,74,83,648** **Maximum value: 2,14,74,83,647**
him_projectmanager	**PM**	Lookup	True	**Targets:** **systemuser**
him_totaltimeentered	**Total Time Entered**	Integer	True	**Minimum value: 2,14,74,83,648** **Maximum value: 2,14,74,83,647**
him_technology	**Technology**	Picklist	True	**Options:** **1: .Net** **2: ASP.NET** **3: SharePoint** **4: Dynamics CRM** **5: Dynamics Ax** **6: Dynamics GP** **Default: 1**

Data model for project tasks

The following table provides fields for project task entity:

Logical Name	Display Name	Type	Custom ?	Additional data
him_userstory	**User Story**	Lookup	True	**Targets:** **him_userstory**
him_startdate	**Start Date**	DateTime	True	**Format: DateOnly**
him_description	**Description**	Memo	True	**Format: Text** **Max length: 2,000**
him_taskid	**Task Id**	Integer	True	**Minimum value: 0** **Maximum value: 2,14,74,83,647**
him_assignedto	**Assigned To**	Lookup	True	**Targets:** **systemuser**

Logical Name	Display Name	Type	Custom ?	Additional data
him_projectid	**Project**	Lookup	True	**Targets:** **him_project**
him_enddate	**End Date**	DateTime	True	**Format: DateOnly**
him_name	**Task Name**	String	True	**Format: Text** **Max length: 100**
him_taskstatus	**Task Status**	Picklist	True	**Options:** **4: Live** **1: In Progress** **3: Not Started** **2: Completed** **Default: 1**
ownerid	**Owner**	Owner	False	

Data model for issue entity

The following are the list of the fields which is used for issue entity:

Logical Name	Display Name	Type	Custom Attribute	Additional data
him_taskid	**Task Id**	Lookup	True	**Targets:** **him_projecttask**
him_issuenumber	**Issue Number**	Integer	True	**Minimum value: 0** **Maximum value: 2,14,74,83,647**
him_issuetype	**Issue Type**	Picklist	True	**Options:** **1: Minor** **2: Major** **3: Show Stopper** **Default: 1**
him_assignedto	**Assigned To**	Lookup	True	**Targets:** **systemuser**
him_name	**Name**	String	True	**Format: Text** **Max length: 100**
him_project	**Project**	Lookup	True	**Targets:** **him_project**

Logical Name	Display Name	Type	Custom Attribute	Additional data
him_issuestatus	**Issue Status**	Picklist	True	**Options:** **1: Fixed** **2: Open** **3: Reopen** **Default: 2**
ownerid	**Submitted By**	Owner	False	

Data model for timesheet entity

The following table provides list of the fields used for timesheet entity:

Logical Name	Display Name	Type	Custom?	Additional data
him_userstory	**User Story**	Lookup	True	**Targets:** **him_userstory**
him_description	**Description**	Memo	True	**Format: Text** **Max length: 2,000**
him_task	**Task**	Lookup	True	**Targets:** **him_projecttask**
him_timesheetcode	**Timesheet Code**	Integer	True	**Minimum value: 0** **Maximum value: 2,14,74,83,647**
him_starttime	**Start**	DateTime	True	**Format: DateAndTime**
ownerid	**Owner**	Owner	False	
him_name	**Name**	String	True	**Format: Text** **Max length: 100**
him_totalhours	**Total Hours**	Integer	True	**Minimum value: 2,14,74,83,648** **Maximum value: 2,14,74,83,647**
him_end	**End**	DateTime	True	**Format: DateAndTime**
him_project	**Project**	Lookup	True	**Targets:** **him_project**

Data model for user story entity

Following are the fields that we need to setup for user story entity:

Logical Name	Display Name	Type	Custom?	Additional data
him_story	**Story**	Memo	True	**Format: Text** **Max length: 2,000**
him_code	**User Story Id**	Integer	True	**Minimum value: 0** **Maximum value: 2,14,74,83,647**
him_status	**Status**	Boolean	True	**True: Approved** **False: Draft** **Default Value: False**
him_name	**Name**	String	True	**Format: Text** **Max length: 100**
him_project	**Project**	Lookup	True	**Targets:** **him_project**
ownerid	**Owner**	Owner	False	

Index

product catalog enhancement 24-26
Service Level Agreement (SLA) 30
synchronization, between CRM and
    Outlook or Exchange 30
welcome screen, disabling 28

O

OData
  about 100
  URL 100
  versus Modern SOAP 112
OData endpoints 10
OData, query options
  $expand 102
  $filter 101, 102
  $orderby 102
  $select 101
  $skip 102
  $top 102
  about 101
  reference link 103
offline drafts 280, 281
online region URLs
  reference link 183
OnLoad event 89-93
on-premise server, Microsoft Dynamics
    CRM 2015
  server edition 3
  workgroup edition 3
on-premise versus online, Microsoft
    Dynamics CRM 2015
  about 4
  availability 5
  CRM add-ons 6
  customization 6
  database access 4
  extension 6
  integration 5
  new updates 5
  security 5
OnReadyStateComplete event 96
OnSave event
  about 93
  reference link 93

optimistic concurrency feature
  about 194
  reference link 194
option sets
  about 48
  Global 48
  Local 49
organization data services
  about 166
  working with 103-106
organization service 166
organization web services
  about 171
  associate method 179
  console application, testing 182
  create method 171-173
  delete method 179
  disassociate method 180
  execute method 180, 181
  retrieve method 176
  RetrieveMultiple method 177, 178
  update method 174, 175
Outlook client, Microsoft Dynamics
    CRM 2015 7

P

paging
  reference link 185
parameters
  passing, to plug-ins 218
  using, in custom workflows 222
platform layers 161
plug-in assemblies, CRM database
  reference link 206
plug-in event execution pipelines
  about 201
  main-operation 202
  post-operation 202
  pre-operation 202
  pre-validation 201
plug-in events 202
plug-in images 215
plug-in registration
  about 204, 205
  assembly storage 206
  plug-in mode 205

S

sample plug-in
  writing 203, 204
scripting method, business process flow
  reference link 16
SDK.REST.js
  reference link 103
security
  about 76
  field-level security 77
  record-based security 77
  reference link 196
  role-based security 76
security, CRM online
  URL 5
security management
  reference link 78
server-side business rules
  versus client-side business rules 118, 119
Service Level Agreement (SLA) 30
Show error message 15
Site Map structure
  reference link 39
SOAP 106
SOAPLogger
  used, for creating SOAP request 106-111
SOAP request
  creating, SOAPLogger used 106-111
SOAP.SDK.js
  reference link 112
SOAP, using 2011 WCF endpoints 10
Social Listening component 2
social media integration
  reference link 256
Social Pane 61
software requisites, Microsoft Dynamics
      CRM 2015
  Internet Information Services 8
  Microsoft SQL Server Reporting Services 8
  reference link 8
  SQL Server 2008 64-bit 8
  Windows Server 8

solution
  about 40
  components, adding to 44, 45
  creating 43, 44
solution compatibility
  reference link 42
sub areas
  reference link 39
Sub Grid 62-64
synchronous plug-ins
  versus asynchronous plug-ins 200, 201
synchronous processes 122
synchronous workflows
  creating 146-148
System Administrators 37
System Customizers 37

T

tablets
  CRM, accessing on 277
TabStateChange event 96
teams
  records, sharing with 264, 265
  setting up 262-264
timesheet entity
  data model 310
tracing
  using 194, 195
Training Catalog
  setting up 70-76
training request entities
  data model 299-302
Training Solution Design 34-37
Training Solution Scope 33, 34

U

UI namespaces
  about 88
  methods 88
  methods, reference link 89
unmanaged solutions 40

**upgrade options, Microsoft Dynamics
CRM 2015**
all 2007 endpoints, cleaning 10
in place 9
migration upgrade 9
support, for Microsoft Dynamics CRM 4.0
object model 10
user story entity
data model 311

V

validation
applying, plug-ins used 216, 217

W

**web client, Microsoft Dynamics
CRM 2015 6**
Web resources
about 82
creating 84, 85
Data (XML) 83
Image (GIF) 83
Image (ICO) 83
Image (JPG) 83
Image (PNG) 83
Script (Jscript) 83
Silverlight (XAP) 83
Style Sheet (CSS) 83
StyleSheet (XSL) 83
Webpage (HTML) 83

welcome screen
disabling 28
whole numbers
about 51
formatting options 51
Windows
URL, for download link 273
**Windows Communication Foundation
(WCF) 162**
Windows Workflow Foundation
URL 122
Workflow Foundation (WF) 122
workflows
about 142
activating 143
automatic execution events 143
Available to Run 143
job retention 143
scope 144

X

XrmToolBox
about 68, 155
references 68

Thank you for buying
Microsoft Dynamics CRM 2015 Application Design

About Packt Publishing

Packt, pronounced 'packed', published its first book, *Mastering phpMyAdmin for Effective MySQL Management*, in April 2004, and subsequently continued to specialize in publishing highly focused books on specific technologies and solutions.

Our books and publications share the experiences of your fellow IT professionals in adapting and customizing today's systems, applications, and frameworks. Our solution-based books give you the knowledge and power to customize the software and technologies you're using to get the job done. Packt books are more specific and less general than the IT books you have seen in the past. Our unique business model allows us to bring you more focused information, giving you more of what you need to know, and less of what you don't.

Packt is a modern yet unique publishing company that focuses on producing quality, cutting-edge books for communities of developers, administrators, and newbies alike. For more information, please visit our website at www.packtpub.com.

About Packt Enterprise

In 2010, Packt launched two new brands, Packt Enterprise and Packt Open Source, in order to continue its focus on specialization. This book is part of the Packt Enterprise brand, home to books published on enterprise software – software created by major vendors, including (but not limited to) IBM, Microsoft, and Oracle, often for use in other corporations. Its titles will offer information relevant to a range of users of this software, including administrators, developers, architects, and end users.

Writing for Packt

We welcome all inquiries from people who are interested in authoring. Book proposals should be sent to author@packtpub.com. If your book idea is still at an early stage and you would like to discuss it first before writing a formal book proposal, then please contact us; one of our commissioning editors will get in touch with you.

We're not just looking for published authors; if you have strong technical skills but no writing experience, our experienced editors can help you develop a writing career, or simply get some additional reward for your expertise.

Microsoft Dynamics CRM 2011 Cookbook

ISBN: 978-1-84968-452-1   Paperback: 406 pages

Includes over 75 incredible recipes for deploying, configuring, and customizing your CRM application

1. Step-by-step guide to deploy Dynamics CRM 2011 components, configuring claim-based authentication and IFD deployment.

2. Focus on Dynamics CRM 2011 server maintenance and optimization techniques.

3. Learn advanced Dynamics CRM 2011 administration techniques.

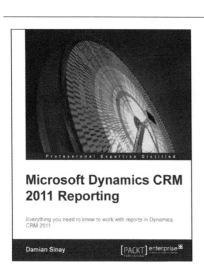

Microsoft Dynamics CRM 2011 Reporting

ISBN: 978-1-84968-230-5   Paperback: 308 pages

Everything you need to know to work with reports in Dynamics CRM 2011

1. Create reports with SQL Reporting Services for CRM.

2. Empower your reports with the different Report Wizards and dashboards.

3. Troubleshoot and optimize your reports for better performance.

Please check **www.PacktPub.com** for information on our titles

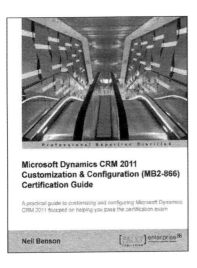
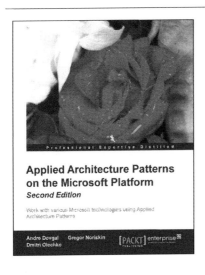

Made in the USA
San Bernardino, CA
27 November 2016